CONTEMPORARY YOUTH CULTURE

CONTEMPORARY YOUTH CULTURE

An International Encyclopedia

Volume 1

Edited by Shirley Steinberg, Priya Parmar, and Birgit Richard
Christine Quail, Assistant Editor

GREENWOOD PRESS
Westport, Connecticut • London

Library of Congress Cataloging-in-Publication Data

Contemporary youth culture : An international encyclopedia / edited by Shirley
Steinberg, Priya Parmar, and Birgit Richard ; Christine Quail, assistant editor.
     p.   cm.
   Includes bibliographical references and index.
   ISBN 0-313-32716-5 (set : alk. paper) — ISBN 0-313-33728-4 (v. 1 : alk. paper) —
ISBN 0-313-33729-2 (v. 2 : alk. paper)   1. Youth—Social conditions—21st
century—Encylopedias. 2.Youth—Social life and customs—21st century—
Encylopedias. 3. Popular culture—Encylopedias. 4. Subculture—Encylopedias.
I. Steinberg, Shirley R., 1952– II. Parmar, Priya. III. Richard, Birgit.

   HQ796.C8154   2006
   305.23509′045—dc22   2005025482

British Library Cataloguing in Publication Data is available.

Library of Congress Catalog Card Number: 2005025482
ISBN: 0–313–32716–5 (set)
      0–313–33728–4 (vol. I)
      0–313–33729–2 (vol. II)

First published in 2006

Greenwood Press, 88 Post Road West, Westport, CT 06881
An imprint of Greenwood Publishing Group, Inc.
www.greenwood.com

Printed in the United States of America

The paper used in this book complies with the
Permanent Paper Standard issued by the National
Information Standards Organization (Z39.48–1984).

10 9 8 7 6 5 4 3 2 1

All photos by Christine M. Quail, PhD
SUNY Oneonta

In celebration of a most amazing young woman,
Shiri Berg, you lived your youth to the fullest
Shirley

To Mayah, my love and future
Priya

To my darling Heinz-Hermann with hugz
Birgit

Contents

Contents

Poetry and Lyrics

Preface

WHY STUDY YOUTH CULTURE?

Shirley R. Steinberg

The notion of youth as we know it has not existed very long in historical time. Such an understanding is central to the conversation about contemporary youth and the forces that shape and reshape what has been called youth in the early twenty-first century. Youth does not float in some timeless and placeless space, above and beyond the influence of historical and social forces. Like any other human dynamic, youth is shaped by macro-social forces such as ideology. Although individual response to such forces may be unique and self-directed, it is not simply free to operate outside the boundaries drawn by such social influences.

Thus, we posit that youth is a social construction, and based on this assertion we set out to examine the forces that are presently constructing it. Many times, scholarly observations of youth have been content to leave the definition of youth uncontested and separate from larger social forces. Thus, over the last few decades, youth has been viewed as "non-social" or "pre-social," more the province of developmental psychologists with their universalizing descriptions of its "normal" phase. Such academic approaches, although pursued with good intentions, have not served the interests of youth and those who seek to help them. By undermining an appreciation of the diversity and complexity of youth, such viewpoints have often equated difference with deficiency, and sociocultural construction with the natural. The complicated nature of youth, youth study, youth psychology, social work for youth, and adolescent and youth education demands more rigorous forms of analysis. A new era of youth has been emerging since the end of the Second World War, noticed by relatively few people who make their living studying or caring for youth. Although scholars are putting more time into the study of youth, it is still not part of the mainstream discourse of most youth-related fields of study and practice. This shift has been shaped in part by the development of new information technologies and the so-called information explosion resulting from them. Information technologies are not the only factors reshaping youth, but they are very significant in this process. Because of this significance, it was argued that those with the financial resources to deploy such technologies have played an exaggerated role in reconstructing youth. This, of course, is why it is essential to study corporate ideologies and influences vis-à-vis youth culture. Because of the profound changes initiated by a variety of social, economic, political, and cultural forces, many analysts maintain that we can no longer make sense of youth by using traditional assumptions about its nature. Even though youth differs profoundly around the world, we can begin to discern some common trends in industrialized and to some degree in industrializing societies. With increasing numbers of one-parent families, the neo-liberal withdrawal of government from social responsibility for the welfare of children and youth, the transformation of the role of women in society, and increased access to information via new information technologies, the world of children and youth has profoundly changed over the last couple of generations.

In respect to changes in access to information it can be argued that young people now in the era of the new (postmodern?) youth possess huge amounts of information about topics traditionally viewed as the province of adults. Some scholars have argued that youth often have more information than adults in these domains because of the time many have to access TV, radio, the Internet, music, and other media. One of the traditional ways suggested to differentiate between youth and adults has involved knowledge of the world. In light of recent changes in information access it is safe to conclude that traditional distinctions between youth and adulthood may no longer be relevant.

Such factors not only change the way we categorize youth and adulthood but change the nature of the relationship between them. Such changes hold profound consequences for parenting, teaching, social service casework, youth psychological counseling, and other youth-related fields. In the context of parenting, evidence indicates that many youth have gained more influence in the life of the family. In such families negotiation, engagement, and more open and egalitarian forms of interaction have replaced authoritarian, hierarchical parent-child relationships. One can identify this loss of traditional forms of parental control in families operating in a variety of social and cultural contexts.

In a new private space created by youth, young adults use their access to information and media productions to negotiate their own culture, albeit within the ideological confines of the productions to which they are privy. Acting on this prerogative youth find it increasingly difficult to return to the status of passive and dependent entities that the iconography of innocence demands. This conflict, the empowerment and new agency that many youth sense in the context of the new youth versus the confinement and call for higher degrees of parental, educational, and social authority of the ideology of innocence, has placed many children and youth in confusing and conflicting social situations. The types of efficacy and self-direction they experience, for example, outside of school creates personal styles and modes of deportment that directly clash with the expectations of them possessed by numerous educators. The outcome of such interactions is not surprising, as the self-assured, adult-like countenance of particular youth is perceived by educators as insolent and disrespectful.

In conversations with youth and educators the recipe for conflict is apparent. Concurrently, this same recipe for conflict is present in the interactions of parents and youth in the social context created by the new adolescence.

When this social context is juxtaposed with the tendency of Western societies, U.S. society in particular, to view youth as economically useless, we begin to understand the sense of confusion and frustration felt by many young people. While the labor market demands that they delay their entry into the workforce to a later and later age, youth are seduced by the material desires of a consumption-based view of selfhood and educated by an information environment that opens the secret knowledge of adulthood to them far earlier in their lives than previously considered appropriate.

Thus, youth in this new social context receive conflicting signals about their role in society, about what it means to be adolescents. In the literature on youth in the early twenty-first century we are beginning to observe debates about the future economic role of young men and women. Those who embrace the innocence paradigm advocate the protection of youth from economic participation. Those who celebrate the changes leading to the empowerment of youth discuss the reemergence of the useful young person. Do not confuse this latter position with a lack of concern for the abuse of youth through the horrors of child and young adult labor. With both parents working outside the home, many argue, new domestic responsibilities may fall to children and youth that will further change their social role in the family. Recognizing this shift, advertisers are already beginning to advertise home appliances and food in young people's magazines.

In the new adolescence the distinction between the lived worlds of adults and youth begins to blur. Certainly youth and adulthood are not one and the same; however, the experiences of adults and youth are more similar now than they were before. Even the materials and artifacts of childhood play in the late years of the twentieth and first years of the twenty-first centuries come from the same informational networks that adults use in their vocational lives. Corporate producers, marketers, and advertisers, recognizing these dynamics before other social agents, have reduced the prior target market segmentations based on chronological age to only two (1) very young children and (2) all other youth. Abandoning divisions suggested by developmental psychology, such business operatives realize how blurred age categorization has become.

It is important to note that despite this blurring of the lines that separate youth and adulthood, youth has not simply collapsed into adulthood. Indeed, the new youth, the contemporary youth, seems to distinguish itself from adulthood on the basis of an affective oppositional stance in relation to it.

In this encyclopedia, this concept of oppositionality provides a central insight into the ways that contemporary youth have manifested their differences.

Why indeed, call this an encyclopedia? If we had been given infinite time and resources, we still could not have included every important issue, concept, behavior, and culture of youth. In fact, we had trouble finishing this encyclopedia, even with this large set of entries. We did not intend to exclude any youth, nor were we able to include every youth. What we did was to survey what scholars in the area of youth studies deemed interesting to youth in this time and in North America. We hope that along with researchers and parents, that students, youth themselves, will enjoy and use this collection. And we want to add to it. We invite all readers who believe they have additional information or new entries to contact us at the email address at the end of this preface. We intend to keep our study of youth culture contemporary, and that means we will continually update our work. As we have found as we study youth, what is *in* today, is most certainly *out* tomorrow.

Unlike a traditional encyclopedia, we have included entries that are not entirely scholarly. Some of the pieces are autobiographical, some are poetic, and some are created to be a reference. The authors are experts and participants in the cultures they describe, and are engaged in the act of studying contemporary youth and the many cultures and subcultures that are included in that study. We organized the entries conceptually, in that we chose the sections and order in a way we hoped would make sense to the reader.

The Encyclopedia of Contemporary Youth Culture is organized in five sections. As we organized the volumes, we were determined to create sections that reflected what was important to youth (**Sections Two, Three, and Four**). We surrounded those sections with **Sections One** and **Five**. **Section One: Studying Youth Culture** sets the tone for the reader to inquire into the reasons for the study of youth culture as a discipline and area of interest. Authors discuss youth in general, as a culture and as a cultural group. They place youth within the larger population and designate youth as an essential demographic group. Authors also discuss the globalization of youth cultures, and different concerns, issues, and problems that youth face. In **Section Five: Teaching and Learning In and Out of School** we present essays that discuss the education of youth, both within and out of formal school settings. By placing this section at the end, we hope that it presents pedagogical choices for teachers and students to continue creating a curriculum that is driven for youth and with youth.

Section Two: Media Culture and Youth addresses the culture that drives the youth of the twenty-first century. Constantly changing, media has exploded in to a world that is interpreted by youth entirely differently than by adults. Driven by MTV, clubbing, music, video, advertising, television, video games, Manga and Anime, instant messaging, cellular phones, the World Wide Web, Disney, and the relentless kinderculture of adolescence, today's youth are experts on the operation and purposes of media. Unlike adults, youth are immediately drawn to media and know how to operate, consume, and disseminate it. Largely North American, European, and Japanese in origin, youth media literacy has become the predominant theme in understanding contemporary youth. Unfortunately, many school curriculums are determined to avoid or ignore youth media culture, isolating students and reinforcing their belief that adults really are *out of it.*

Section Three: Youth Identities and Subcultures looks at ways in which youth have created their own self and group expression. Identity has played an essential role in the development of young men and women through every generation. Identity seems to be that which an adolescent insists on having and yet, something which she or he continually searches for. Even though the essays are titled with the major theme of the piece, each essay seems to blend the essentials of youth culture: music, physical looks, sexuality, fashion, sports, and dating/dance activities. This section looks at both the whimsical and serious parts of youth identity, and places adolescents within a chosen identity or culture. From the early influences of the Teddy Boys to the sex bracelets of today's middle and high schools students, identity must be considered in order to consider youth.

Section Four: Politics and Youth Activism is the most unusual section in an encyclopedia of this type. To so many, the construct of youth is negative, a *stage* in which to get through quickly, and a group that must be controlled and kept busy. In this section we examine the amazing accomplishments and organizations that youth have created and promoted in order to achieve identity, social justice, and awareness. How proud we felt as editors, to create a section that proclaimed the majesty and brilliance of groups of young men and women who refuse to allow corporate or governmental preferences to dictate their lives. In an era that has become increasingly tense at the global level, we celebrate the youth who have insisted on taking their futures by storm, and creating realities that will usher in a better world. We do not attempt to judge youth, nor to particularly identify with each movement. In taking the words of The Who's *My Generation* to heart, we "don't try to dig what they (we) all say." Celebration is not appropriation, nor critique, we present youth culture as we see it, hear it, and feel it.

The three editors of this book come to this project from strong youth cultures of our own. As the oldest, I (Shirley) have been fighting the fact that I am not still eighteen years old. While being a teenager was hard, really hard, (remembering the Vietnam War, the draft, and battling conservative parents), I also watched the Beatles' first performance on *The Ed Sullivan*

Show, saw *Buffalo Springfield* on stage in 1965, and never woke up in the morning without the sounds of KHJ Los Angeles beating through my brain. Rock and roll was the formation of my consciousness. My clothing, language, and thoughts revolved around it. As a person from the sixties, I am continually shocked that I am not *still* that teenager. Remnants appear when our "kids" (all over 23) insist that I turn down the music, that they find it deafening. I like that…it means I still have *it*.

Birgit is the curator of an amazing archive of youth culture in Frankfurt, Germany. Interestingly, she may be one of the only curators of a museum that uses many of her own things as artifacts. Self-described as a sort of Goth punk in the eighties, Birgit wears the piercings and hair that remind us all of where her heart lies. I recall a favorite day with Birgit as I climbed through the archives and she would grab a piece of clothing or pointed black boots and tell me where she wore them and the color of her hair that day. She took her culture seriously, and it became her life's study.

Priya comes from the post-MTV culture. Raised in Central Pennsylvania, she grew up listening to mainstream rock, pop, and hip hop; yet it was hip hop that raised her consciousness. As a teenager she felt she connected to the messages that the music sent. An East Indian by ethnicity, the small, white, rural town in which she lived created a marginalized persona who didn't have a peer group with whom she could identify. Hip hop became an escape for her and created a voice. Priya now grounds her scholarship and pedagogy in hip hop, and that which gave her a voice as a teenager now has helped her establish her work as a writer and teacher.

We present this encyclopedia to you, not as a complete work, or a definitive set that defines all youth culture, but as a work in progress, much like contemporary youth culture is itself. We relish our lives as former youth, and we celebrate the lives of the youth of today. Our hope is that readers will both identify and understand young men and women, and that this encyclopedia will encourage the field of youth studies to flourish and grow; and, most importantly, we invite youth to participate in this study and conversation.

We thank the contributors of *The Encyclopedia of Contemporary Youth Culture.*

We have been privileged to work with a global spectrum of writers who regard the study of youth as a passion. We have placed selections of spoken word poetry throughout the encyclopedia, written by gifted high school students. We cannot thank you all enough for giving part of yourselves to the success of this encyclopedia.

Shirley R. Steinberg

Please write us with suggestions, questions, or continued conversations at: nycresearch@aol.com

Section One

STUDYING YOUTH CULTURE

Life

Kesha Manragh

What is life? Is it a sin?
This is how my story begins.
I see my fellow peers out on the street,
Out hustling and starting battles they can't defeat.
Looking at me, you think everything's okay?
You need to look what's within and not what's on display.
'Cause I never give up, I just do what's right for me,
Everyone got problems, just take a minute and see.

Materialistic things, that's not what makes us up,
What makes us is intelligence and personality, now that's wassup.
We all need to stop discriminating, segregating, or even just hating,
'Cause we have dignity, integrity, or even prosperity.

Emotions running through my mind,
I see so many people self-conscious they can't find.
Who they are and what they want to be,
Life has so many aspects for us to see.
Sometimes I feel that the world wants to bring me down,
But I remember to stay true to myself and stay on top of the ground!

OH PUHLEEZE!
LEARNING YOUTH CULTURE

Rebecca A. Goldstein

Assuming that youth culture is deviant or hostile without really exploring how, why, and where it comes about prevents teachers and others who work with young people from engaging in serious exploration of how youth culture challenges and sustains larger cultural norms and shapes young people's identities. Many Western definitions of youth culture present young people in terms of what they are not—they are not children, they are not adults, and they are not economic or social contributors to the wider society—rather than focusing on what they are. Those who work with young people need to explore the roles media, music, fashion, education, family, and society play in the creation of youth culture to better understand how youth culture shapes the identities of young people. In doing so, they will realize that youth culture reflects many of the hidden values of the larger culture while simultaneously presenting possible alternatives.

To learn about youth culture requires the acknowledgment that the term itself is socially constructed in relation to culture itself, is the creation of people, and is defined by who has power and who does not. There are many perspectives that we can take when talking about culture/youth culture. Some argue that only one culture exists in a given society, and that it transcends time, politics, and races, classes, and genders. From this perspective, culture is simply the combination of traditions and values, including family roles, foods, language, rites of passage, the arts, and so on, and it is passed down from one generation to the next. Accordingly, those who follow this perspective believe that youth culture is merely an extension of the wider culture—one that questions and challenges the wider culture, but also reaffirms that culture on many levels. In this sense, culture can be seen as stable, unchanging, and more or less coherent.

Still others believe that our understandings of culture are in fact much more complex and contested. The late Edward Said noted, "Cultures . . . can not seriously be understood without their force, or more precisely the configurations of power, also being studied." In other words, each culture, as an entity, has the ability to assert a certain amount of force on those who live within its imaginary bounds. Further, each culture has the ability to shape other cultures. Those who take such a perspective also believe that some cultures are more dominant than others, that is, they are able to assert more power over individuals who live within a given society, and in fact such cultures function to maintain the privilege of some while exploiting others. Still others comment that those who are members of the dominant class within a given society define culture, and thus, culture reflects dominant class needs, beliefs, traditions, and values. From this perspective, it makes sense that a subordinate youth culture exists to challenge the dominant culture of society, because a youth culture will challenge and resist the dominant, even though it may end up changing nothing. Further, how that youth culture is defined comes about as a result of the dominant class.

For the sake of this discussion, I would like to take the perspective that culture, which includes the traditions, language, practices, beliefs, education, and politics of a given group, is in fact historically specific, and very much concerned with which group has the power to define and be reflected in that culture. Indeed, cultures change over time as new influences are introduced and others are removed. Further, race, class, gender, ethnicity, and language shape how one experiences or lives culture. And culture itself is influenced by the people who engage in its practices; for this and many other reasons, culture and, in turn, youth culture, can be considered to be socially constructed, that is, created and sustained by the people who live it. However, it is important to note that culture is not simply a benign entity that floats around out in society. Because people *live* culture, that is, engage in and with the production of culture, culture can be both productive (helpful) and destructive (harmful) to those living within a given society.

This brings us to youth culture. Is youth culture an extension of the wider culture of a group or society? Is it a resistance to and breaking with the old? Do those who engage in the practices of youth culture reject the power inherent in the culture of the previous generation? Or, is youth culture an amalgam of the old and the new, so that certain elements of the wider culture are reflected alongside new elements? The answer to this question is influenced by one's experiences, beliefs regarding how the world works (e.g., ideologies), who one believes has the most power to construct and control culture, and, most likely, by one's age. It is true that certain practices within a given youth culture may be similar to other cultural movements (e.g., the raves of the 1990s and the love-ins of the 1960s). But it is important to understand each of these practices within their particular time period because not only might they be a response to particular historical moments, they may also be responded to differently because of when and how they occur.

MEDIA, MUSIC, AND FASHION

There are few places clearer than in the media, music, and fashion where struggles over the role of youth culture in a given society are manifested. In Western society, the media (television, the news, magazines, movies, etc.) both defines youth culture and is defined by it. Evening news reports tell people young and old what is wrong with young people today, and often presents the most extreme examples of youth culture, bad or good. Stories about students "wilding" (most often black or Latino inner-city males) and committing horrible crimes, although infrequent, are the top stories on the evening news. A serious reporter (most likely white and, depending on the station, male) tells of the latest "crisis" to afflict young people. Rarely does the media focus on something good about youth culture (for instance, teens are waiting longer to have sex; drug use is down, as is violent crime). The public very quickly learns that youth culture is deviant and dangerous because television says it is so, even though the statistics tell people otherwise.

Print media such as newspapers and magazines are no better with the messages they send to and about youth culture. Few days go by without some sensational headline appearing on the front page of local and national newspapers reporting on the latest tragedy concerning, or wrong perpetrated upon or by, youth. In the United States, the public is told of young women having sex, getting pregnant, abandoning their babies, and so on. Stories about young men relate that they are engaging in reckless behavior: steroid and other dangerous drug use, binge drinking, dangerous driving, aggressive behavior—in spite of the fact, as I noted earlier, that such behaviors are not nearly as prevalent as the public is led to believe. In spite of this truth we are told to fear the teen mother on crack who can't take care of her child, because if parents are not careful it could be their daughter. And, the public is waiting for the next group of adolescent men to use guns on their classmates to express their blind rage.

In contrast, popular magazines such as *Seventeen, Young Miss, Ebony, Cosmogirl, Teen People, FHM, Vibe, YM, Maxim, Stuff,* and others tell young men and women (and their more mature counterparts) how to appear more attractive, more successful, and more popular while simultaneously cautioning young people not to go too far. Quite literally, youth culture is being encouraged on the inhale and being condemned on the exhale. Examining

5

any magazine that is read by many adolescent women reaffirms the standards of beauty and heterosexuality of the dominant culture, and yet these same magazines present ambivalent as well as contradictory stories to challenge the dominant culture's perceptions of adolescents in the United States. In some cases, these magazines present youth culture as little more than the latest fad in fashion, so that the culture itself is nothing more than consumerism. In others, young people speak back, and attempt to define themselves against the backdrops of the larger dominant culture in any given society or community, in order to point out the ways they differ from the perception of them in that dominant culture.

Nowhere is America's ambivalent relationship with youth culture more apparent than in popular film. Movies such as *The Breakfast Club, Boyz n the Hood, Baby Boy, Thirteen, Mean Girls,* and *Real Women Have Curves* present youth culture in varying ways. The now-classics, including *The Breakfast Club* and *Boyz n the Hood*, present normative images of youth culture, both white and black. In *The Breakfast Club* viewers are presented with a variety of different members of youth culture: the geek, the jock, the princess, the basket case, the loser, and so on, and the message is that no matter where you fit in the social strata of different youth cultures, the adults are still able to exert incredible pressure regarding the present and the future. Those who watch *Boyz n the Hood* see the violence and the stereotypes of black men, women, and families, and are compelled to believe that what they see on the film is the truth. Even the more recent movies mentioned above tell similar stories. But there is one important thing to note about these movies: they all present particular images of different youth cultures that actually mask the relationships between different youth cultures and the larger dominant culture. All of these movies present youth culture as a personal experience, nothing more than an individual teen's struggle against the adults who populate her or his world. And, whether it's about music or fashion, teens are pitted against the adult world and how media portrays them.

Media evidence of the problems with youth culture takes many forms and pays particular attention to popular music and fashion as if they are the sole defining elements of youth culture. Rap, rock and roll, metal, and techno music are all criticized for different reasons. The music of different groups of youths is more or less viewed as violent, sexist, anti-authority, and as promoting drug use, sexual promiscuity, and a host of other social ills. Of particular note is the fact that the media and concerned adults automatically assume that any and all young people who listen to such music blindly follow what the medium says, and in fact engage in social practices as a direct result of such music. In other words, if a young person listens to gangsta rap he or she will go out and shoot someone, do drugs, have unprotected sex, buy the latest sexually revealing clothing, and follow any other suggestions in the songs.

The same thing goes for students who listen to techno or trance music, though the media won't necessarily focus on if and when such young people might engage in violence. Instead, these normally clean, cute (read white) young people will go to a rave, and fall victim to predators who spike their drinks with GHB (gamma-hydroxybutyrate, known as the date rape drug) or ecstasy. And if they choose to ingest such drugs, they will engage in wild orgies that endanger the very fabric of society, or so the media tells the public in the United States. So-called Goth kids are also at risk, though the media portrays them in a much more negative light than their rave counterparts. First, young people who listen to Goth music are viewed as being angry (not necessarily untrue), which can be clearly seen by the music they listen to (think Marilyn Manson), their clothes (think lots of black and chains), and their hair and makeup. Even though the genres of music are representative of different youth cultures, their differences are more or less reduced down to one crucial difference: it does not reflect the dominant culture.

In addition to music, clothing and fashion also present a very interesting contradictory example of the relationship between media and youth culture. What's interesting about fashion is how young people, because of their youth, are both viewed as the ideal in fashion and are an anathema. Particularly in the United States, the quest to stay young is seen everywhere, but it is nowhere more evident than on the catwalks of the major fashion houses, on prime–time TV, and in the latest music videos. New styles need to be fun, young, and hip/def/phat/bad. To be young is to be sexy. Many fashion designers examine how the famous and the young wear their clothes and use this as their inspiration. At the same time, adults are outraged by the clothes that young people choose to wear: too much skin, not enough fabric, pants hanging down too far, too tight, too loose, "gang" colors. As a result, young people who engage in youth cultural practices are actually punished for simply being who they are. For all intents and purposes, they are condemned regardless of their choices.

SOCIETY AND FAMILY

Western society and many families today make an assumed connection between youth culture, adolescence, and schools. Many adults view adolescence as a period of emotional and physical upheaval, and at this time more than any other, these same adults assume that young people are trying to figure out who they are and where they fit into the wider society. From this perspective, youth culture can be viewed simply as an expression of developmental struggle that will resolve itself when young people mature into adults. That is, from the time people are born, they will pass through a series of stages cognitively, emotionally, and physically as they mature from babies into adults. The goal, of course, is to mature into well-mannered, successful, and emotionally stable adults who will take their place in the dominant culture and society. All of this happening is not so simple, for many reasons. How young people become adults in certain cultures is not only characterized by rites of passage that delineate moving from childhood to adulthood; how young people become adults is also very much shaped by the expectations reflected in the dominant culture in which they live. Rites of passage such as Holy Communion, Confirmation, and the Bar or Bat Mitzvah signal for many Judeo-Christian cultures that young people in those societies have crossed one of many major thresholds; these traditions symbolize passing from nonmembership to membership into a given society and culture. In this case, the previously mentioned rites mark important entrance into religious culture and membership. In others, the rites of passage are related to physical maturation or age, including the onset of puberty, learning to drive, the first kiss, and being able to go to the movies without a parent. Regardless of how such rites of passage come into play in any given society, it is important to note that each society sanctions particular rites of passage while discouraging others, even though such societies expect adolescence to occur in some culturally specific manner that is more complex than simple biology.

At the same time that Western society values these rites of passage, it also views the family as the primary socialization force in preparing children to enter school and take their first steps as members of the larger society. Even so, many families are vilified for not ensuring appropriate values and controlling their children. The irony of this, of course, is the assumption that only the nuclear family can ensure the survival of society, and the dominance of youth culture in the lives of adolescence is viewed as the result of the family's failure to properly instill good values. When the family fails in its responsibility, then the schools will pick up the burden of instilling those values. In fact, during many of the "great waves" of immigration (I would argue it's been one big one), one of the commonly accepted views of the purpose of public schools, particularly those in urban areas, was to acculturate immigrant youth into the culture of the United States. In other words, immigrant adolescents were expected to attend crowded public schools in which they were to learn the English language, how to get employment appropriate for their station in life, and how to think, dress, eat, and be American. If the schools should fail, then society will fail. As a result, many schools today continue to be viewed (and view themselves) as the last best hope to protect young people from the dangers of the outside world, by both teaching them about the dangers of drugs, sex, and other questionable activities, and simultaneously making sure that young people learn to follow the rules and be good Americans.

The arguments over the purposes of education—whether to inculcate young people into society or to provide access to knowledge in order to ensure equity for all—often reduces the struggles over youth culture to administrative and disciplinary issues. Dress codes require students to conform and often result in punitive actions for young people. Language use, headphone use, and wearing a hat all become activities to constrain. In fact, many teachers and schools continue to view their main purpose as saving students from themselves and the negative habits they learn from home and their peers. The reality is that such conflicts have more or less always existed between adults and young people. When the Puritans first came to Plymouth Rock, the reason they started schools was to teach young people to read so that they could maintain their religious grounding in the community. If we fast-forward to today, public education, although now not directly related to instilling religious values (though in parts of the United States religion is a regular part of the curriculum, in spite of the Constitution), continues to serve a similar, equally important role in society. By constraining what students wear, the music they listen to, the books they read, their behaviors, and other aspects of their lives, public education as an institution not only serves to pass on the values of the dominant culture, but it also serves as a space where young people can come to gather to challenge dominant culture.

LEARNING YOUTH CULTURE: ADOLESCENCE AND IDENTITY CONSTRUCTION

Students learn a great deal about who they are and what their futures might hold from the schools they attend and the people with whom they have contact both inside school and beyond. For this reason alone, adults who work with young people need to explore and understand youth culture and its influence on how young people come to understand who they are and who they are not. We need to ask, "What is the relationship between identity and youth culture?" At its most fundamental, a person's identity exists in part because of the culture(s) into which one is born. Thus, one's identity is also a reflection of the elements and things of value within that culture. How a society views youth culture has an impact on the identity development of youth. That impact extends beyond the question, "What's the matter with kids these days?" Take, for instance, the cultural belief in many Western cultures that teens today are irresponsible, fickle, and falsely believe they are invincible and immortal. Many adults not only believe that this is a reflection of youth culture, they believe that it *is* youth culture. There is little or no acknowledgment that many young people work long hours at school or jobs, take care of siblings, contribute to their family economic situations, and maintain deep commitments to the things that are important to them, and that for some young people, the issue is not that they are invincible, it is whether they will live to the age of eighteen or not. Such realities are not indicative of irresponsibility; they are a sign of maturity that is often overlooked by many adults. And yet, many still view youth culture as a function of an extended adolescence rather than an expression of the lived realities of young people today.

What's funny about how people think about identity and youth culture is that even though people are all different, many assume that the trajectories of identity and youth culture are the same for all young people. In fact it differs greatly; where one is from, one's parents, race, class, gender, sexuality, language, and many other factors all shape both identity and youth culture. Thus, perhaps the concern should not be saving or remediating (that is, fixing what is wrong with them) young people in the hopes of eliminating youth culture; perhaps it should be understanding how youth culture evolves and how young people can be viewed as empowering and strategic. In fact, assuming that there is something wrong with young people and youth culture in the first place often prevents adults from being able to see what it is that young people are capable of doing.

Adults, who live and work with young people, if they are to better understand youth culture and its potential productive power, must learn to cross cultural borders. In other words, they must learn to navigate between the dominant culture in which they live and the youth culture with which they come into contact. It might appear to be a daunting task to learn how to see youth culture, and to see it in a positive light. But young people do it every day as they travel from home to school and into the workplace. Many have learned how to live in a world filled with conflicting messages, that vilifies them and reveres them at the same time. Coming to a better understanding of how so many young people are able to do this, and why some find it so difficult, will enable adults to think differently about what young people do and think, and why.

So, how do adults begin to learn about youth culture? First and foremost, adults can start by listening to the young people who surround them. They need to hear what young people are listening to, hearing, saying, thinking, and feeling. Many adults say they listen, and that is true. But it is also necessary that adults talk less. Instead of telling young people how hard it was when they were growing up, or giving sage advice never asked for, adults need to simply close their mouths and hear what it is that young people have to say. In addition, adults need to listen with an open mind to the music that imbues youth culture with the many rhythms that provide a pulse to the culture. Not only will listening to the music that young people listen to provide adults with crucial insight into what is important within varying youth cultures, but it can also serve as an entry point into different youth cultures. Each generation seems to have its own musical expression; listening to the latest can only help adults find the commonalities and differences.

Adults also need to avoid engaging in making prescriptive statements and policies that presume young people's guilt. The expectation that young people are going to engage in poor behavior because of their age or place in youth culture may cause adults to live in a state of waiting. After all, if one believes that teens will go bad, it's only a matter of time until one does. At the same time, adults need to start paying attention to what is happening in young people's lives, and stop shrugging off certain statements and reactions as "a phase." It's only a phase until it's a tragedy. Adults who learn to appreciate the strengths and challenges of youth culture will not only be able to advocate better for those with whom they work; they will also become the role models young people look to for guidance when they can't find the answers from their peers.

Resources

Altheide, D. L. (2002). *Creating fear: News and the construction of crisis*. New York: Aldine de Gruyter.

Benhabid, S. (2002). *The claims of culture*. Princeton, NJ: Oxford University Press.

Bourdieu, P. (1993). *The field of cultural production: Essays on art and literature*. New York: Columbia University Press.

Kincheloe, J. L., & Steinberg, S. R. (1996). *Thirteen questions: Reframing education's conversations* (2nd ed.). New York: Peter Lang.

Kliebard, H. M. (2004). *The struggle for the American curriculum, 1893–1958* (2nd ed.). New York: Routledge.

Lesko, N. (2001). *Act your age! A cultural construction of adolescence*. New York: Routledge/Falmer.

Males, M. M. (1999). *Framing youth: 10 myths about the next generation*. Monroe, ME: Common Courage Press.

Said, E. (1993). Orientalism. In A. Gray & M. McGuigan (Eds.). *Studying culture: An introductory reader* (pp. 42–53). New York: Edward Arnold.

Williams, R. (1993). Culture is ordinary. In A. Gray & M. McGuigan (Eds.). *Studying culture: An introductory reader* (pp. 5–14). New York: Edward Arnold.

YOUTH SUBCULTURES, POSTMODERNISM, AND THE MEDIA

David Muggleton

The first part of this entry presents an overview of both the postmodern and the CCCS (the Centre for Contemporary Cultural Studies at the University of Birmingham) theories of the relationship between British youth subcultures and the media. Despite important differences between these two perspectives, they nonetheless share the view that the forces of media and commerce lead to the inauthentication of what were previously resistant, radical, and authentic subcultures. What they also share is a failure to provide empirical evidence of how the young people themselves define and make sense of their own situation as subcultural members. The second and third sections of this entry, therefore, examine extracts from two of my own interviews with members of "spectacular" youth subcultures in order to understand their own subjective perceptions of how the media impact upon their status as authentic subcultural members. I argue that various forms of media play an important role in both the self-construction of their authenticity and their perceptions of other members as inauthentic.

AUTHENTICITY AND INCORPORATION

The seminal work on British youth subcultures that emerged during the 1970s from the CCCS (the Centre for Contemporary Cultural Studies at the University of Birmingham) has been subjected since the early 1990s to a sustained and fatally damaging critique by a new "post-CCCS" generation of subcultural researchers who find its premises increasingly irrelevant for the changed cultural conditions of the new millennium. Yet, for nearly twenty years, from the time of its publication until the emergence of what might loosely be termed a "postmodern" agenda for youth studies, the work of the CCCS remained virtually unchallenged in its position as the dominant, neo-Marxist paradigm for British subcultural research. One major theoretical point of disagreement between the CCCS and more recent postmodern positions has concerned the role allocated to the media in the construction of youth subcultures. Since the 1990s, work on subcultures influenced by the general climate of postmodern theory has been increasing willing to recognize that "spectacular" youth style subcultures are necessarily positioned in a symbiotic relationship to the forces of media and commerce. Yet the approach of the CCCS was predicated upon precisely this claim for "working-class purity"—their concepts of authenticity and resistance depended for their very existence upon the assumption of both a media- and market-free subcultural space.

Those who wish to understand youth subcultures should be careful, however, not to present a caricature of the CCCS position, for they did provide some acknowledgment (albeit partial and limited) of the impact that the media and culture industries had upon the emergence of a succession of UK post–World War II deviant youth styles. For example, John Clarke and his fellow contributors in the 1976 collection *Resistance Through Rituals*, in arguing for the recognition of a material base for youth styles, were adamant that marketing to youth was essential to the development of subcultures. In a rather different way, Dick Hebdige's discussion of the punk subculture in *Subculture: The Meaning of Style* a few years later made a case for the ideological interplay between youthful articulations and media messages. Yet what *was* very much downplayed in both these analyses was the concrete process by which the formative ideas, images, and raw materials of subcultural styles were actually mediated to young people via the forces of marketing, advertising, and commerce.

Undoubtedly, the main reason for this relative absence in the literature was the attempt by the CCCS authors to impute a radical agenda to stylistically innovative working-class youth. In such an analysis, "authentic" subcultural styles were theorized as collective, cohesive, and ritualistic forms of resistance to bourgeois hegemony, their radical meanings expressed visually through *bricolage*—the process by which commodities, the raw materials, from the dominant culture are appropriated and recontextualized to express oppositional meanings in a new stylistic ensemble. This notion of stylistic radicalism made sense only if contrasted with a portrayal of the rest of working-class youth as passive consumers, duped by advertising and marketing into accepting the dominant media images and meanings of mass teenage fashions. Hence, in order to regard subcultures as the culturally pure unmediated innovations of a small nucleus of working-class youth, it was necessary to exclude from this narrative of radical authenticity any potentially negative, manipulative role that could be allocated to media influences.

The point at which the CCCS do become interested in analyzing the role of the media in rather more detail is where Clarke and Hebdige examine the process of "defusion and diffusion"—the eventual incorporation of authentic subcultural styles back into the mainstream. Through defusion, the subversive potential of style is sanitized: the subcultural "folk devil" is ridiculed or trivialized by the popular press; the commodification of subcultural forms turns gestures and signs of refusal into "inauthentic" popular fashions; mod, skinhead, or hippie becomes no more than a pure "market" or "consumer" style. Diffusion is the actual geographical and social dispersal of the style from the original nucleus of innovators to new and mass publics, mediated through television and tabloid reports. In both cases, the process assumes a clearly defined, self-contained subcultural resistance movement, untainted by the world of media and commerce until its discovery, dissemination, and dissipation by the institutions of dominant society. Hence, despite his earlier discussion of the "shared ideological ground" existing between youth subcultures and the dominant culture, Hebdige is still able to refer elsewhere in his book to the, now infamous, "distinction between originals and hangers-on," thereby "contrasting the active creativity and imagination of a small number of innovative subculturalists with an apparently passive, manipulated societal majority or mainstream, including those who adopted subcultural styles after the moment of incorporation."

By drawing an explicit distinction between subcultural resistance and media incorporation, the moment of creativity and the point of recuperation, the social formation and the ideological apparatus, the CCCS work on subcultures displayed a high modernist conception of the relationship between the media and society in that the former is theorized as distinct from, and a mere ideological reflection of, the latter. In subcultural studies since the early 1990s, however, this mode of thinking is no longer tenable, and this is mainly due to the influx of postmodernist theory within work on youth culture. If modernity was an epoch characterized by a rigid demarcation of the social and cultural-ideological spheres, then postmodernity has supposedly entailed the breaking down of such hitherto rigid boundaries. Theorists of the postmodern propose that the social sphere has become saturated by the cultural, with reality increasingly constructed through an endless play of media images. With typical postmodern hyperbole, Jean Baudrillard has gone so far as to claim that society has now "imploded" into the media, or that in this society of the "simulacra" (a model without any original) there is no longer any external social reality to which images refer. With the absolute power of the media in a postmodern era, signs refer only to each other "in an 'aesthetic' hallucination of reality"—a hyperreal.

Despite the vague generality of such arguments, the exposure of post-CCCS youth researchers to this mode of postmodern grand theorizing has at least encouraged many of them to foreground what was previous excluded from youth subcultural theory: the central role for the visual media as vital component in the very construction of subcultural identities. Hodkinson provides a particularly good empirical study of how a number of the above media forms, also including online discussion groups, impact the formation and reinforcement of the gothic subculture. Media impact should be understood here, therefore, as not only influencing the point of entry by individuals into a previously existing subculture, but also as creating and sustaining the very notion of a substantive subcultural group identity itself.

Given the predilection in postmodern theory toward a celebration of the inauthentic, mediated, and superficial experience, it is not surprising that some theorists of youth culture view a postmodern, image-saturated, information-based society as having negative implications for subcultural authenticity. Steve Redhead, for example, proposes that "post-punk subcultures have been characterized by a speeding up of the time between points of 'authenticity' and 'manufacture,'" whereas Angela McRobbie much more emphatically states how "the 'implosionary' effect of the mass media means that . . . there is now an 'instantaneity' which replaces the old period of subcultural incubation."

The problem with such accounts as these, however, is the implication (retained from the work of the CCCS) that the increasing power of the mass media merely hastens the process of subcultural incorporation into the mainstream. Hodkinson provides an important break with this mode of thinking in two ways. First, he examines how certain media and commercial forms are internal to a subculture's development in that they are produced by and for gothic affiliates themselves. These forms therefore display a relative autonomy from non-subcultural commercial enterprises and their attempts to market gothic artifacts to a wider audience. Second, even these external or non-subcultural media do not incorporate or destroy previously authentic subcultures; rather, they are essential to the subculture's authentic creation and formation from its very inception. Clearly, Hodkinson's revisions to both the CCCS and postmodern positions imply a rather different set of implications for subcultural authenticity.

FOLK DEVILS AND MORAL PANICS

Two significant weaknesses exist in both the CCCS and postmodern perspectives on youth subcultures: (1) the scarcity of firsthand empirical evidence for their claims in the form of detailed case studies of subcultures, and (2) their employment of a totalizing theory in terms of which the object of study is interpreted Even otherwise impressive empirical studies of specific youth subcultures do not directly engage with the question of how the members of subcultures themselves subjectively perceive their relationship to the media and its relevance to their own definitions of authenticity, in the sense of what makes someone a genuine or proper subcultural member. Through interview extracts taken from my own fieldwork with members of various subcultures in Brighton, England in the mid-1990s, I therefore aim in the remainder of this essay to address three interrelated questions: (1) How do subculturalists view the role of media and commerce in the construction of their own identity?; (2) How do they view the role of the media in the construction of others?; and (3) Are different media allocated distinct roles in the above processes?

> *Matt:* *If you actually look at the photographs of the Sex Pistols gigs there is like not a punk in the audience, they have all got long hair. They have all got, like . . . if you look at the real photographs, nobody knew what a punk was, there was no uniform. There wasn't a punk uniform. Maybe I might be wrong. There might have been people who actually thought they were punks, but um, I'm not so sure, you know, I think punk became a label possibly after Johnny Lydon, Johnny Rotten said . . . er . . . told . . . er . . . Grundy to f*** off.*

In the first extract we find Matt, who in this part of the interview is engaged in the process of authenticating his punk identity by reference to his initial involvement having occurred prior to the labeling process by which punk was publicly named and identified by outsiders to the subculture. What is at issue here is the way that insiders and outsiders to a particular youth grouping hold different perceptions on subcultural identification, classification, and labeling. Not only does Matt's inception predate the point at which punk became a uniform, he was initially unaware of his identity as a punk. As corroborative evidence he points to photographs of the Sex Pistols' gigs. It is clear that these must be the gigs that took place before the end of 1976, before punk became a focus of mass media attention. The people in the audience in these photographs not only fail to look like what the mass media call punks, they are more likely to resemble hippies or, at the very least, sport the general youth fashion of the time ("they have all got long hair"). As Matt points out, at this period in time "nobody knew what a punk was."

What is significant is how the mass media are deemed to be fully responsible for the sudden transformation of this situation. The watershed is precisely identified as the Bill Grundy interview with the Sex Pistols. Broadcast on Thames Television in the early evening of December 1, 1976, this infamous encounter and the following morning's tabloid press coverage of the incident brought national notoriety to the group specifically and provided the catalyst for a fully fledged moral panic about punk rock in general. It is only after this event, Matt claims, that punk became labeled, the style became identifiable as a uniform, and people began to think of themselves *as* punks. This not only clearly defines the subculture's identity, but the perceived movement toward homogeneity sharply demarcates it from the remnants of residual cultural movements such as hippie. This further implies that those who became punks in the wake of this event are inauthenticated, not only through their uniformity of look and easily manipulated rapid conversion (attributable to one specific instance of media exposure), but by the very fact of media-influenced affiliation itself. As Osgerby has perceptively argued, "any sense of a coherent punk 'movement' or punk 'identity' was largely the outcome of media simplification and commercial marketing strategy."

In one obvious sense, Matt's observation follows the pattern of events set out by the CCCS work: the mass communications media are evacuated from Matt's own (authentic) inception, but construct those who enter the subculture after the Grundy interview as, for all intents and purposes, inauthentic followers. Yet, as the Osgerby quotation suggests, this appears to reverse the CCCS construction of subcultural cohesion. Rather than self-contained and clearly defined subcultures being diffused and dissipated by media attention and commercial exploitation, authentic inception is characterized here by a lack of cohesion and demarcation, with the media playing a homogenizing and clarifying role. McDonald-Walker, for example, has discussed how the media hype surrounding the 1960s mods and rockers clashes helped construct the notion of "the biker" as a negative, categorical stereotype. It might appear that Matt's views are more consistent with those expressed by Stanley Cohen in his seminal text on the media coverage of the mods and rockers, *Folk Devils and Moral Panics*. As Trowler and Riley say of this work, "its principal theme [is] that youth subculture must be seen as a media creation rather than as a reaction by the working class section of youth to their economic and social environment.". Similarly, according to Thornton, "scholars of 'moral panic' assume that little or nothing existed prior to *mass* media labeling [emphasis in original]."

These, it must be said, are somewhat oversimplistic readings of Cohen, who was careful to stress in the final chapter of his book that a conventional socio-structural account is required to explain the origins of such subcultures. It would be more accurate to see this as an origin in which the media are not allocated any explicit or significant role. Only in the process of societal reaction do the media really come to prominence, the effect of which is to homogenize and polarize the two subcultures. Matt appears to be proposing a more radical version of Cohen's thesis whereby mass media coverage does not simply intensify weakly drawn differences between already existing groups, but *actually creates the very notion* of a subcultural identity itself.

MASS, NICHE, AND MICRO MEDIA

That media effects are imputed to others is unsurprising, given the oft-made equation between mass media influence and a lack of capacity for critical and independent thought in those so swayed. This does, however, suggest the need to examine whether subculturalists have in mind different types or forms of media, and if these are regarded as having varying implications for the construction of authenticity or inauthenticity. Relevant to such an analysis is Sarah Thornton's study, *Club Cultures*. In the section on her discussion of the media, Thornton poses two questions. First, in what way are the media involved in the actual development of subcultures? Second, how do subcultural ideologies—the subjective perceptions of subcultural members—construct the role of the media?

In answering the first of these questions, Thornton takes issue with Cohen, who defines media solely in terms of the regional and national press. She argues instead for an internally differentiated understanding of the media, distinguishing between micro, niche, and mass media. Thornton makes three claims by which to justify her divergence from the CCCS view of the media as merely effecting the incorporation of hitherto resistant subcultures. First, negative and sensationalized mass media coverage does not act as a mechanism of defusion and diffusion, but on the contrary can help to render subcultures subversive and increase their longevity. Second, niche media—the music press and style magazines—are often staffed with people previously or currently subcultural members themselves. Such media actively help to compose and structure stable subcultural entities from real yet nonetheless nebulous movements and cultural fragments. Third, micro media, such as fanzines, listings, posters, and flyers, are also integral to the networking process of assembling individuals as a crowd for a specific purpose and imbuing them with a particular identity.

Clearly, Thornton's conclusion, that media produce and name subcultures, does not allow any space for a nonmediated subcultural identity. This is a point that, on one level, a number of my interviewees are happy to concur with, for as one interviewee, Oliver, put it, "everybody's influenced by the media." However, this is precisely to raise Thornton's second question of how subculturalists position the media (or different aspects of it) in relation to their own affiliation. In much the same way as my own interviewees, Thornton's informants proclaimed their authenticity through comparisons with two types of reference group. The first was against a feminized nightclub mainstream in which respectable working-class "Sharon and Tracey dance around their handbags." The second was against a subcultural "Other"—inauthentic clubbers known, somewhat bizarrely, as "Acid Teds." There are really, then, two aspects to Thornton's second question: How do her clubber informants regard their own relationship to the media? And, how do they see the role of the media in the construction of these inauthentic Others?

Predictably, in line with Matt, we find that Others are denigrated as mass-media-influenced. Sharon and Tracey, who personify the mainstream, set their cultural standards by the prime-time BBC television program "Top of the Pops," while Acid Teds, and their feminized equivalent "Techno Traceys," take their cues from the top-selling British tabloid newspaper *The Sun*. And as we might also have expected, the clubbers invert this relationship when referring to themselves, disparaging the mass media (a sure sign of selling out), yet championing micro media such as fanzines as an authentic, grassroots means of communication. This varying regard given to different aspects of the media can, in fact, be detected in Matt's earlier comment. Note how Matt characterizes the visual evidence of those first gigs as "the real photographs," thereby suggesting their authenticity, presumably in relation to the falsity of the mass media. Yet this is too easy a conclusion to leap to. Such remarks may be more of a comment on the people portrayed and constructed by the media than it is on the media themselves. As Widdicombe and Wooffitt have shown, a distinction between genuine and false members can often be mobilized as a common-sense construct by subculturalists themselves as a means of self-authentication.

It would also be necessary to see how subculturalists deal with the complications that arise when, unlike Matt, they would find it difficult to claim that their own inception preceded not only media attention but the very naming process of the subculture itself. Let us look then at another interview statement, which deals not with punk, but with mod.

DM: I mean—you know—the difference between being genuine or whatever you want to call it and not being a fad-follower. And yet I'm wondering that someone else might see you as a fad-follower and what your defense would be. Because I can't see what it is that you have which fad-followers don't. Or at least, I don't know what it is.

Oliver: Yeah, I see what you mean. I don't know, because I got into dressing like this through sort of hanging around with people like it. And although everyone's going . . . you know, there's been that piece in that music paper, Select, about the mod revival, and there's like Blow Up, which is a mod club, and everything like that . . . but I don't know. I was sort of dressing quite sharp before I read about those, and it's more about watching Quadrophenia or something like that.

This extract opens with a reference to the distinction between real members and mere followers. Here, I put it to Oliver that there is nothing that obviously seems to place him in the former group rather than the latter. We can observe in this extract how three potential admissions of inauthenticity are counteracted through their framing within claims for authenticity. First, Oliver states that his style has emerged though peer-group interaction. This could be interpreted as an admission of a simple and inauthentic copying of others rather than an attempt at *bricolage*, but the point of this statement is to highlight how the style came about through face-to-face contact rather than the influence of the media. Secondly, he does not deny knowledge of the contemporary mod revival, nor of his interest in associated media coverage. Yet he plays down any possible accusation of influence by chronologically placing his initial involvement as having preceded such developments ("before I read about those"). Note also that he does not acknowledge "mod" as a group label relevant to his identity, but merely says that he was "dressing quite sharp." His alternative source of influence ("it's more about watching *Quadrophenia* or something like that") also provides the third potential admission of inauthenticity. Not only is this an explicit acknowledgement of media influence, but a particularly significant one given that *Quadrophenia* is not merely a cult film amongst mod affiliates, but was popular in major cinemas at the time of its release. It could conceivably be regarded as more akin to a mass-media text than *Select*, the music paper whose influence is mitigated, and which Thornton would clearly regard as an example of niche media.

But as Oliver is attempting to situate his involvement as having occurred before the, then current, 1994 mod revival, mitigation need take place only with regard to contemporary media influences. As *Quadrophenia* was originally released in 1979, it would normally be cited as having helped precipitate the 1980 mod revival. Although we would therefore have expected 1980 mods to have at the time denied such an influence, Oliver would then have been only eight years old, and too young to be involved. It is precisely this point that allows him to cite the film as an influence rather than, say, current music papers, for he can now safely claim he saw it well before the origins of the 1994 revival. In other words, there are significant time lags between the 1980 revival and his own viewing of the film, and from then until the emergence of the 1994 mod subculture. This minimizes the likelihood of others who were similarly influenced becoming mods through viewing the film at the same time as Oliver, and emphasizes his individuality and authentic origins. The point is the manner in which the age of the film, Oliver's personal biography, and the dates of the two revivals intersect, providing a historical conjuncture that allows this particular person to cite this specific film at this moment in time while retaining his authenticity in relation to a media-influenced collective other.

CONCLUSION

By examining interviews with subcultural members themselves, it can be demonstrated that many of these affiliates fully recognized the pervasiveness of the media and the inevitability of its influence on people's lives. Yet media effects were most usually attributed to others or retrospectively to a point in one's own past in order to authenticate a more recent situation. Neither did subculturalists consistently differentiate along a scale of decreasing authenticity between micro, niche, and mass media. This is because claims for authenticity are primary, which the media can then be illustrative of. In other words, one's own heterogeneity and originality is first contrasted to the relative lack of such qualities in a subcultural or conventional Other or past situation. Various media are then positioned and defined as mass or otherwise on the basis of this contrast. Their relative massness is therefore derived from the homogenization of the Other, not in terms of any predefined formal qualities. This means that admissions of media influence by subculturalists are most likely to take the form of mitigation. The claims for authenticity that they seek to establish are, moreover, explicitly or implicitly conditional upon the mass media-influenced inauthenticity of others.

Note

This chapter is a fully revised and updated version of pages 131–140 of *Inside subculture: The postmodern meaning of style*, by David Muggleton.

Resources

Baudrillard, J. (1983). *Simulations*. New York: Semiotext.

Burke, R., & Sunley, R. (1998). Post-modernism and youth subcultures in Britain in the 1990s. In K. Hazlehurst & C. Hazlehurst (Eds.). *Gangs and youth subcultures: International explorations*. New Brunswick, NJ: Transaction.

Clarke, G. (1982). *Defending ski-jumpers: A critique of theories of youth subcultures*. Occasional Paper 71, CCCS, University of Birmingham.

Clarke, J. (1976). Style. In S. Hall & T. Jefferson (Eds.). *Resistance through rituals: Youth subcultures in post-war Britain*. London: Hutchinson.

Clarke, J., Hall, S., Jefferson, T., & Roberts, B. (1976). Subcultures, cultures and class: A theoretical overview. In S. Hall & T. Jefferson (Eds.). *Resistance through rituals: Youth subcultures in post-war Britain*. London: Hutchinson.

Cohen, S. (1973). *Folk devils and moral panics*. St. Albans, UK: Paladin.

Hall, S., & Jefferson, T. (Eds.). (1976). *Resistance through rituals: Youth subcultures in post-war Britain*. London: Hutchinson.

Hebdige, D. (1979). *Subculture: The meaning of style*. London: Methuen.

Hodkinson, P. (2002). *Goth: Identity, style and subculture*. Oxford: Berg.

Jameson, F. (1991). *Postmodernism, or the cultural logic of late capitalism*. London: Verso.

McDonald-Walker, S. (2000). *Bikers: Culture, politics and power*. Oxford: Berg.

McRobbie, A. (1994). *Postmodernism and popular culture*. London: Routledge.

Muggleton, D. (2000). *Inside subculture: The postmodern meaning of style*. Oxford: Berg.

Osgerby, B. (1998). *Youth in Britain since 1945*. Oxford: Blackwell.

Redhead, S. (1991, January). Rave off: Youth subcultures and the law. *Social Studies Review*, 92–94.

Thornton, S. (1995). *Club cultures: Music, media and subcultural capital*. Cambridge, UK: Polity.

Trowler, P., & Riley, M. (1985). *Topics in sociology*. Slough, UK: University Tutorial Press.

Weinzierl, R., & Muggleton, D. (2004). What is post-subcultural studies anyway? In D. Muggleton & R. Weinzierl (Eds.). *The post-subcultures reader*. Oxford: Berg.

Widdicombe, S., & Wooffitt, R. (1995). *The language of youth subcultures: Social identity in action*. Hemel Hempstead, UK: Harvester Wheatsheaf.

A CRITICAL GEOGRAPHY OF YOUTH CULTURE

Robert J. Helfenbein

Critical geography is the school of thought that seeks to understand how the construction of space and place can be used to reinforce structures of power. A critical geography of youth culture tries to understand how youth are defined, constrained, and liberated by spatial relationships. To understand such a complex set of issues, one must begin with definitions.

Space and place—what's the difference? In most conversations, the two terms are used interchangeably, as in "I need my space!" or "everyone needs a place to hang out." But to geographers, the difference between the terms is the basis of their entire field of study. Geographers begin to think of *space* as the physical attributes of the world around us. This is what most of us think of as geography: things like mountains, rivers, and deserts. Geographers point out that something like a national border certainly represents the spatial but is man-made, can change all the time, and may have varying levels of importance. Space, therefore, can be natural and man-made with the key characteristic that humans interact with and within its constraints.

Place, on the other hand, is a particular form of space—one in which people have put meaning onto its particular location or characteristics. Everyone has places that are special to them for a variety of reasons, good and bad. Recent thinkers in geography have become interested in how a space becomes a place and what that might mean for the people involved. When those processes involve an exploration of power and identity the field of study for these thinkers is called critical geography.

Power, for critical geographers, is always a key component in spatial relations. Think, for example, of how at certain times of the day students can only be in certain parts of the school property; simply being in a particular area can mean big trouble from adults. This shows how those that have power—in this case, teachers and administrators—can define the limits of where youth can and cannot go. This happens all the time in society. But young people do it as well. Think in this case about how a school cafeteria is divided up. Although there are usually no rules as to who sits where, students typically think of certain areas as their own or, sometimes dangerously, clearly belonging to another group. Critical geographers would think about all the factors that come into play in the process of making those spatial divisions for students and then think about what those separations might mean in the development of their identities.

Identity—commonly expressed in the question, "Who am I?"—involves how young people come to see themselves as individuals and as members of larger society. Critical geographers suggest that this process of identity formation always happens in spaces that both construct and limit possibilities and the places that have already been invested with meaning. A critical geography of youth culture would insist on including all the varying forces that act on youth as they come to know themselves and their place in the world. Although most education scholars would suggest that the process of identity formation takes place in dramatic ways during the period of adolescence, most contemporary thinkers describe the process of identity as one that is continual, ever-changing. This is to say that for critical geographers, place and space play a role in setting the limits for a young person's process of identity and simultaneously reflect and come to have meaning in the interaction with the identities of those young people. Some might suggest that the question of "Who am I?" needs to begin with the spatial twist of "Where am I?"

The geographies of schools serve as a point to begin looking at youth culture and its intersections with power and identity. Beginning at the smallest scale, some scholars study the physical geography of classrooms themselves and map out how the teachers interact with students, how the students interact—or don't—with each other, and how bodies themselves are arranged and arrange themselves. Expanding the scale, other researchers study school buildings and architectural layouts to see if the experiences of students are in some way controlled by the physical nature of a school campus. Many of these thinkers, for example, suggest that racial segregation continues to happen in desegregated schools through the tracking of students through certain classes and therefore through certain parts of the building. Other researchers still offer an analysis of schools that begins with the unequal system of school funding based on property value and the taxes the states collect. How neighborhoods themselves are segregated and how resources spread out across school systems might be the basis of their study. Critical geography, interested in coming to understand human interaction in all its complexity, would insist on an analysis that includes all these scales at once.

While schools might be a place to start such study, they should not be the markers of where to stop. Many studies of youth and education tend to stop at the doorway of the school failing to recognize how young people both bring the world of their home and neighborhood into the school every day but also how events in the school day are carried outside the four walls of school buildings. Very often, youth culture is simply divided into studies of school experiences and studies of rebellion—or what some call "deviance." A critical geographer thinks that division is too simple an explanation or even description of the lives of young people. Critical geography also insists that trying to understand students' experiences in schools must include some understanding of the spaces and places that the students bring with them—in other words, we must know where kids are coming from.

Youth in the contemporary world continually interact with a complex variety of forces that not only create possibility for them but also set limits on their behavior. Indeed, the notion of youth itself has geographic characteristics as the term means different things in different places. The roles that young people play in society vary according to the norms of the geographies they inhabit and it then follows that youth take up, negotiate with, or resist those norms in multiple ways that reflect those spatial contexts. For example, what may be rebellious behavior for youth in Chiapas, Mexico may have little resemblance to rebellion in South Korea; place matters. Furthermore, youth cultures increasingly intersect in a global economy. Fashions worn in U.S. public schools not only reflect the fads and trends of youth in Paris or Milan, but also often originate in the sweatshop labor of young people in Indonesia or Nicaragua. Other cultural forms such as pop music, interactive video games, and anime also show how the borders between youth are open and interactive.

The inclusion of youth labor in this description is not incidental as many theorists insist on bringing to light the participation of young people in the global economic system. In the industrial North—a term referring to the countries with the highest stage of consumer capitalism such as Britain, the United States, and Japan—youth culture plays an important role in their ever expanding economies. Young people are increasingly seen as consumers and their culture as a market. In the South—those countries who still depend on agrarian and industrial forms of economy—the labor of young people is exploited to produce goods for sale in the global system. In both instances youth culture operates under the constraints of economic operations and the opportunities for the development of identity respond to the structures of power that have particular characteristics in particular places.

Finally, it has been suggested by some critical geographers that if an individual or group enjoys some degree of power they then must be able to have some control of space. If this is true, then some study of the spaces that are controlled by youth should become a part of our study of human geography. How students divide up the spaces of schools and neighborhoods shows how structures of power are at work within those groups and speak to how the culture of those young people works. Assumptions about youth and what was once termed deviance no longer sufficiently explain the behaviors, cultures, or geographies of young people. Rather, critical geography offers another insight into the particular ways in which identity is formed as a process, how structures of power operate on young people, and how youth culture responds to the places in which it resides.

Resources

Aitken, S. (2001). *Geographies of young people: The morally contested spaces of identity*. New York: Routledge.

Harvey, D. (1996). *Justice, nature, and the geography of difference*. Cambridge, MA: Blackwell.

Hubbard, P., Kitchin, R., & Valentine, G. (Eds.). (2004). *Key thinkers on space and place*. Thousand Oaks, CA: Sage.

Massey, D. (1994). *Space, place, and gender*. Minneapolis: University of Minnesota Press.

Soja, E. (1989). *Postmodern geographies: The reassertion of space in critical social theory*. New York: Verso.

GLOBAL YOUTH

Bart Vautour

Global youth are those who have always been subject to, and saturated by, the logic of late-capitalist globalization. This does not mean that all young people have been affected by globalization in the same way. For example, differences among today's young people are not completely unlike the differences among young people from a pre-globalized era. In other words, members of the global youth still live different lives (not occupying the same positions within international divisions of labor, culture, religion, class, race, age, and gender identification), but globalization has insisted upon common hyper-mediated and technologically charged ways of knowing. "Global youth" is important, as a category, because it allows us to look at youth through another framework or lens. Although the more accepted types of classifying youth culture (such as class, race, and gender) are still important, the use of another grouping to consider contemporary youth culture gives us a theoretical framework that allows us to explore the current or emergent formations of youth cultures as global formations. Also, an attempt to consider youth culture as a global phenomenon is an attempt to include youth in the current accounts of global change. This global change has caused a new politics of experience in youth culture. It is important to note that emerging global youth practices have already produced many cultural products and networks that are historically unprecedented.

Not too long ago, philosophers and cultural theorists were talking about something called postmodernism. It was difficult to get a grasp on what exactly they were talking about. They wrote books about how the world worked in completely different ways. They tried to point to a crisis and a shift in the way we lived. Many people rejected what these people were writing about. Some people said they were just playing complicated word games. What does this have to do with today's youth? Youth of our current moment—of the new millennium—are the first generation to *live* the precepts of postmodern theory—they have emerged along with it. Given that today's youth play out postmodernity in a quasi-naturalized way, and do not simply wax eloquent on something that (twenty years ago) seemed to be merely abstract language games, new tools that account for the now not-so-extra-ordinary (yet still indeterminate) ways young people live their lives are needed. These tools are needed to work at drawing-out and recognizing a set of fresh and unprecedented historical happenings and new social specificities. As an example of this, we could point to the fact that prior generations have had to adapt to a wired-life and reorient themselves to an increasingly technologically mediated workplace. The global youth do not have to adapt to these conditions. Rather, the global youth have grown with these conditions and these hyper-mediated conditions are part of the way today's youth come to understand and navigate their way through the world. For the first time, we do not need to return to postmodern theory to hear about people living fractured and indeterminate lives. Now, we can see it in the way that youth experience their lives.

Today's youth are the quintessential inhabitants of postmodern and global life because they are the first generation to live integrated with the changing spheres of cyberspace, and hyperreality where media culture, laptops, stem cell research, and other emerging technologies are radically altering all aspects of life. Things like entropy, chaos, indeterminacy, hybridity, replication, and hyperreality are no longer only notions they might come across in a university seminar, but actual relations of their lived experience. In this sense, the global youth are more attuned to a higher level of interactivity than any previous generation.

Traditional accounts of youth cultures have tended to have a local focus. The local practices of youth, which have largely been the main concerns of youth studies, remain extremely useful for determining immediate issues and concerns in site-specific contexts. One example of this sort of localized work is reflected in the large contribution to the study of youth cultures that came from the work of the Centre for Contemporary Cultural Studies (CCCS) in Birmingham, United Kingdom. This type of theoretical work has, for the most part, a distinctly British accent. As the rather well worn story goes, Cultural Studies is said to have arisen in Britain sometime around the late 1950s. The work of Cultural Studies can be traced back to various organizations associated with working classes in Britain. The work of the CCCS carved out a space that allows us to reproduce a thorough study of sidelined social formations and their cultural practices. Recent accounts of youth culture, however, hint at dissatisfaction with the work of the CCCS on the grounds of its inability to be directly translated into an age of hyper-globalization. This early work on youth subcultures has been criticized for focusing on a single determinant—class—and not contributing a model that addresses the multiple alliances and multiple determinations that abound in our current historical moment.

While admitting that the many theoretical tools used by the subcultural theory of the CCCS remain important, there are various areas overtheorized, others undertheorized, which question the continued relevance of their work for our current context. It may be the case that the CCCS's account of youth subcultures offers unsuccessful explanatory tools that often make it difficult to understand the complexity of current cultural practices that are caused by the indeterminate effects of a globalized cultural economy.

In the United States, the type of academic work that accounts for youth has tended to fall under the category of American Studies. This version of youth studies, as the name suggests, has focused on the locality of the United States. It is not difficult to recognize the gaps in any account of current youth practices that remains within national boundaries.

There is an interesting shift here, from the locality, which is implicit in the work of the CCCS as well as the American studies that focus on youth, to cultural practices produced in part by the indeterminate effects of a globalized cultural economy. One explanation for this shift could be that the early work, which has an explicit focus on locality, is historically based in a milieu prior to the hyper-globalization that has characterized the most recent *fin de siècle* both culturally and academically. The meaning of "local" has morphed many times over since the moment when the CCCS work was being produced. The workings of globalization have necessitated a re-articulation of the local; however, the theoretical grounds from which subcultural studies emerged (which were a reflection of the cultural practices they were writing about) have potentially turned into a sort of orthodoxy.

The important distinction to be made here is that it would be too simple to define global practices in opposition to a nostalgic notion of what constitutes local practices. If we were to consider global as the opposite of local, accounts of global youth cultures would be working through much the same framework as the older models that have focused on local practices. The effects of globalization have been infused with local practices to such an extent that we can no longer make easy distinctions between local and global. Today's youth have the option of acting out a local practice in a very global way. They also have the ability to act out global phenomena in a distinctly local way.

One way this change has manifested itself is through a shift away from youth cultures as something distinctly urban to a view of youth cultures that work through other geographies. For example, it might be useful to think about the Internet as a type of geography. Like traditional types of geographies, the Internet is a place that is navigated and explored. It is a place where communities are formed in nodes and turf wars are fought. These communities have all the characteristics of local communities except that they happen across vast distances. These recent networked geographies need not be limited to on-line culture. The way that electronic music gets played today is another example.

When we hear electronic music in a club or in the spatially constructed "houses" of youth culture, we often hear a localized style of mixing sounds that have global origins. In other words, even though places like London, New York, or Ibiza have distinct and discernable ways of producing music, it must be recognized that these localized styles utilize many different sounds in the process of remixing already produced material. Although those with discerning ears can tell that a certain type of music conforms to certain criteria, it does not mean that the sounds that the music is created with have uniform criteria. There might be traditional Cree vocals mixed with Brazilian beats and put together in a form that we might identify as "UK Garage". In this sense, youth are using global products in localized performance. To push the music metaphor even further, interested listeners need not be located in the United Kingdom to have access to UK Garage. The performance of a certain style of presentation has also moved beyond the locale of its origins. For example, UK Garage can be heard in clubs around the world. UK Garage can also be heard coming out of speakers attached to any computer in the world. Both production and reception are no longer tied down to any one site.

As noted above, global youth still live their lives in very different ways. It would be a grave mistake to try to say that all youth occupy a level playing field in today's world. Certainly they do not, in any way, occupy a level playing field. While some youth have reaped the benefits of globalization in terms of high standards of living and upward mobility, others have suffered because of globalization. While some young people in the so-called developing world have been forced into working at an early age and in poor conditions to produce such things as shoes or computer hardware, youth in the so-called developed world wear those shoes or use that same hardware for either their high-paid work or increased periods of leisure. Of course these are radically different situations but there is a vital connection to be made between young people in drastically dissimilar circumstances. The connection is globalization.

The logic of capitalist globalization has been far reaching in incorporating militarism and neo-liberal economics as well as insisting upon hyper-mediated and technologically-charged ways of living in the world. Young people have different levels of access to the products that exist because of globalization, but globalization nonetheless has effect on their daily lives. Like any form of dominance, far reaching corporate globalization has a potential to overreach and provide foundations for resistance. An example of this is the "anti-globalization" or "globalization from below" movement that has arisen in recent years. Young activists have been able to subvert, tactically, the projects of neo-liberal capitalism by utilizing and re-articulating the very infrastructures late-capitalism has worked so hard to spread and sustain. For example, if governments and corporations have taught us that they are able to boycott trade with their ideological enemies in order that they might force economic collapse, young activists around the world have shown that they can boycott global corporations that support exploitive labor practices or disastrous environmental practices.

The term "overreach" resonates with the moral-panics that have sought to classify youth in a negative sense. This is the case where youth is only talked about as a problem. "Overreach" can be classified generally as an effort to contain and regulate, but the effort reaches, stretches, or strains itself beyond its strength, beyond its aim. In large part, it is the classifications constructed on conservative principles that help to invigorate those very classifications as operative resistance. Put another way, in the effort to exert control over devious and *grand-delinquent* youth, youth have thrived on being viewed as threatening to the social status quo—they have made it *work* for them. By the way of this working and excess productivity, conservative (and more or less liberal) moral-panic has tended to function as a self-fulfilling prophecy. In reaction to this overextension youth have become scavengers, taking the products that global capitalism has thrown at them and reinventing these selfsame products in ways that go beyond the best interests of the global corporate order, which allowed for the spread and distribution of the products in the first place. In the case of music, the global youth have taken the products of the corporate music industry—with help from the increasing spread of technological literacy—and appropriated and reconfigured how these products get circulated.

Given the various effects of globalization, it cannot be said that the lives of young people are *determined* by the global corporate order. Rather, the effects of globalization *overdetermine* the global youth. Overdetermination is a way of thinking about the multiple, often opposed, forces active at one time in any cultural circumstance, without falling into oversimplified ideas of these forces being simply contradictory. When we think about the global youth as overdetermined—dealing with many different things at once—we realize that young people are not just the puppets of globalization. Instead, we begin to see that the global youth are able to mix and modify both the products and consequences of corporate globalization.

Resources

Besley, A. C. (2003). Hybridized and globalized: youth cultures in the postmodern era. *The Review of Education, Pedagogy, and Cultural Studies, 25*, 153–177.

Best, S., & Kellner, D. (2000). Contemporary youth and the postmodern adventure. *The Review of Education, Pedagogy, and Cultural Studies, 25*, 75–93.

Brennan, T. (2003). Global youth and local pleasure: Cuba and the right to popular music. In D. Fischlin & A. Heble (Eds.). *Rebel musics: Human rights, resistant sounds, and the politics of music making* (pp. 210–231). Montreal: Black Rose Books.

Clarke, T., & Dopp, S. (2001). *Challenging McWorld*. Ottawa: Canadian Centre for Policy Alternatives.

Green, C. (2001). *Manufacturing powerlessness in the black diaspora: Inner-city youth and the new global frontier*. Walnut Creek, CA: AltaMira Press.

Klein, N. (2002). *Fences and windows: Dispatches from the front lines of the globalization debate*. Toronto: Vintage Canada.

Leistyna, P. (Ed.). (2005). *Cultural studies: From theory to action*. Malden, MA: Blackwell.

Muggleton, D., & Weinzierl, R. (Eds.). (2003). *The post-subcultures reader*. Oxford: Berg.

Nayak, A. (2003). *Race, place and globalization: Youth cultures in a changing world*. Oxford: Berg.

Skelton, T., & Valentine, G. (Eds.). (1998). *Cool places: Geographies of youth cultures*. New York: Routledge.

Thornton, S. (1995). *Club cultures: Music, media, and subcultural capital*. Cambridge, UK: Polity Press.

Ghetto Life Pt. 2

Alex Tate

Here's some information I have to provide
From what I've learned in my ghetto life
Blacks going on killing sprees
While others try to be free
I don't care what any of ya'll do
As long as it doesn't include me

Poor people try to get some money from you
While ho's in the streets do things
You won't believe what they'll do
To get money too
By protecting yourself
By caring a knife
Duh, this is the hood, a.k.a. the ghetto life

My mama always told me
That everything that glitters ain't gold
And she should know
Because she's been in da hood
Since she was 2 years old
In da hood, don't hang wit da wrong people
Or you'll learn that they're just plain evil.

The ghetto life is where it's at
From people smoking crack
Always having to keep their pockets fat
Take it from me
Or soon you'll see that you'll have to protect
Yourself in the streets

HIP HOP GLOBALIZATION AND YOUTH CULTURE

Jennifer Kelly

The term "youth culture," directs us to the cultural aspects of youth. Further, the word "culture" refers to "that level at which social groups develop distinct patterns of life, and give expressive form to their social life and material experience." The study of youth cultures in general has long been associated with the theoretical field of British cultural studies through the 1970s ethnographic work of theorists (Dick Hebdige, Paul Willis, Stuart Hall, and Angela McRobbie) at the Birmingham Centre for Contemporary Cultural Studies (CCCS). Within the CCCS, Hall and Jefferson's edited collection *Resistance through Rituals*—a major study of youth cultures—laid the foundation for the recognition of youth as a social category and youth cultures as worthy of study in their own right. The stated object of this seminal text was to explain youth cultures as "a phenomenon, and their appearance in the post war period." Further, these early British cultural studies theorists recognize that youth culture has the capacity to educate youth to think, feel, and desire. So for example, youth relate not only to the music that they listen to, but relate also through the music in such a way that they develop a sense of cultural membership and orientation to morality. In contrast to present day emphasis, much of the early 1970s youth cultural analysis produced by the CCCS was centered on lived experiences of white working class males. As such racialized and gendered experiences were constructed as peripheral to the main concern of class, with sexualities totally out of bounds. Although the experiences of black African Caribbean youth were included in such seminal work as Hebdige's *Subculture and the Meaning of Style*, they were nonetheless regarded as background against which to read white working-class experiences; very much an Other against whom social anxieties could be displaced and oppositional identities constructed.

Since the 1980s and 1990s this situation has changed so much that for many cultural studies theorists the experiences of youth of African descent have been at the forefront of theorization of youth culture through examination of hip hop and its most enduring child: rap music.

Over the past twenty years, youth culture in general, and North American mediated black youth culture in particular, has been dominated by the social formation of hip hop culture. Although its mythic origins are associated solely with the African American community in the New York Bronx, its roots and routes are much more complex and draw on a combination of

African American, Caribbean, and Latino based influences. Social, economic, and political factors were also at play in the United States during the early years of the cultural formation of hip hop. In support of this complex analysis Tricia Rose argues that much of this early development of hip hop was undertaken against the backdrop of a "post-industrial city. . . that shaped their cultural terrain, access to space, materials, and power." Further, as a cultural formation, hip hop is heterogeneous rather than homogenous consisting of the intertextual relationship between rap, graffiti, and break dancing. Although over the past few years the influence of graffiti and break dancing has waned, they were, in the early stages of this cultural phenomenon, thriving aspects of hip hop's formation. Perkins suggests that the decline of break dancing was a consequence of corporate America's raid on hip hop culture, alongside the growth of a video medium that replaced "authentic break dancers" with "'video hos,' 'fly girls' and 'fly boys.'"

Technological changes in the late twentieth century and early twenty-first have enabled access to the social spaces previously bounded by time and geographic borders; a process identified by John Thompson as mediazation—a flow of images across time and space. If the importance and degree of permeation of digital technology and mediazation needs reinforcing one only needs to note the actuality that this is a generation of youth that cannot remember a time without televisual images and the consequences of living within an age of electronic media. The social and cultural effects of the breaking down of time-space barriers between geographic regions—a process whereby social interaction is no longer face-to-face interaction within the same physical locale—are a concern as well. Thus, the breaking down of geographic and state constructed economic barriers via the growth in information and media technology affects social relations within society. This breaking down of geographic barriers has been described contrastingly as a "shrinking of time" (Harvey) or "time-space distanciation" that implies a stretching of time and place (Giddens). Whereas the latter theorists might not agree on whether space is shrinking or time is stretching, they would concur that this increased broadcasting of media to extended audiences not only "create new and unpredictable forms of connection, identification and cultural affinity, but also dislocation and disjuncture between people, places and cultures." In some ways, what we are viewing is the development of horizontal communities—people who are connected through media rather than necessarily geography.

As with analysis of all cultural formations this growth in the ability of youth in various geographic regions to access U.S.-based youth cultural forms cannot be analyzed purely through an emphasis on culture and meaning-making but needs to also recognize the influence of political economy and the ways in which economic and cultural globalization in the United States is linked to expansion of economic borders in order to maximize profits. Such profit making is linked to a globalization of capital, markets, and technologies. Social critic Naomi Klein's book *No Logo* illustrates quite clearly this relationship between youth culture, growth in access to technology, and what we now euphemistically call "branding"— the use of bodies to advertise clothing labels. In examining these trends Klein has been able to periodize how these pioneers of branding took opportunity of trade liberalization and labor law reforms in order to expand their manufacturing base overseas and to increase an emphasis on youth style. As Klein argues, "what these companies produced primarily were not things, they said, but *images* of their brands. Their real work lay not in manufacturing but in marketing." If one examines youth empirically it is evident how these specific economic configurations affect their everyday reality. The world that they attempt to *think through*, to make sense of, is one that is formed through the economic. So it is interesting to note not only

Over-sizing jeans means a belt

how school youth are willing to pay an exorbitant amount for a "brand" item of clothing but also nuanced ways in which access to such branded goods can be converted to "surplus value" that can be used to contour and produce subjectivity. So it is that empirical (and often ethnographic) research on youth reveals that one can travel from New York to Auckland, to Lagos and see the inflections of hip hop youth culture on local youth. Bearing in mind the powerful influence of youth culture on adolescents, this dominance of U.S.-based mediated cultural products is interesting when placed in a relation to a new geographic location, and also the ways in which branding has become linked to black male bodies. Hence access to representations of blackness that youth of African descent could either identify with or contest, the U.S. media would seem to exert a hegemonic hold over such conceptions in North America and the African diaspora.

The ability to produce and reproduce certain types of subjects often occurs through discourses and differing types of texts or language—print, photos, talk, and so on. So along with the growth in the ability of youth to access media technology and simulation has come an expansion of the "language" that is available for use in social interaction. Hence youth culture offers not just sites of pleasure, but also a source for what Paul Willis aptly identifies as symbolic creativity—the "ways in which young people use, humanise, decorate, and invest meanings within their common and immediate life spaces and social practices." This media-induced blurring of the boundaries between the local and the global has led to the reconceptualization of social experiences, knowledge, and identity as produced through the dominance of hip hop cultural formation. For many youth, this world of changing representations of culture and media that extends beyond geographic boundaries has become an important symbolic carrier for discourses of identity and "reality." It is through this process that media becomes the key mechanism for centralizing cultural power via cultural reception and the articulation of ideology into social formation. So it is that some theorists argue that youth culture has been one area in which mainstream white culture has been able to provide an ideological framework of symbols, concepts, and images through which we understand, interpret, and represent "racial differences." However, while hip hop culture has had an effect on all youth; youth of the African diaspora have been at an interesting intersection in terms of its representations and consumption.

Hence, the ability of the United States to disseminate its cultural forms around the globe via digital pulses has an effect on the formation of black youth identity as well as the social construction of racialized understandings and identities not just for its close neighbor Canada but many other nation states in Europe, Latin America, and Australasia. These shared racialized understandings are not individual responses but are constructed intersubjectively—shared to a degree by all members of a culture or subculture. Within these practices of consumption youth draw on media culture in order to represent and give meaning to everyday experiences and their identities. It is within this social space of symbolic activity that one can identify the ways in which youth receive and appropriate media culture.

Periodization is important in any analysis of youth culture and in examining hip hop culture and rap music in particular such periodization becomes even more acute. While many agree that the development of hip hop culture in the 1970s Bronx New York was a hybrid formation that had the potential to be oppositional; with changing times and its increased commodification during the 1990s this resistant potential has diminished. This change in the way in which oppositional meanings can be produced is reinforced through the representations of a specific variant of rap—namely gangsta—that the media produces and universalizes as the particular. Periodization of rap also appears consistently though discourses produced within rap. Empirical research indicates that such discursive practices construct a space of contestation that allows youth to position themselves in relation to discourses that reinforce binaries around the descriptors "old school" or "mainstream rap." Such dualism becomes symbolic as youth negotiate meanings in relation to their constructions of the "real" and authentic. Through this emphasis on authenticity and style "authenticity" has been constructed as one more style wherein values of truth and authenticity are regarded as set up in the dress codes and style of singing performers. Identification has come to the fore as an important aspect of the ways in which discourse which positions genuine rap as based upon "real" experiences in life and the "hood" and therefore more "authentic" than rap, which is based upon fantasy—a genre that is geared to a mainstream market and is produced purely for sales. Such discourses not only create a binary between mainstream rap and authentic rap, but further reinforces the argument that rappers speak with the authentic voice of personal experience.

It is evident that hip hop culture and rap has become not just commodified but also a resource for the reinforcement and production of stereotypical black subjectivity. Representations are not constructed in isolation, but often work in relation to other social formations in order to develop what Stuart Hall identifies as a "regime of representation." The films that are watched, the magazines that are read, and the music that is listened to offer an insight into the ways in which youth are able to create meanings from the varying media representations that they encounter. In examining youth culture one is struck by the degree of ideological "trace" that is evident in terms of these various cultural forms. So it is that critics such as bell hooks contend that the promotion of gangsta rappers reinforces the same old stereotypes about black men as hypersexual and predatory.

Illustrated in this process of representation is the way in which intertextuality is important in relation to meaning making, in other words the ways in which the historical and contemporary meanings can be aligned with broader discourses. Recognition of the alignment of meaning within a broader discourse allows one to analyze how the marketing and branding of black male bodies in particular is made easier because of the existing discourses that produce black subjectivity. So it is credible for discourses to produce black males as hypermasculine because of the centuries-old representations of black males that metonymically link them to physicality and body rather than intellect and mind. Similarly hip hop culture is represented as a male sphere where women are "hos" and "b****es" despite the attempt of female rappers to reverse such representations. Discourses of commodification highlight the ways in which blackness as a signifier articulates within a wider capitalist economic structure to produce racialized meanings in relation to rap.

Although rap music as a culture attempts to fix the meaning of blackness empirically this has proven problematic as youth of African descent fragment the presumed homogeneity through the lens of class, gender, and sexuality, as well as geographic region. Examination of these discourses illustrates the ways in which youth orient themselves to and within the discourses as well as the ways in which they use the discourses in their everyday lives. What is evident is that black identification is associated with specific discursive practices and is intertextual in nature. Use of phrases such as "acting black" problematizes the fixity of blackness and instead illustrates the contested nature of mediated black youth culture; how youth recognize that blackness is not fixed but is to some extent constructed through discourses. So it is that we can recognize at least two competing discourses that try to fix meaning around blackness: blackness as Black Nationalism and blackness as youth cultural style. Recognition of these changing discourses around the meaning of blackness for youth is evident in Paul Gilroy's book *Between Camps*, where he indicates the present-day triumph of blackness as style among youth.

Intellectuals and social theorists are an important part of any discursive formation and with rap they have played a role in mediating the reception and normative assumptions underlying its production. In particular, post-structural theories provided a receptive opening for early forms of rap as oppositional; such openness has to be rethought. As with all social and cultural formations one cannot assume that there exists within rap an essential meaning that remains fixed ahistorically. Further, this initial openness to rap as rebellious musical expression has allowed it to get away with various transgressive formations that consequently enable the free-flow of sexist and racialized discourses. In a similar vein the role of women in hip hop culture is a theoretically contested positioning. In some ways examination of youth culture as oppositional has reinforced the earlier critiques by theorists such as McRobbie and Jenny Garber that subcultural activity takes place primarily on the streets; a space that often remains taboo for girls. Further the alignment of youth culture with maleness and the "spectacular" aspects of hip hop has meant that much of the research emphasis has been on male consumers of rap music. Thus while it would be problematic to return to a simple and deterministic cultural imperialism model as favored by "mass culture" theorists such as Adorno and Horkheimer we nonetheless have to recognize that consumption is not innocent but is taking place within an ideologically driven capitalist framework. Keith Negus argues that music production and consumption is a business based upon a profit margin, and should be understood as a commercial enterprise driven by the profit margin. Thus any understanding of rap music has to take into account that music production is not purely a matter of aesthetics. It becomes part of a wider capitalist production, something to make money from. As such, production of rap becomes intertwined with racialized and aesthetic meanings that lead to positioning on issues that might, on the surface, be perceived as not related.

Resources

Giddens, A. (1990). *The consequences of modernity.* London: Polity Press.

Gillespie, M. (1995). *Television, ethnicity, and cultural change.* London: Routledge.

Gilroy, P. (2000). *Between camps*. London: Allen Lane, The Penguin Press.

Hall, S. (Ed.). (1997). *Representation, cultural representation, and signifying practices*. London: Sage.

Hall, S., & Jefferson, T. (Eds.). (1976). *Resistance through rituals: Youth subcultures in post-war Britain*. London: Hutchinson.

Harvey, D. (1989). *The condition of postmodernity*. Oxford: Blackwell Publishers.

Hebdige, D. (1979). *Subculture and the meaning of style*. London: Methuen.

hooks, bell. (2004). *We real cool: Black men and masculinity*. New York: Routledge.

Kelly, J. (2004). *Borrowed identities*. New York: Peter Lang.

Klein, N. (2000). *No logo: Taking aim at the brand bullies*. Toronto: Vintage Canada.

Negus, K. (1996). *Popular theory in music: An introduction*. Cambridge, MA: Polity Press.

Perkins, W. (Ed.). (1996). *Droppin' science: Critical essays on rap music and hip hop culture*. Philadelphia: Temple University Press.

Rose, T. (1994). *Black noise*. Hanover, NH: University Press of New England.

Thompson, J. (1990). *Ideology and modern culture*. Stanford, CA: Stanford University Press.

Walcott, R. (1995). *Performing the postmodern: Black Atlantic rap & identity in North America*. Unpublished doctoral thesis, University of Toronto, Toronto, Canada.

Willis, P. (1990). *Common culture*. Milton Keynes, UK: Open University Press.

LANGUAGE AND IDENTITY IN YOUTH CULTURE

Stacey Duncan

So what about language? As a shared system of communication we know that speakers within the same culture, or cultural group, and others who know the system participate. Every culture and sub-culture has a way of communicating, or talking to one another. Thus, at least in the abstract, language is a system of knowledge that produces communication, allowing knowledge to be passed back and forth between individuals. Conversations between two people who do not speak the same "language" can be difficult if there is no common or shared system of knowledge to refer to, for example, when the youth and their elders try to relate. We also know there are some universal and shared traits of languages, but humanity is a species most definitely varied in its language capabilities. This is obvious on a global scale when we consider just the difference in sound between say English and Japanese, but what about the not-so-obvious speech of say hip hop culture. For example, to the outsider the distinction between the lyrics of East versus West Coast rap may be unclear babble but to the insider the difference is just as obvious as the message. To dismiss something because it is unclear does not mean it is invalid. The notion here is that in Western society our hypermedia driven popular culture is a shared system of knowledge, a context that within our own cultural and subcultural spaces we communicate through. The way people think, especially about themselves and others, is in many ways guided by the language they speak. Through language, we self-identify as well as identify ourselves as part of a group.

Since the days of ancient Greece there has been debate about the relationship between language and thought, and how much one influences the other. The principle of linguistic relativity looks at the importance between thought and a language's organization or structure. Basically, how we understand reality, express ourselves, and behave with respect to it is because of the grammar of the language in question. Benjamin Lee Whorf coined the term "the principle of linguistic relativity" in the late 1930s in his essay *Linguistics as an Exact Science*, yet it is to this day more widely known and misunderstood as the Sapir-Whorf hypothesis, even though they were colleagues, Edward Sapir and Whorf did not coauthor such a hypothesis. With respect to issues of language, culture, and identity, the principle of linguistic relativity provides a unique lens into the worldview and perspectives of individuals and groups at micro and macro levels. What does this mean for learning, especially in a world of hypermedia, where language and communication take on alternative forms?

We can look at words as having meaning to the extent that they are engaged within a particular system of other words. An example could be the specialization of language in business, economics, politics, science, or technology, but by this definition so is the rhetoric of youth. After all there are regional and specialized dictionaries now: *The Hip Hoptionary, How to Talk American,* as well as numerous slang dictionaries. In the history of Western thought, the notions of universality and its opposite relativity have been presented as an either/or system where either you look at things by analyzing their differences or their similarities. This has the potential to provide a holistic understanding of reality if both sides were to come to the table, actually talk about the differences and similarities, and perhaps find a degree of complementarity, where differences and similarities are equally valued. Unfortunately, much of what we have seen is that one side claims superiority over the other and in this case, the differences are not considered as meaningful as the similarities thereby ignoring the voice of the voiceless in our society.

The idea behind the principle of linguistic relativity is that our Western individual and group ways of looking at the world, or our reality, is because of Indo-European language domination. It was through his research on the Hopi language that Whorf found that there was a relationship between the language (what they said) and culture (what they did) of the Hopi, which he then found as well in the Western or European languages and culture. It is clear that in the course of conversation, different speakers may represent elements of the same nonlinguistic context differently, they can share the same experience but not express it in the same way. That is, each speaker takes up a different referential and ideological perspective concerning the situation. Language then not only helps shape thought by directing specific attention to some aspects of experience rather than to others, but is also a mirror or reflection of our thoughts.

Exploring its vast array of knowledge for what it is truly worth, it is here that the principle of linguistic relativity might be a useful framework for looking at the patterns of popular culture that dominate our media driven society. Everyone has a variety of identities (not multiple personalities), and we use these identities depending on where we are situated within a social scene, like when we are in a classroom versus a sporting event. The media and popular culture are ultimately connected to the daily ways we express our social connections and construct our social identities. Thus, communication is a culturally conditioned way of speaking. If culture is the practice of group life, then cultural communication is the practice of expression within that group, stated or illustrated through representing symbols of identity, language being one of many.

Language then is not first and only a means of communication, but an interactional social accomplishment. It is a representative arrangement, a way of ordering and directing the hyper-abundance of information that overwhelm us, especially in this modern age. Since the beginning of the youth culture after World War II, a synergetic mutual dependence has developed between them and the media. The popular or media culture now provides its own terminology that represents particular individual and cultural beliefs and values. These can be broken down depending on which medium we are talking about, for instance art, music, film, television, or literature. For example, there are areas that reflect personal, local, national, and global beliefs and awareness. It is via these areas that a worldview is constructed for many youth that have been immersed in it since birth, and why it is so important to understand their language and not dismiss it as meaningless because it cannot be readily understood.

Although the language of youth may seem to be trivial because of its relationship to popular culture, a worldview can be identified and heard because it is a reflection of metaphors we live by. Every expression of difference or similarity in identity exists within all ways of communicating and more than ever in this age of globalization, it is through language and culture that we learn to read the world. The principle of linguistic relativity can provide a lens for understanding the way language patterns affect our beliefs of reality from the way the youth resonate with popular culture to the reasoning and science of Western civilization.

This concept may provide a point of convergence, a union that can strengthen our individual consciousness and reunite our cultural consciousness. This means that individually we need to know who we are and how we express who we are in different cultural contexts and what that personally means, as well as how our identity is situated within a local and global communal context. The diversity of cultural communication becomes by nature important to our symbols of identity. The time has certainly come for Western culture, communication, and identity to find its balance as well. Since language makes up a large portion of our thinking it is important to realize how communication includes the concept of self in our social interactions, and how such social interactions can negotiate the individual and social dimensions of selves in human relationships. In essence, our social agreements create meaning to our concept of self and identity, and these contracts are culturally fulfilled. The problem is that it is not fully recognized on an individual or local level, much less global.

So, if we know relativity is true, and our general thoughts about reality are not all there is to respect, we can begin to look at the relationship between language, culture, and identity. Multiplicity is more personal and cultural than ever before for it is a multicultural world we live in, extraordinary by the diversity of combined associations. Everyone may experience universals in living, but we have and will continue to do it differently across cultures, and even individually. Understanding the way our worldviews are influenced by language and the patterns that maintain those beliefs can create a bridge of awareness between the generations and cultures of our humanity. Cultures might not still be confined in the conventional way, but are nevertheless distinct and abundant, and mutually connected in this enigmatic web of life. Further research and analysis in this area requires an inclusive and relativistic process, demanding more than just discourse, but an applied nonconformity of our social conditions.

Language and culture are complementary, for you cannot have one without the other. In our social environment where all knowledge is dynamically interrelated among objects and beliefs, languages and cultures, people and places, and an environment where every connection cannot be recognized or understood; social definitions (regardless of our habit to stick to the usual and established) cannot be conclusive or finalized. Our popular media culture is a dominant form of communication and our ways of thinking about language, culture, and identity have to be as fluid and relative as possible.

Resources

Bennett, A., & Kahn-Harris, K. (2004). *After subculture: Critical studies in contemporary youth culture*. New York: Palgrave MacMillan.

Epstein, J. S. (Ed.). (1998). *Youth culture: Identity in a postmodern world.* Malden, MA and Oxford, UK: Blackwell.

Kellner, D. (1995). *Media culture: Culture studies, identity and politics between the modern and the postmodern.* London and New York: Routledge.

Ulrich, J. M., & Harris, A. L. (Eds.). (2003). *GenXegesis: Essays on alternative youth (sub)cultures.* Madison: University of Wisconsin Press.

Whorf, B. L. (1964). Languages and logic. In J. B. Carroll (Ed.). *Language, thought, and reality: Selected writings of Benjamin Lee Whorf* (pp. 233–245). Cambridge: MIT Press.

———. (1964). Language, mind, and reality. In J. B. Carroll (Ed.). *Language, thought, and reality: Selected writings of Benjamin Lee Whorf* (pp. 247–270). Cambridge: MIT Press.

———. (1964). Linguistics as an exact science. In J. B. Carroll (Ed.). *Language, thought, and reality: Selected writings of Benjamin Lee Whorf* (pp. 220–232). Cambridge: MIT Press.

LANGUAGE AND TALK

David Poveda

Researchers on language development often consider that by adolescence human beings have mastered most of the grammatical rules of their language and, therefore, beyond this age significant transformations in language development do not occur. However, the way we use language continues to change throughout our lives. We learn new ways of talking and become familiar with special kinds of written texts through education, training, and work. We live with diverse groups of people who have different ways of speaking—accents, expressions, localisms—that we, consciously and unconsciously, incorporate into our own language use. In later childhood we become aware that the ways we talk, dress, and behave are how we show who we are to the rest of the world. Through speaking, choosing what to wear, and behaving differently according to the situation, we express a wide set of personal identities, social characteristics, and values.

Adolescence and youth are periods of life, especially in industrialized nations, in which these processes are especially visible because during

41

adolescence we work hard to construct new identities and personalities. Transformations in language use can be seen as part of a broader effort to develop a particular *youth style* that along with language, includes forms of self-presentation (dress and body care), investment in academic and non-academic activities (sports or computers), or musical preferences (house or grunge.) Appropriating a style of one's own has important social functions that help adolescents and youth build their own identities. All youth styles help set apart, as an age group, adolescents and youth from children and adults, but especially from adults. Adolescents work to achieve more autonomy and responsibility than they were allowed during childhood but do not want to be identified with their parents and other surrounding adults. Creating a distinctive age style helps achieve this. Yet, adolescent identity is not primarily built in opposition to adults. Rather, relationships with other adolescents are the major influences in adolescent identity development. Consequently, groups of adolescents and youth develop different and complex styles that help them to be seen as different kinds of youth. These distinctions are simultaneously constructed on both global and local levels. On one hand, broad categories exist (such as "punk," "hip hopper," or "raver") which allow adolescents to identify common traits of these styles across many countries in the world. On the other hand, youth styles are tied to the social networks to which adolescents and youth actually belong and in which they participate. These peer relations define distinct local styles (for example, the high school "burnouts" or "nerds") that relate to how ethnic, gender, class, and geographical distinctions are played out in each particular context.

Language has a role in the development of these youth styles and social activities. The invention of new words, the development of new systems of communication and the use of particular forms of talk are three aspects of language that are integral to the formation of youth styles.

INVENTING AND USING NEW WORDS

Probably the most easily identifiable and commented aspect of adolescents' talk is how they invent new words or transform the meaning of available words to refer to particular objects, situations or activities—a process described in linguistics as *lexical innovation*. This accumulation of vocabulary is what is often thought of as slang. Yet, just as it is surprising to count the number of new terms used by youth, it is their fate that many new terms become quickly outdated and cease to be used by successive cohorts of adolescents. The use of particular words illustrates clearly the two social functions of style: separation from adults and distinction from peers.

A common definition of slang considers it a vocabulary related to taboo topics and activities. Coining new words is a way of protecting certain activities and events from adult surveillance. In this way, lexical innovation is especially active in areas that are illicit or usually censored by parents and adults, such as alcohol and drug consumption. In many countries we can find a large number of terms to refer to each particular drug and especially to states of intoxication. For example, in American English "baked," "blasted," and "blitzed" are terms for the state of intoxication. In Iberian Spanish some similar terms are "puesto," "tostado," or "pedo." However, these terms only serve their purpose if they change rapidly, since current adults were once young and would easily identify the terminology if it did not change. For example, "stoned" is clearly considered an outmoded term by contemporary North American youth.

Lexical innovation does not only occur in relation to taboo topics, it also takes place within the context of activities in which youth may specialize as part of their identity and construction of style. These activities may not necessarily be censored by adults (for example, role-playing games or making music) or may be considered more or less illicit depending on the context (for example, skateboarding or graffiti). Engagement in these leisure activities introduces adolescents and youth into particular social networks and peer groups that distinguish each other in terms of their investment in particular areas of youth culture. Also, participating in them demands learning new skills, behaviors, or rules, and also a specialized vocabulary, a jargon, related to each particular area of expertise. For example, each of the labels and adjectives relating to different musical sub-styles or the terminology for different aspects of songs and song composition are part of the specialized vocabulary of music fans. Consequently, individual adolescents can be distinguished from each other through their familiarity with the specialized vocabularies that result from individual connection with different activities and styles.

Slang and jargon knowledge can be used as measures of an adolescent's real involvement with the youth styles to which that particular individual declares affiliation. The relationship between vocabulary and involvement may be of interest to researchers since often it is easier to access and observe youth vocabulary (for example, drug terminology) than the actual activities that may be hidden from adults (for example, actual drug use). Peers also use this relationship to assess each individual's vocabulary, along with other aspects of appearance and behavior, as a means to distinguish the experts from the novices or even the more contentious pretenders. For example, when an individual "gears up" to act and talk as a "hip hopper" but is found laughable by peers because the peers do not see her or him as a real "hip hopper."

In summary, lexical innovation is an aspect of youth language and talk that, in comparison to other aspects, is accessible and flexible; vocabulary reflects the dynamics of peer groups both in relation to each other and to adults.

DEVELOPING NEW SYSTEMS OF COMMUNICATION

Another feature of language use in youth is the development of new systems of communication or *codes*. A code can be considered a more complex system that is not limited to a vocabulary and includes other levels of language and rules of production. Communication systems produced through graphic representations that go beyond conventional writing and include aspects such as shape, texture, and color to transmit meaning are part of youth cultural productions. In comparison to the lexical level, codes may have a more gradual development, but also tend to be more stable through time, allowing for certain key features of the code to be present in different reinterpretations of the system.

One reason this stability occurs is because innovative youth codes often become familiar, through media and commercial appropriations, to both youth and adults of successive generations and become conventionalized. A classic example of a youth code is graffiti painting and writing. For several decades now, throughout many cities of the world, graffiti has spread as a form of cultural expression, tying linguistic messages with other visual elements. However, graffiti has also been incorporated to mainstream culture, recycled for commercial purposes, and in certain circles is even seen as a legitimate form of artistic expression. This does not mean that graffiti is not still practiced by adolescents and youth, but its potential subversive meaning is constantly being transformed as graffiti has become more acceptable and mainstream.

Other examples of youth codes, in this case with a closer tie to literacy, are fanzines: underground and non-commercial publications that specialize in different topics of interest to youth (particular musical tendencies, such as "hard-core," or various political orientations). Each family of fanzines, as print mediums reflective of particular youth styles, develops its own representative ways of using non-conventional writing, a special vocabulary and mixing written texts with other graphical representations—photographs, colors, symbols. However, again many original elements designed in fanzines have been taken up by commercial media and publications that have as target audience adolescents, youth, and even young adults, but which most often are not produced by adolescents or youth themselves.

A final example of the development of a code in which adolescents have played an important role is the different adaptations that conventional writing has experienced when used in mobile short message systems (SMS). In this instance, the code can be considered the result of very practical constraints, each graphic symbol has a cost and, therefore, adolescents have attempted to develop conventions that are both cost effective and informative. In the case of SMS, adolescents can be considered the innovators of the code but their innovations do not necessarily carry other social and cultural meanings (or at least not as many as graffiti or fanzines), since they are quickly incorporated by message system users of all ages. Nevertheless, when the conventions of the SMS code are transposed to other writing activities, the origin of the code becomes more visible. On one hand, in recent years (at least in Spain) teachers have complained about the new family of writing mistakes and problems that their students are producing as a result of applying abbreviations and transformations common to SMS in school writings where these conventions are neither appropriate nor necessary—at most, academic writing tasks have a maximum number of words, not graphic symbols, per text. On the other hand, commercial messages (and even public campaigns) that are not tied to the constraints of SMS, may nevertheless present their written announcements using features of the SMS code when the intended audiences are adolescents and youth.

In summary, youth language is not limited to oral aspects but has also produced different kinds of communicative systems that combine transformations of writing with other graphic and visual elements. Also, since the production of these codes tends to be a more stable process, they have allowed for different forms of contact with the adult social and economic world.

ENGAGING IN CERTAIN FORMS OF TALK

The final aspect of youth language to be discussed is the production of language as part of routine social interactions. At this level the interest centers on stretches of talk longer than words and sentences, what is normally described as *discourse*. Focusing on discourse is important for several reasons. First, language actually takes place not as isolated words and sentences, but as an organized whole (discourse) through which people carry on with social life. Second, each of the aspects discussed above (vocabulary and codes) occur within discourse. New words are invented and used as part of larger speech activities and codes are constructed in a combination of writing, graphic production, and talk about the task. Third, while vocabulary was examined in terms of adolescents' group and individual knowledge, and codes were seen as more abstract cultural products, discursive production is the level where most clearly each individual's skills and verbal styles are displayed.

Often it is possible to identify in the peer group one or more individuals who stand out for their verbal skills. Friends who are good storytellers or those who are always fast with their retorts are looked upon for their contributions to the peer group's language repertory. These individuals, described as *sociolinguistic icons* by discourse researchers, are usually at the forefront of innovation of youth language and set the standard of performance in complex speech activities, whether these are rather well known and routine (for example, "playing the dozens" within an African American community) or are less articulated but identifiable (such as Valspeak in California).

Also, it is at the level of forms of talk where the relationship between aspects of language and other components of social identity, such as gender, ethnicity, class, geographical location, or institutional role, is more explicitly exploited. Some researchers approach this relationship as a mathematical value, a correlation between a fixed social category, such as class, ethnicity, or gender, and some feature of language, such as vocabulary, but most often a specific feature of accent—a contraction, a change in grammar. In this way, existing correlations can be claimed to be meaningful regardless of whether speakers are aware of their presence.

However, through the purposeful construction of specific forms of talk, adolescents and youth can make explicit associations between the way they are choosing to talk at a given moment, the meaning they are trying to convey to the activity, and their own identities within the activity. In this way, discourse makes visible the relationship between talk itself, speakers, and social values or beliefs associated to that particular way of talking. For example, a study of a multi-ethnic group of British teenagers showed how teenagers of several ethic groups (Pakistani and white Anglo) used mock variations of Stylized Asian English (SAE) during detention or in class to address adults in school and subvert the institutional relationship between pupils and teachers. In this case, SAE use recalls the colonial relationship between the British and their subordinate Indians and Pakistanis, a relationship which is not considered appropriate in contemporary British schools and made adults uncomfortable. In a similar manner, among themselves, teenagers of all ethnic origins (white Anglo, Pakistani, and Afro-Caribbean) used and adapted several features of Creole, which has its origins in British Black English, since this was the form of talk more clearly associated with a cool street culture to which all teenagers wanted to belong.

In summary, discourse reveals adolescent and youth verbal creativity at work. Youth discourse provides a means for researchers to examine how this creativity may be used to question and exploit the complex relationships that exist between language, social values, and aspects of personal identity such as gender, ethnicity, social class, or geographical location.

In conclusion, an overview of different aspects of youth language and talk provides evidence of very sophisticated skills put into action. Therefore, popular accounts of how adolescents' language is degrading and how this, in turn, will degrade overall language quality should be questioned. These panics are voiced every other decade and only prove that youth are succeeding in using language to socially demarcate themselves as an age group in very complex ways.

Resources

Androutsopoulos, J. K. (2000). Non-standard spellings in media texts: The case of German fanzines. *Journal of Sociolinguistics,* 4 (4), 514–533.

Bucholtz, M. (2002). Youth and cultural practice. *Annual Review of Anthropology,* 31, 525–552.

Chambers, J. K. (2003). *Sociolinguistic theory* (2nd ed.). Oxford: Blackwell.

Eckert, P. (2000). *Linguistic variation as social practice.* Oxford: Blackwell.

Rampton, B. (1995). *Crossing: Language and ethnicity among adolescents.* London: Longman.

PROBLEMATIZING THE "PROBLEM" TEEN: RECONCEPTUALIZING ADOLESCENT DEVELOPMENT

Kathryn Herr

THE SOCIAL CONSTRUCTION OF THE PROBLEM OF TEENAGERS

In the United States, youth, particularly teenagers, are often defined in the negative. It is not uncommon to hear about the "youth crisis" or "the youth problem." Headlines in local and national newspapers report incidents of adolescent violence and the public has come to believe that these are very common occurrences. Youth involvement in areas such as crime and violence is proportionally very small and is, in fact, on the decline, yet these facts do little to puncture popular public perception that believes otherwise.

An image persists in the United States of an adolescent age cohort that is troubling to the general society. The life stage of adolescence[1] has inaccurately been described as a period of "storm and stress" where teenagers are seen as difficult and contrary. Another common description is that adolescents are prey to "raging hormones," where their bodies overrule their minds, leading them astray; this characterization belittles the capabilities of adolescents in terms of growing into their own bodies and judgments.

Adolescents in general are seen as a problematic population, with the problems said to reside within that age cohort rather than in the society that has created them. This image persists despite data that indicate that most teenagers' relationships with their parents and other authorities are much less stormy than has generally been thought. Rarely are adolescents seen as viable partners or creative collaborators in the construction of the social fabric of society. They are more likely defined by what they are not—neither child nor adult. While the United States may stand out in its particular negativity toward the next generation, some couple this with a youth image problem around the world. It is thought that adolescence may well be the most maligned and misunderstood age group in the larger culture.

The actual life stage of adolescence is socially and historically variable, dependent on the coming to adulthood within the context of current economic circumstances, social norms, and policies. Today there is an increased period of adolescence because of prolonged preparation for the workplace and the increasing numbers of college-bound youth. Previously the transition to adulthood was fairly straightforward because of the stable nature of the occupational world. While in the past meaningful roles were learned in the workplace, today's adolescents have few opportunities to demonstrate responsibility and participate in meaningful societal roles.

A sense of rolelessness in current society is one of the most common dilemmas of adolescents. This is particularly problematic given fundamental needs among youth to find a sense of belonging and to feel a sense of worth as a person. Available jobs for teenagers have changed from one where it was possible to learn skills (farming, crafts, factories) to an employment landscape made up of sales and service (fast food for example). This latter category of jobs is typically educationally irrelevant and the jobs themselves are often age-segregated, limiting the kinds of apprentice types of interactions with adults that have previously been available.

In the past, adolescents frequently followed their parents' footsteps into the labor market, growing into a world they were assuming that reflected established class and gender-based relationships. They had an awareness early on that their familial and societal roles would be similar to that of their parents; adults provided adolescents with applicable role models. In short, the work world, which previously was an area that helped to prepare adolescents for the transition to adulthood, rarely provides that kind of opportunity or support today.

Beyond this, changes in the modern family have meant that interactions with siblings and parents that used to be routine are not as available today. Because of contemporary economics, parents typically work more hours outside the home and have less time for family life. Extracurricular activities and other organized activities serve as substitutes for interactions that routinely occurred in the family. David Elkind, a scholar of child development and family life, makes the case that each family member is now expected to be independent, achievement-oriented, competent, and able to go it alone.

These shifts in social structures that helped foster the transition to adulthood leave youth vulnerable to the manipulation of other forces. For example, mass media attempts to sell identity scripts to youth, often based on stereotypical gendered and sexualized images. In addition, today's teenagers are seen as an important segment of the consumer market and this consumer role plays into adolescents' sense of self-identity. Youth use consumer goods for both a sense of fitting in and standing out, both of which play a role in identity development.

Significant changes, then, have taken place in the context in which youth are growing up. There seems to be a consensus that these changes threaten adolescents' capacities to grow in positive ways. Rather than focusing on societal shifts that fray the "social container" for today's adolescents, more often youth themselves are villanized. Within a discourse of "personal responsibility" and accountability for one's own actions, attention is diverted from a society that may or may not support its youth, to the youths themselves and "youth problems."

"Kid fixing" has become a growth industry in the United States, with a focus on intervention of one kind or another for individual offenders or deviants. Mental health practitioners make solid profits offering therapy to privately insured youth. For those at the other end of the economic spectrum, often coupled with minority status, confinement of youth in prisons continues to grow dramatically. Numbers of youth correctional facilities increased many times over during the last decade and the youth treatment industry is worth billions of dollars per business year. The irony of these interventions lies in the desire to remove individual youth from society to keep other members of society safe; the question of how society might put youth at risk begs to be asked but goes unaddressed.

WHO ARE ADOLESCENTS?

The answer to this depends on the socio-historical era in which the question is located. Two hundred years ago in the United States it was not uncommon for urban youth, by ages twelve or thirteen, to move directly from school into the workplace. Their work was seen as an integral part of the family's survival. They often moved into these adult roles before they had experienced puberty. In this era, the idea of an extended period of adolescence, marked by a space in between childhood and adulthood, was unheard of. By the early 1900s, stricter child labor laws were in place and the school years were extended. Youth of this era had fewer adult responsibilities. They were less likely to spend their days with adults since they were out of the workplace and in school. The stage of adolescence was born.

Also over the past two hundred years, children have been reaching puberty at younger ages. This is thought to be the result of better nutrition and hygiene and the control of many infectious diseases. The average age of menarche dropped during this time from sixteen to twelve. Ironically, this change has occurred simultaneously with a postponement of adulthood. Adolescents are going to college in increasing numbers, thereby prolonging a period of dependence and preparation for the future. The past fifty years have seen the widest separation ever experienced between the timing of sexual maturation and the assumption of adult roles such as marriage. Between the physical and social shifts, adolescence can currently be said to span ages ten or eleven through college students in their twenties. Some describe adolescence as a "waiting period" since they have few responsibilities or meaningful roles; they are not yet seen as "full citizens" of the country.

Of course, adolescents are not a monolithic group and the portraits offered of them need to be stratified across gender, racial, and social class lines. So, while more adolescents are going to college, minority and inner-city, low income youth face many more barriers to attending school. For example, well known statistics indicate that inner-city, African American young males are more likely to end up in lock-up than in a college classroom. At the same time, those without a college education face a difficult economic future. For past generations, unionized employment was available, allowing a middle class lifestyle despite a lack of higher education. These kinds of jobs have increasingly disappeared and have been replaced with more service type jobs, the foundation for those characterized as the working poor.

The United States is one of the leading multiethnic nations in the world. Although a majority proportion of the elder population of the country is white of European ancestry, over a third of youth under eighteen are nonwhite or are of Hispanic origin. This plurality of youth has been on the rise since the 1970s and every indication is that it will continue to increase. In some urban areas, the phenomenon of a minority majority youth population has become increasingly common.

Because the period of adolescence has been extended, it is common to divide it into two developmental periods, early and late adolescence. Early adolescence is usually seen as the ages ten to fourteen and is regarded as an increasingly significant developmental period. Early adolescence is a time of physical, sexual, and psychological awakening, a time of such change that it has been equated with the rapid growth of an infant who enters toddlerhood. This incredible physical growth coincides with major changes in the social lives of early adolescents as they move from elementary school to middle school.

Identity issues permeate the whole adolescent period, with adolescents addressing the questions "Who am I?" and "Who can I become?" For early adolescents, it is thought that they first engage these questions through affiliation with others their age. They take on a "group identity" where through their choices of affiliation they are essentially saying to other members of their group: "I am like you." Early adolescent culture is permeated with the presence of "cliques" that reflect these choices.

Later adolescence, ages fifteen and up, brings youth closer to the issues and eventual roles of adulthood. During this time, it is expected that an adolescent would begin to form a sense of self that is distinct from friends and family. While sharing some traits and beliefs in common with both of these important groups, at the same time an adolescent may exert his or her differences from them. This sense of distinctness is a hallmark of adolescent behaviors. There is also an emphasis on future thinking during this time, where adolescents begin to envision life possibilities, or conversely, begin to lose hope in a personal future for themselves. These choices are reflected in choices such as planning for college and dropping out of high school.

THEORETICAL FRAMING OF ADOLESCENCE

A theory of adolescent development is, in part, about creating a portrait of the "normal" adolescent's pathway of growth. At the same time, predominant developmental models are a reflection of societal values that a culture wants to instill in its youth. While designed to illuminate the experience of adolescence, developmental theory also becomes a guiding frame for shaping youth into roles seen as acceptable and necessary to sustain a given culture.

In the United States, the work of Erik Erikson has, for the past several decades, been a major theoretical construct in terms of defining "normal" development across the lifespan. He theorized that at each stage of development there were "tasks" for an individual to resolve. The resolution could be a positive building block for the next stage or, if the resolution was not successful, it could become more difficult to tackle the next developmental task. The task that Erikson describes for adolescence is the formation of a sense of identity. Part of this work includes forming an occupational identity. If the task of forming a sense of identity is not resolved successfully, Erikson believed it would lead to identity confusion or the inability to assume a productive role in the American culture.

The belief was that successful identity development was predicated on the earlier task of "industry," experienced during the end of elementary school and into middle school. During this stage individuals get a sense of their own capabilities and the rewards that can come to them in the society in which they live. For example, success in school can help a young student see herself as someone who is capable and who has a bright future. This is sometimes referred to as the time where individuals learn the "rules of the game" and how to play it.

Many theorists, Erikson included, stress that the pathway to identity development is separation from others, to form a distinct sense of self. Typically called individuation,[2] this phase is described by terms such as autonomy, self-reliance, and independence. Valuing of individuation has both permeated our culture as well as been cultivated by it. Expressions like "stand on your own two feet," "self made man," or "he pulled himself up by his bootstraps" sum up the sense of this concept. It is seen as preparing the groundwork for individualistic competition in both educational and economic settings.

In this framework, the process of development is one of disconnection and differentiation, first from the mother and later from mentors, teachers, and other important adults as well as from the natural world. Only later in the life cycle, after the adolescent develops a strong sense of self, is intimacy seen as possible. Prior to this, intimacy and empathy can be as experienced as threats to autonomy, agency, and self-determination.

This process of becoming one's own person involves two complementary and essential aspects of the identity development process: the sense of developing one's *personal identity*, where the adolescent reflects on one's talents and weaknesses, to bring to bear on a sense of *social identity*, that is, what the adolescent brings to the socio-historical context in which the person grows and develops. The idea is to form a sense of an integrated identity which comes from bringing a consistent sense of self and one's individual talents into congruence with the creativity needed to further construct and sustain the traditions of the society in which one resides. The role of society and the previous generations is to spell out the societal history, traditions, and symbols that youth need to consider as they grow toward their adult selves and roles.

In reviewing the key points of Erikson's theory of growth and development then, the pathway is a linear one, building on successful resolution of tasks in previous stages, toward individuation and adulthood; the individual is shaped in relation to his or her society and the ideas that that society espouses for its own perpetuation. The individual is being prepared to take part in an ongoing regeneration of societal values and goals. As stated earlier, current values in this Western framework include self-reliance, independence, autonomy, and self-actualization. A model of separation and individuation as the developmental pathway for youth can serve well the goals of a capitalistic society where "success" depends on self-reliance, competition with others, and self-enhancement.

The model described by Erikson, then, becomes a virtual prescription of what should happen or is expected to happen as youth grow and develop. This model has become part of the norming of youth, shaping them into their expected roles for the "good of society." Yet a parallel conversation bemoans a sense of alienation in our Western culture and a lack of community. This sense of alienation has been linked to the traits of individuated identity: look out for self and advance beyond those seen as competitors. In addition, a case has been made that this sense of a psychological separation from others leads to a quest for power over others and power over natural resources. Not much in this conception of identity prepares adolescents to take their place *in community*, whether with other human beings or in a sense of sustaining the planet.

Erikson's model of adolescent identity development is not without its detractors who offer both critique and alternative conceptualizations of developmental pathways. For the past twenty years, Jean Baker Miller and others at the Wellesley Stone Center have offered a lens where growing into a sense of self comes about in relation to others. In the "self-in-relation" viewpoint, an adolescent grows into a sense of self through relating to others in mutual, life enhancing ways. Affiliation with others is valued more highly than self-enhancement. The groundwork for this sense of relatedness is laid in infants' relationships with their caretakers when the infants' needs are reliably met.

As the theoretical model continued to be developed, Miller and the other scholars at the Wellesley Stone Center renamed their approach from self-in-relation to the Relational/Cultural Model. From this perspective, they put forth the idea that in addition to laying a foundation for trust in the world as a nurturing space, the infant is also beginning to develop an internal sense of self as a being-in-relationship; this is characterized as a dynamic interaction where each pay attention to the other's mental state and emotions. Miller and others believe that this early interaction lays the foundation for the ongoing development of relationships. This experience helps to cultivate the intrinsic inner awareness and responsiveness to the continuous existence of others and the expectation of mutuality in relationships.

The difference in this conception of the self is that the sense of being a "relater" empowers the adolescent to act for oneself as well as for the general welfare of others. The Relational/Cultural model involves an important shift in emphasis from separation to relationship as the basis for self-experience and development. Further, relationship is seen as the basic goal of development: that is, the deepening capacity for relationship and relational competence. The Relational/Cultural Model assumes that other aspects of self (e.g., creativity, autonomy, assertion) develop within this primary context.

The idea is that one comes to know more about oneself through affiliation and attachment to others. In taking care of the relationship between them, each can feel pleasure in their own as well as the other's competence. Relational energy is seen as empowering each to a sense of agency-in-community. From this perspective, being in relationships also involves the capacity to identify with a unit larger than the single self and this is coupled with a motivation to care for this new, larger unit.

This sense of being able to identify with a larger unit, and a sense that one's own development occurs in relationship with others, redefines affiliation from a threat to autonomy and individuation to one of mutually enhancing growth in community. Events that seemed threatening from a separation/individuation model are redefined and are seen instead as satisfying, motivating and empowering. From this model's framework, one's intellect and initiative are not self-serving but rather requires a simultaneous responsibility for the care and growth of others and the natural world. Miller sees the possibility of redefining notions of power away from domination, mastery or power over, to a "power with" or "power together" model; this shift implies the capacity to produce change in arenas larger than those for one's own self aggrandizement.

Erik Erikson primarily studied the developmental pathway of males and then generalized his findings to the total population. In contrast, the Relational/Cultural theorists have written primarily about the development of girls and women. Their premise is not that there is a fundamentally different developmental pathway for girls and boys as much as that the cultural constructs and socialization around maleness and femaleness are different.

Miller has pointed out that while all begin life in relationships of deep attachment, boys are encouraged to move away from this way of being. They are actively encouraged to suppress certain relational sensitivities such as crying when seeing someone in pain or experiencing sadness or pain themselves. Instead boys are taught a stance of "toughness" and invulnerability. The idea is that they are being socialized to be good competitors, where empathy for others or being "soft" could be a drawback in an alienated, competitive work world.

Through this kind of socialization the importance of affiliation recedes in boys' lives and they psychically organize themselves around a striving for individuation. In essence, in Western culture, a boy is not encouraged to continue the development of his "being-in-relation." It is thought that he has the same relational needs for connectedness as his female counterparts but has been deterred from the further acknowledgment of them. While girls are encouraged to continue to develop their sense of others, empathizing with and caring for them, boys are systematically diverted from this through our social constructions of maleness and manhood. Gradually the importance of affiliation is displaced in boys' lives and they psychically organize themselves around a striving for individuation. Relational/Cultural theorists see this displacement as a loss both for the individual boy as well to the larger societal structure.

Girls and women in Western society then become the "carriers" of various aspects of the human experience. Traits such as connection, affiliation, and mutual relations, while important for the functioning of a culture, have been undervalued along with their female "carriers." It is thought though that in seeking to understand development from a perspective different than that of Erikson's pathway to identity through individuation, models of the "self" are opened to encompass more fully the range of human possibilities and a different sustaining vision of the society in which those selves are expressed.

Theory is a socio-cultural creation, bound in historical context and time. The work of Erikson is in congruence with dominant discourses that are all about preparing adolescents to eventually, successfully, take their places in the economic structure of the U.S. Miller and others suggest that the very notion of a successful life could be redefined to encompass values of affiliation, relationship, and connection to a larger community in which one finds oneself. What remains insidious for youth is that individualistic notions of success are still the popular measuring stick whereby they will be seen as "making it" or as failures; it is the discourse whereby they may be seen as "at risk."

WHO IS "AT RISK?"

There is a growing discourse and literature addressing "at risk" youth. The term has become commonplace in describing a whole segment of youth who are seen as in danger of not assuming constructive adult roles in society, who may sour their life chances long before they reach adulthood. In the U.S., current trends in risky behavior by teens are tracked—substance abuse, risky sexual behaviors, delinquency, etc.; these are quantified to develop a schema of "common characteristics" of high-risk youth. The work on high-risk youth typically frames youth problems from a deficit model; youth problems are treated as private and personal failings, essentially a "blaming the victim" mentality. This youth risk discourse is set within a larger belief system of meritocracy, that is, all successes are individually earned rather than a possible benefit of being in a privileged place in society. According to this point of view, if individuals are not "making it," it is their own individual failure.

In contrast, many children of privilege receive and internalize both tacit and explicit messages concerning their "right" to see their privileges perpetuated. Youth of privilege often benefit from having parents who are "successes," that is, are highly educated, have accumulated wealth and resources that allow them to provide opportunities to their children. Whereas many nations have committed strong public policies to the welfare of families, and consider the care and welfare of the young a basic social right, the United States has yet to do so. Families in the U.S. are virtually on their own in terms of providing care for their children and are judged according to the same standards of success of failures as individuals are, that is, how much private wealth they can accumulate to "take care of their own." The definition of "at risk" used implicitly points to what kinds of interventions will be considered. Most often the term reflects an individualistic notion of social and educational failure rather than pointing the lens at a larger societal realm that creates inequity and perpetuates privilege.

BEYOND TRANSITORY TO UNIQUE CONTRIBUTIONS

Adolescents are often seen as on their way to becoming—hopefully productive adults who will have something to offer to society. The life stage of adolescence, then, is seen from a transitory view rather than as a valued period in and of itself. Invisible in this view are the contributions adolescents currently offer the culture. Rather than a preparation to contribute, the suggestion is that during this growth period to adulthood, adolescents have much to offer a culture in their own right.

Part of the thinking in terms of adolescents preparing to be adults is the idea that they will continue to perpetuate the culture, carrying on the norms that have been important in any given society. While adolescents are shaped and socialized by cultural norms, and internalized throughout their development, at the same time they appropriate and reinvent the culture. This is done through their interactions with adults as well as fellow adolescents. The suggestion made by some theorists of adolescents is that they affect and are affected by major societal events and developments. In this way they participate in the evolution of a culture, perpetuating it while also remaking it, encouraging new shapes and growth.

Adolescents have always made contributions to society but the nature of this has changed. These were more easily seen during the days when the country was agrarian or prior to the current era of an extended adolescence. Their concrete contributions to the family's economic welfare were easily evident. In the current era, formal schooling is the "work" of adolescents. This should not be seen as a break from the times when they were more productive but rather the current iteration of this productivity. An educated citizenry is an investment in the economic health of any modern society.

MONITORING ADOLESCENT WELL-BEING

Some have issued a call to move beyond fragmented interventions and turn instead to a more comprehensive inquiry into the underlying conditions that create the experiences of youth on the margins. Shifting away from calculating characteristics of youth "at risk," others are suggesting a monitoring of youth well-being. Just as the framing of "at riskness" as an individual problem implicitly points to the directions considered for interventions, assessing the environment for youth's well-being raises new possibilities for analysis and intervention.

Any social problem that can be broken apart to highlight how a social problem is disproportionately represented in a culture could begin to shed light on interventions at a larger level. If the suggestion is that success in school is the current work and contribution of adolescents to our culture, it could be of benefit to explore what groups are currently not succeeding in school and ask who is leaving school prior to finishing. Much data suggests that educators are currently serving middle and upper class, Caucasian students well, but leaving behind other diverse segments of the population. This is particularly important in light of data trends that indicate our schools and society will be increasingly diverse. Those currently most disadvantaged in schools include Latinos and African Americans.

From a monitoring well-being perspective, the goal becomes not so much one of individuals succeeding or failing, although that of course, is important. But rather, what kind of societal interventions, in this case in schools and our educational systems, would provide an environment that allows diverse students to succeed. This moves away from the judgment of an adolescent as a success or failure to a questioning of how we as a society have failed a particular group; it also allows shifts on a societal level as a remedy beyond pathologizing those who do not succeed in the current educational arrangements. We would move as a society beyond individualistic terms of success to one where we join in cultivating the success of others and appreciating their contributions to the larger society. From this lens, our sense of relatedness to each other would allow a fostering of each other's success rather than seeing it as a threat to our own.

Notes

1 Adolescence is regarded as a period of development between the ages of eleven and the early twenties; it is seen as a time when youth are preoccupied with identity issues, asking questions such as "Who am I?" and "Who can I be?"

2 Individuation is defined as the progressive sense of becoming an independent, autonomous being.

Resources

Davis, N. (1999). *Youth crisis: Growing up in the high-risk society.* Westport, CT: Praeger.

Erikson, E. (1968). *Identity: Youth and crisis.* New York: W. W. Norton.

Jordan, J. V., Kaplan, A. G., Miller, J. B., Stiver, I. P., & Surrey, J. L. (1991). *Women's growth in connection: Writing from the Stone Center.* New York: Guilford Press.

What's Your Way Out?

Kyle Adams

As I sit and stare into the back of my mind
I tend to reflect on the year 19 double 9
At a young age I figured how to get mine
Which leads to bigger dreams in time.

I dreamed ghetto dreams of being rich
Dreams of leaving out this B****
It frustrated me so much
to see poverty and then a jail house bus
Now it's 20-04 with the cops stay harassing us!

My dreams have changed to become a billionaire
With a Master Company Name
Yeah it's time to flip the game
Education by any means necessary
You should of heard the same
Obstacles in my way like
Bush winning the election, seems I'll be the
selection for his master plan for perfection

But you see this very spot will be the reason
Why I've reached the top
Haters I'm coming up so don't fuss
Wanna come grab your metro card
And get on the bus

ADOLESCENT RITES OF PASSAGE

Lynn M. Hoffman

Although all adolescents in our society eventually navigate their passage from late childhood to adulthood, few universally accepted benchmarks or markers guide their journey or indicate that they have accomplished their goal. Our culture lacks a systematic way of transitioning adolescents into adulthood, and we do not identify a set of achievements that would mark that status. As a result of weakening institutional ties, contemporary adolescents must look elsewhere to mark their passage from childhood to young adulthood. Part time jobs and driving now supply adolescents with proof of their growing independence. Classic school rituals and events contribute to the high school's role as a four-year rite of passage experience, although they are rarely connected to academics. Some researchers believe that a state of elongated adolescence exists because we do not have a clear, unquestionable way to identify the point at which an adolescent becomes an adult.

In primitive societies, passage into adulthood is more closely aligned with physical maturity. Children of a certain age participate in detailed rituals and ceremonies painstakingly constructed by adults that are observed with great interest by all members of their society. Participants emerge from these proscribed rituals as adult members of their society. These ceremonies and rituals contain the three required stages of a true rite of passage. First, there is the separation or preliminal stage in which the participants and those around them recognize that a change in the usual sets of social relations is coming. Next, there is a transition or liminal stage in which adolescents, under the supervision of adults, engage in the activities and learning that is required to pass to the next stage. Upon completing the transition phase, adolescents enter the third passage stage, the incorporation, reaggregation, or post liminal stage. Completion of a prescribed ritual may not instantaneously produce the desired status change. However, participation in the ritual creates anxiety in individuals as they recognize the growing expectations and responsibilities associated with their changed status. Individuals experiencing this state of anxiety are particularly susceptible to the symbols and signs attached to the rituals they are undergoing, and they grow into their new status over time.

In 1909, Arnold Van Gennup, an expert in rite of passage research, noted the importance of separating the attainment of physical maturity from social maturity, especially in modern societies. For example, in the United States, the average age of menarche has declined from fifteen years old in the 1840s to about twelve and a half years today. Although endowed with the physical capacity to reproduce at age twelve or younger, few would consider middle school girls to be adults. Existing rites of passage ceremonies, limited as they are, help adolescents attain the social maturity that is more elusive and less specifically identified in American society. In our society, traditional marriage is a rite of passage that tends to confer adult status to the married couple. In keeping with the three stage process embedded in a rite of passage experience, the successful proposal can be considered the separation phase, in which each person identifies the other as the future spouse, foregoing other possible mates. The engagement is the liminal phase. The couple engages in a variety of preparations and ceremonies during this period such as purchasing engagement and wedding rings, introducing the intended spouse to friends and relatives, planning a wedding and reception with the advice and support of parents and others, meeting religious requirements for the wedding, choosing a place to live and the furnishings to occupy the new space, and attending wedding showers given by friends and family. The marriage ceremony corresponds to the third phase of the passage experience, in which the two individuals are publicly reincorporated into society as a married couple. This culminating stage consists of several formal properties, including repetition of format, content or occasion; an element of acting, in which the movements and words are not spontaneous; special behavior, including actions that do not normally occur, or occur in different ways; order, meaning that the event is organized with a beginning, middle and end; staging, with special presentations and sensory stimuli to increase the attention and concentration of participants and observers; and finally, a collective dimension, in which the rite has a social meaning or message for all attending. A traditional wedding ceremony in our culture is filled with these elements.

As late as the 1950s, marriage reliably marked the beginning of adulthood for a majority of people just emerging from adolescence in our society. Immediately after high school, or shortly thereafter, later adolescents married and started families of their own. Societal shifts since then have encouraged the further education of women, and permitted extensive new career and lifestyle options that have pushed the median age of first marriage to 25.3 years for women and 27.1 years for men, increased from 20.3 years for women and 22.8 years for men in 1950. The median childbearing age for women has also increased from 21.4 years in 1970 to 25.1 years in 2002. In the absence of previously universal early marriage and family creation as markers of adulthood, other events have taken on special importance as adolescents seek adult status.

The rite of passage experience changes the status of the individual from within and without, in the eyes of other community members. Such rites require the participation, guidance, and witness of adults in the society. However, a number of recent societal shifts have served to isolate adolescents from the day-to-day world of adults, minimizing their influence and opportunities for interaction. The predominance of nuclear families over extended ones and the increasing geographic distance between nuclear families and their extended family members have reduced the regular, intimate contact that children once had with grandparents, aunts, uncles, and cousins. The prevalence of two career parents working outside the home for extended hours reduces the amount of regular contact between parents and children. New economic realities drive single parents to work two jobs or double shifts, further limiting contact between them and their children. Divorce or unwed parenthood often limits children's access to one parent or the other, usually the father. Frequent moves, safety concerns, a desire for privacy, and limited time at home have contributed to the disintegration of bonds among neighbors, eliminating yet another source of regular contact with adults for modern adolescents. Finally, children in our society participate in an extensive schooling experience often beginning with some form of day care or pre-school, leading into kindergarten which is increasingly a full day experience, into twelve more years spent primarily in the company of peers. A university experience adds four years or more to the adolescent's experience of almost total segregation with peers from the world of adults. As a result of these societal changes that serve to limit contact with adults in the community, adolescents have significant time and energy to expend on peers. Left increasingly to their own devices, adolescents are especially vulnerable to influences of the mass media and the emotional and material consumption of all that the mass media provides. In this new environment, adolescents lack recognized avenues to demonstrate to the society at large that they are ready to assume adult status; the unavailability of adults contributes to their dilemma.

MODERN RITES OF PASSAGE

The acquisition of a driver's license is perhaps one of the earliest and most universally accepted benchmarks of pending adult status unrelated to school in our society. An adolescent is separated from all younger adolescents upon the event of the sixteenth birthday, which allows the acquisition of a learner's permit to drive a car under the supervision of a licensed driver. The student practices driving during the transition phase while studying the details of the driver's manual. After passing a written test and a driving test, the adolescent is certified to drive, achieving a mark of responsibility and independence in our society. Living through one's first car accident and taking responsibility for possible driving errors, along with insurance claims and repairs, causes some adolescents to feel like adults.

For a segment of the adolescent population, working outside the home at a part time job and earning one's own money is another step toward adulthood. Some girls look forward to a Sweet Sixteen Party that can range from a sleepover with a group of favorite girlfriends to an elaborate semi-formal dinner dance attended by relatives and friends of both sexes. Among Mexican girls, the quinceaneros combines a religious ceremony with an elaborate dinner for friends and families to celebrate a girl's fifteenth birthday. This celebration has moved away from its original intent of signaling to eligible young men in the local community and their families that the honored girl is now ready to be married. In the Jewish tradition, boys prepare for their bar mitzvah, also combining a religious ceremony to recognize a young adolescent boy's new adult status in the faith community with an often lavish dinner for relatives and friends. In Christian communities, adolescents are confirmed in their faith, a sign that they are mature enough to make a personal commitment to it. Boy scouts and girl scouts work through an elaborate system of gaining experiences and participating in community service to acquire badges and move from one level to the next. For boys, becoming an Eagle Scout, usually in late adolescence, marks the culmination of this process. Finally, leaving home and living on one's own, either with friends or a sexual partner, signals to outsiders that one is truly grown up. For some adolescents, this process is concurrent with attending college, in itself a modern rite of passage for a portion of the adolescent population. Some adolescents have indicated that getting personal mail, usually as part of the college recruitment process, helps them feel grown up, as does experiencing the unexpected death of a peer. Living through trying times, such as a high school renovation or multiple bomb scares, also appears to catapult adolescents into feeling like adults.

HIGH SCHOOL AS A FOUR-YEAR RITE OF PASSAGE EXPERIENCE

As early as the 1930s, August Hollinshead noted that the high school was the only formal institution in the community that seemed to contain rituals marking students' passage from adolescence to adulthood. In Elmtown, as Hollinshead called the small town he studied, high school was the place where teenagers worked at growing up. In the process of completing high school, students gradually freed themselves from the direct oversight of their parents, selected their friends and often, a mate, or determined the qualities desired in a mate, chose a career path, and obtained the education required to pursue it. Many of the important rite of passage rituals marking the leaving of childhood and entrance into adulthood continue to be left to the high school to accomplish. In fact, in contemporary society, many perceive the high school's primarily focus to be the maturation of its students, rather than the acquisition of their academic skills.

In 1969, Jacquelyn Burnett described high school as a four-year rite of passage experience that starts with initiation for freshmen and extends to graduation and the senior trip, or Senior Week, in students' final year of high school. In between, students look forward to the junior ring ceremony and dance and the junior and senior proms, all rites of passage in themselves. In many high schools, the junior prom is held in each school's lavishly decorated gym or cafeteria; the senior prom, only for senior students and their dates, is held off campus, often in a local country club or restaurant. In rural schools, prom is often a junior and senior class affair, also held in the gym or cafeteria transformed according to a selected theme by members of the junior class. Exquisite gowns and flowers to match for girls, formal attire for boys, and expensive dinners, pictures, and special transportation combine to create lavish, once in a lifetime events for participants. Its rituals, including a specialized format, dress, and expectations are designed to be a life changing experience for each adolescent who attends. Some high schools design a senior class trip as a culminating experience for students just before graduation. In schools that do not legitimize such an adventure as part of the curriculum, seniors often organize a ritual senior trip independently; gathering in droves at a prearranged destination such as nearby seashore town after school has ended. Both prom and senior trips serve to set adolescents apart from their daily routine and propel them into a unique situation apart from family, resulting in a change within the individual as a result of the experience. Curiously, the high school rarely offers a rite of passage experience for sophomores, or second year high school students. Also, while graduation marks the completion of the high school program, the only rite of passage reflecting academic excellence in modern high schools is often the induction into the National Honor Society, an experience reserved for a small percentage of the student population. Participation in rituals helps to alter students' perceptions of themselves, their relationships to others, and to the community. The rituals described, recognized by adolescents and adults and steeped in emotion described signal a change in status, or a step toward adulthood, for the participants. Adults, as spectators in student activities, in which students play, perform, or organize major portions of events, contribute to the socialization process of the adolescents.

Adolescents unengaged in school or traditional community organizations find other mechanisms to signal their passage to adulthood, although they are usually accomplished without the intersession of adults. For example, initiation into a gang represents a sort of rite of passage for some adolescents, if only among one's peers, and pregnancy or fathering a child can be interpreted as proof that the adolescent is now an adult within some segments of society.

Resources

Burnett, J. H. (1969). Ceremony, rites, and economy in the student system of an American high school. *Human Organization*, 28 (1), 1–10.

Hoffman, L. (2002). Why high schools don't change: What students and their yearbooks tell us. *The High School Journal*, 86 (2), 22–37.

Hollingshead, A. (1975). *Elmtown's youth and Elmtown revisited*. New York: Wiley. [Orig. published 1939.]

Marcus, G. E., & Fischer, M. M. J. (1986). *Anthropology as cultural critique: An experimental moment in the human sciences*. Chicago: The University of Chicago Press.

National Center for Health Statistics. (n.d.). Retrieved September 25, 2004 from http://www.cdc.gov/nchs/default.htm

Santrock, J. (2003). *Adolescence* (9th ed.). Boston: McGraw-Hill.

Sizer, T. R. (1992). *Horace's school: Redesigning the American high school*. Boston: Houghton Mifflin.

U.S. Bureau of the Census. (n.d.). Retrieved September 28, 2004 from http://www.census.gov

Van Gennup, A. (1960). *The rites of passage*. Chicago: The University of Chicago Press. [Orig. published 1909.]

ON YOUTH AND PSYCHOLOGICAL INVESTMENT

Anthony M. Roselli

The complexity of contemporary youth culture seems to demand a closer look at the issue of young people's willingness, or lack thereof, to invest in the external agendas presented to them by organized, mandated activities. Before we examine this phenomenon—psychological investment—let us consider the context of one major mandated activity, namely schooling until the age of sixteen.

There is ample evidence that schooling frequently fails to cause a high degree of engagement on the part of pre-adolescents and teens. Indeed, if engagement requires a conscious cognitive act then psychological investment in school, in general, is put at risk. Many researchers have studied the issue of engagement and the overall conclusion from the findings is similar to what many others casually observe: that school, as an organization, tends to discourage active engagement in its activities and offerings. Is it the school's fault? Are we dealing with perennial and expected rebellion on the part of young people? Or is it something else, something constructed by contemporary society and fueled by nothing more than the dynamic of human interaction?

Before we make a judgment on youth and psychological investment, let us consider how young people themselves might view the academic staples of a typical school program. Then, we might be in a slightly better

63

position to offer an analysis of youth and the psychological processes that must surely be influenced by many external social forces. In fact, some social learning theorists believe that a kind of self-efficacy appraisal occurs exerting an enormous influence on motivation.

Youth experiences organized school activities as unilaterally thrust upon them, not as a set of learning activities negotiated to the satisfaction of both student and teacher. It is traditional that youth comply with the rules of school and yield to the requests of adults who extract authority from the organization. Never is it the case that youth sets the agenda, or that adults acquiesce to the wishes of the learner to change or modify the curriculum. After all, there is a curriculum to be covered and standards to be met. However, the stark impenetrability of the school's authority in matters of curriculum, standards and testing tends to alienate youth and create a passive consumer mentality at best (if not a rejection of the curriculum at worst). Of course, the preceding portrayal of a place called school is not far afield from how John Goodlad described it in his poignant 1984 warning about the shortcomings of schooling in America. Today, however, two decades later we must be even more concerned with the accelerating alienation and disengagement of youth from school, the nature of which acceleration speaks more to a need for attention to the macro-social forces that shape such alienation than to a necessity for revisiting yet again the psychology of disengagement. Simply put, youth's lack of psychological investment might be an evolutionary response to the blurring of lines between the role of youth and that of adult.

Let us return to our discussion of how youth views the academic staples of schooling. Entering school today as a pre-adolescent or teen, a student is confronted with conflicting emotions about self-efficacy, identity, survival, peer pressure, and all other "forces" that impact the social context of the learning environment. It is certain that group dynamics, unpredictable as they may seem at first, create a pattern in school that causes youth to anticipate, over time, a perfectly predictable set of events: teachers instruct on subject matter; students listen, take notes and read. Occasionally there is discussion of the content both with the teacher and with classmates in groups. Under optimal conditions the events unfold without harmful impact on the self. But, in reality, the desired simplicity of the unfolding of teaching and learning is frequently elusive and out of reach. Psychological differences aside, the learner is too often mired in self-doubt and self-criticism because of the organizational imprecision of the teaching and learning process: confusion about meanings of content entangles with an overload of self-efficacy appraisal and leads invariably to a "checking-out," an escape . . . what we have called in this chapter a lack of psychological investment.

Investment in school, psychological or otherwise, requires an habituation to the emerging culture of blurred roles, imprecise curriculum content, confused teaching and unfair tests. Taken together, those mismatched and unreliable features of what constitutes schooling for many youth create overwhelmingly negative conditions that most young people are unable to ignore. The few (5 to 10 percent) who possess a numbness to that milieu (such that their own goals for continued education [i.e., high grades] beyond mandatory schooling are stronger than the moment) do manage to invest enough in order to obtain necessary credentials. Yet, for most the phenomenology of an existential moment in such emotional discomfort is strong enough to divert attention away from immediate learning goals and toward a psychological divestiture from all that is "school." Yet, it is as sad as it is true that all youth possess a natural but untapped reservoir of potent tendency to react with parity, compassion and engagement to the events of schooling. What is requisite to unleash the power is, of course, a pedagogy that equalizes all potential; balances needs with wants; reunites adult with youth on humanistic ground where altruism gains value and disagreement is safe. The kind of school that inspires youth to do "good works" and to put aside self-doubt is as rare as it is desirable. Furthermore, the unavoidable reality of a second natural tendency, that is, to oppose all that is part of the adult world, demands both a reconceptualization of relationships and roles in school, *and* a focused attention to the unmistakable, and different, emerging culture of youth created by constantly changing social, political, and economic conditions. It is not so much that kids are different today as it is that everyone misunderstands the new and evolving rules for carrying out a successful school experience for all youth in these (post)modern times.

So, let us now answer the questions posed earlier: Is it the school's fault that youth is disengaged? Is it youth's way of rebelling? Or, is it something else, something constructed by contemporary society and fueled by nothing more than the dynamic of human interaction? First of all, it is not the school's fault because the school is a microcosm of society—social trends and phenomena trickle into the fabric of a place called school and render it as effective/ineffective as what a functionalist theory in sociology describes as follows: society is a system of interrelated parts and various social institutions perform various tasks that are vital to society's survival. Therefore, and in like manner, a school plays a part in the overall function of a society but it alone cannot be blamed for how youth reacts to schooling. Another sociological concept, conflict theory, sheds light on this functionalist idea and adds the notion of social division, that is, that competing groups vie for scarce resources, power and prestige. Thus, youth's disengagement in school may be rebellion or it may have as its root cause something else, something constructed symbolically or dynamically in some other social institution: the workplace, the family, the place of worship, etc. (Note that we have affirmed the third question posed above). Youth defines reality in ways not dissimilar from adults; jointly with other groups, and other individuals, through a dynamic of human interaction. So, where does all this leave us in terms of an understanding of "psychological investment" of youth?

One revered developmental psychologist who broke from the ranks somewhat more than two decades ago believed in studying behavior in natural settings in order to avoid deeming most behavior "strange." His ideas recall the Sartrian view that we are the sum total of what we do, past and present, and that the inescapable reality is our interaction with others, in real time and in real environments. Bronfenbrenner's courage in putting forth a radical notion of human development allows us, today, to speak of school as an ecology within which youth acts, reacts, and interacts with various subgroups of the school. Remembering that the school itself is embedded in a larger context, that is, society, we can now take a somber, reasoned view of what Emile Durkheim meant when he pointed out in several important books, published posthumously, that education (schooling) is closely linked to other institutions and to current values and beliefs of the society. Therefore, whatever it is that we bemoan about the state of affairs in society today we must realize that youth also has felt the impact. Does this pessimistic view of social dynamics excuse the lack of psychological investment on the part of youth? We should, by now, be at least open to forgiving both adults and young people; to accepting the emerging, and ever-changing culture in which we all must live and work; to dedicating ourselves to understanding the evolving roles of adults and youth in the context of larger social forces . . . What, then, is the judgment to be passed on the question of youth and psychological investment in school, or in society, or in life?

Returning to an earlier point in this chapter (concerning youth's emotive responses to schooling), namely, the conflicted identity that school can arouse due to its organizational features, we might venture to say that identity itself is a concept whose formation comprises both continuing sameness and constant change. Perhaps, it might comfort us, all of us—adults and youth alike, in our quest for more understanding, to appreciate these words: "In the jungle of human existence, there is no feeling of being alive without a sense of identity."

In the end, or at the end of the day, we might all feel re-energized and more committed to each other's health and well-being if we all subscribe to what was outlined earlier in discussing youth and their natural tendency to react with parity, compassion and engagement: if we believe in youth's capacity to do good works and to invest psychologically in spite of many oppositional forces perhaps working against that natural tendency, then we must begin immediately, and continually, to tap into that capacity.

Resources

Alexander, K. L., Entwisle, D. R., & Danber, S. L. (1993). First-grade classroom behavior: Its short- and long-term consequences for school performance. *Child Development, 64,* 801–14.

Bandura, A. (1986). *Social foundations of thought and action: A social cognitive theory.* Englewood Cliffs, NJ: Prentice-Hall.

———. (1997). *Self-efficacy.* New York: W. H. Freeman.

Battistich, V., Solomon, D., Watson, M., & Schaps, E. (1997). Caring school communities. *Educational Psychologist, 32*, 137–51.

Bronfenbrenner, U. (1979). *The ecology of human development: Experiments by nature and design.* Cambridge, MA: Harvard University Press.

Connell, J. P. (1990). Context, self, and action: A motivational analysis of self-esteem processes across the life span. In D. Cicchetti (Ed.). *The self in transition: Infancy to childhood.* Chicago: The University of Chicago Press.

Durkheim, E. (1956). *Education and sociology.* (trans. S. D. Fox). Glencoe, IL: Free Press.

———. (1961). *Moral education.* (trans. E. K. Wilson & H. Schnurer). Glencoe, IL: Free Press.

———. (1977). *The evolution of educational thought.* (trans. P. Collins). London: Routledge.

Erikson, E. H. (1950). *Childhood and society.* New York: Norton.

———. (1968). *Identity, youth, and crisis.* New York: Norton.

Finn, J. D. (1993). *School engagement and students at risk.* Washington, DC: National Center for Education Statistics.

Goodlad, J. (1984). *A place called school: Prospects for the future.* New York: McGraw-Hill.

Kindermann, T. A., McCollam, T., & Gibson, E. (1996). Peer networks and students' classroom engagement during childhood and adolescence. In J. Juvone & K. Wentzel (Eds.). *Social motivation: Understanding children's school adjustment.* Cambridge, UK: Cambridge University Press.

Locke-Davidson, A. (1996). *Making and molding identity in schools: Student narratives on race, gender, and academic engagements.* Albany: State University of New York Press.

Newmann, F. (1981). Reducing student alienation in high schools: Implications of theory. *Harvard Educational Review, 51*, 546–64.

Newmann, F., Wehlage, G. G., & Lamborn, S. D. (1992). The significance and sources of student engagement. In F. Newmann (Ed.). *Student engagement and achievement in American secondary schools.* New York: Teachers College Press.

Nystrand, M., & Gamoran, A. (1991). Instructional discourse, student engagement, and literature achievement. *Research in the Teaching of English, 25*, 261–90.

Skinner, E. A., Wellborn, J. G., & Connell, J. P. (1990). What it takes to do well in school and whether I've got it: The role of perceived control in children's engagement and school achievement. *Journal of Educational Psychology, 82*, 22–32.

Stipek, D. (2002). Good instruction is motivating. In A. Wigfield & J. Eccles (Eds.). *Development of achievement motivation.* San Diego, CA: Academic Press.

STEPFAMILIES IN THE UNITED STATES

Keisha McGhee Love

Sources vary slightly in their definition of stepfamilies; however, the term "stepfamilies" generally refers to a married couple in which there is at least one stepchild in the family unit. Stepfamilies also come in a variety of con-stellations. For instance, stepfamilies can be described as *simple,* in which only one partner in the marriage brings children to the family, or *complex* in which both partners bring children to the family. Due to the high divorce rate and the large percentage of children being born to unmarried parents, the number of stepfamilies in the United States is rapidly increasing. In fact, it is estimated that by the year 2010, stepfamilies will be the most prev-alent type of family in the United States, accounting for over 50 percent of all families in the United States. According to the 2000 U.S. Census Bureau, 41 million people, or approximately 18 percent of Americans, were wid-owed, separated, or divorced. The divorce rate in the United States began dramatically increasing in the early 1960s and continued to rise annually until eventually leveling off in the late 1980s and early 1990s. In 1999, Data Digest reported that the divorce rate in the United States was 50 percent. This means that half of all couples that married would eventually divorce. An estimated 35 percent of children born in the 1980s will experience the divorce and remarriage of their custodial parent during their childhood or adolescent years, and this number is expected to continue to rise with each passing year. Norton and Miller estimate that approximately 70 percent of these individual's parents would eventually remarry, and note the signifi-cant number of stepfamilies that will be formed due to his phenomenon.

According to statistics, roughly 86 percent of stepfamilies are com-posed of biological mothers and a stepfather. Additionally, African Americans account for 32 percent of all stepfamilies. African American children and adolescents are significantly more likely to be a member of a stepfamily than their Hispanic or White peers, who represent 16 per-cent and 14 percent of stepfamily constellations respectively. Despite the rapid growth of stepfamilies across all ethnic groups in the United States, little is known about the dynamics of stepfamilies. Most research related to families has been conducted on intact families (families that consist of both married biological parents residing in the same house-hold) and generalized to stepfamilies. However, research has recently begun to emerge on individuals from stepfamily environments. For instance, studies have shown that second marriages are at a high risk for dissolution because stepfamilies are prone to experience conflict related to several key areas including the disciplining of children, financial concerns, and loyalty concerns.

An example of stepfamily conflict, especially in complex stepfamilies, is the discipline of children. Parents may be comfortable disciplining their own children, but doubt may arise concerning their role in disciplining their spouse's children. This doubt can cause tension and confusion for all members of the stepfamily, especially when the children do not receive the same type of discipline measures from both parents. The utilization of finances may also be a point of contention for parents as they must decide if they will share the financial responsibilities of all the children in the stepfamily, or just their own children. Tension can occur in the stepfamily if one parent expends money on his or her own children, but does not financially provide for his or her spouses' children. Finally, studies have shown that children often times are subjected to emotional stress when they feel a sense of divided loyalty between their non-custodial biological parent and their stepparent. Again, this can lead to tension for all members of the stepfamily unit.

Another area of research conducted on stepfamilies has focused on the well-being of children and adolescents from these family environments in a variety of areas including academic performance, psychological health, social and emotional health, and physical health. There is consistent evidence that children raised in stepfamilies are at an increased risk for developing a host of problems compared to their peers raised in intact families. For example, Hanson, McLanahan, and Thomson found that children in stepfamilies had more behavioral problems in school, showed less initiative towards their schoolwork, and generally experienced a lower quality of life when compared to children in intact, biological families. Similarly, Dunn, Deater-Deckard, Pickering, O'Conner, and Golding studied four-year-old children growing up in stepfamilies and found that these children (and their older siblings) had more emotional problems, more peer problems, and higher levels of hyperactivity than their peers from intact, biological families. Finally, Amato and Keith reported that children from stepfamilies had poorer outcomes in numerous areas such as academic skills, psychological health, and social health compared to their peers from intact, biological families.

Numerous studies have sought to explain why individuals in stepfamilies have poorer levels of health than individuals from intact, biological families, but definitive answers have yet to be reached. For instance, because greater levels of household conflict have been associated with greater psychological and emotional problems, Hanson et al. theorized the greater amounts of household conflict associated with stepfamilies versus intact families would account for the differences in health found between individuals in these different types of households. However, their theory was not supported. Love and Murdock advanced another theory that might explain the discrepancy in health found between individuals from intact, biological families and those in stepfamilies. Studies have shown positive associations between levels of emotional attachment children have to their parents and their psychological, emotional, and social health. Specifically, children that are more closely attached to their parents tend to exhibit greater psychological health (they suffer less from depression, anxiety, and other psychological disorders), they tend to be more emotionally healthy (they are not as prone to experiencing severe episodes of negative emotions), and display greater levels of social health (they have more meaningful friendships/relationships). Love and Murdock found that children in stepfamilies were not as emotionally attached to their parents as children from intact, biological families, and postulated that this lack of attachment would account for the discrepancy in health found between individuals from stepfamilies versus intact biological families. They found that children's emotional attachment to their parents was one factor related to the less favorable outcomes in school, psychological health, and social health for individuals from stepfamilies, but acknowledge there are many other contributing factors to this phenomenon.

Despite studies that have found less favorable outcomes for children and adolescents from stepfamilies, being a member of a stepfamily does not mean individuals will experience negative outcomes. Many stepfamilies function as well as, if not better, than intact, biological families. Several factors have been identified that can facilitate the successful formation and existence of a stepfamily. For instance, early in the relationship, parents should discuss and decide how each parent will discipline children in the family. Additionally, parents should determine how financial matters will be addressed in the family. Parents should also encourage the child's non-custodial biological parent to stay actively involved in the child's life and attempt to minimize issues related to divided loyalty. Moreover, stepparents must be sensitive to the relationship that exists between their spouses' children and the children's non-custodial parent. Parents should also allow children to develop their relationship with their stepparent at their own pace instead of attempting to force the relationship to develop faster than the children or stepparent may desire. Children must respect the stepparent as their biological parent's new partner, and must put forth a valiant effort to bond with their stepparent. Last, improving the levels of emotional closeness between all members of the stepfamily by encouraging open communication and respect can facilitate the smooth formation and maintenance of any stepfamily. More information regarding stepfamilies can be obtained from the Web site of the Stepfamily Association of America.

Resources

Amato, P., & Keith, B. (1991). Parental divorce and the well-being of children. *Psychological Bulletin, 110*, 26–46.

Arnold, C. (1998). Center for Law and Social Policy. Children and stepfamilies: a snapshot. Retrieved May 26, 2001 from http://www.clasp.org/publications/children_stepfamilies.pdf

Carter, B., & McGoldrick, M. (1999). *The extended family life cycle: Individual, family, and social perspectives* (3rd ed.). Boston: Allyn and Bacon.

Dunn, J., Deater-Deckard, K., Pickering, K., O'Conner, T., Golding, J., & ALSPAC Study Team. (1998). Children's adjustment and prosocial behavior in step-, single parent, and non-stepfamily settings: Findings from a community study. *Journal of Child Psychology and Psychiatry, 39,* 1083–1095.

Hanson, T., McLanahan S., & Thompson, E. (1996). Double jeopardy: Parental conflict and stepfamily outcomes for children. *Journal of Marriage and the Family, 58,* 141–154.

Kreider, R., & Simmons, T. (2003). *Marital status: 2000* [Electronic Version]. U.S. Bureau of the Census, Census 2000 Brief, October 2003. Washington, DC: U.S. Government Printing Office.

Love, K., & Murdock, T. (2005). Attachment to parents and psychological well-being: An examination of young adult college students in intact families and stepfamilies. *Journal of Family Psychology.*

Nicholson, J., Fergusson, D., & Horwood, L. J. (1999). Effects of later adjustment of living in a stepfamily during childhood and adolescence. *Journal of Child Psychology and Psychiatry, 40,* 405–416.

Norton, A., & Miller, L. (1992). *Marriage, divorce, and remarriage in the 1990s.* U.S. Bureau of the Census, Current Population Reports, Series P-23, No. 180. Washington, DC: U.S. Government Printing Office.

Stepfamily Association of America. (2000). Retrieved September 18, 2004 from http://www.saafamilies.org/

BLENDING YOUTH AND ORGANIZATIONAL CULTURES

Rebecca L. Carver

Blending organizational and youth cultures is a process of supporting youth in their maintenance and expression of individual identities while facilitating a welcoming experience for the youth within an organization. When successful, blending youth and organizational cultures enables youth to incorporate their roles as members of an organization into positive development of relationships with themselves, others, and their environments.

"Organizational culture" refers to the underlying rules and assumptions about how things work and how people interact in an organization. Organizational culture comprises accepted practices and values that affect how people behave within the organization, and how the organization is presented to outsiders. Most organizations that affect youth are developed and run by adults who, because they are adults, subconsciously impose cultural norms that are based on fundamental aspects of adult culture.

While youth culture assumes many forms and is not static, it is distinguishable from the adult culture in which expectations for youth behavior are often imposed. As an example, youth tend to have a different temporal orientation than what is assumed by mainstream adult culture. Youth are often absorbed in thoughts about the very near future—today, possibly later this week—rather than focusing on long-term goals or long-term consequences of actions. For a young person struggling to get through the day, a message about the importance of learning something today that might have application years down the road is not going to register with the same effectiveness as a message about the importance of completing a task in the next week in order to help relieve somebody's pain or address what the youth perceives to be a critical issue in her or his community. Members of organizations that successfully blend youth and organizational culture typically allow youth to see the immediate or short-term value, as well as the potential long-term value of activities.

The blending of youth and organizational cultures takes place over time, through collaborative work of healthy youth-adult partnerships at deep levels of leadership activity. In organizations that embrace collaborative leadership and the privileging of youth voice in the critical decision making processes, mission statements tend to be embraced by both youth and adult members; productivity is high and aligned with the organizations' missions; inter-personal conflicts are resolved efficiently and without violence; youth and adults support one another; youth develop healthy decision making habits, and grow as productive and contributing members of society.

However, even well intentioned adults often fail to engage youth in leadership roles because the blending of youth and organizational cultures can be difficult. Keys to success include: providing structured opportunities for adults and youth to benefit from ongoing forms of experiential education, attending to youth needs for short-term goals and opportunities to achieve tangible results, limiting rules to a few simple concepts that youth accept as worthwhile, and ensuring that adult behavior is consistent across time and with espoused organizational values.

GETTING YOUTH INVOLVED:

Getting youth in the door is accomplished by showing youth that an organization is welcoming, respectful, and provides opportunities for both meaningful personal growth and social satisfaction. Youth may see the opportunity to enjoy activities they perceive as fun, and they may be more focused on the opportunity to build friendships with interesting peers. Connecting with youth implies presenting attractive options with immediate relevance, as well as any well-meaning long-term benefits that might be received through organizational membership.

Organizations that are successful at attracting and retaining youth participation share underlying goals of fostering the development of *agency, belonging, and competence*, three basic human needs. Developing **agency** refers to a process of becoming more effective as a change agent in one's life and community. **Belonging** refers to a sense of positive connection with other people and the environment in which one finds oneself. **Competence** includes the possession of skills and knowledge and also the ability to apply what has been learned in new situations.

Organizations that foster the development of **agency** provide structures and supports for youth to experience success beyond what they thought was possible in relation to meeting challenges that they perceive as being significant in their lives. Youth often describe this phenomenon as an experience of becoming empowered by overcoming mental blocks, fears, and insecurities, and learning to set higher expectations for themselves.

Organizations foster the development of **belonging** by establishing infrastructure and expectations for meaningful interpersonal relationships among youth, among adults, and across generations. People work hard at these organizations to learn and practice communication skills reflecting active listening, expression of feelings, empathy, appreciation of diverse perspectives, and the effective use of assertiveness techniques. Both youth and adults feel a positive sense of connection to each other and to the mission of the organization in cases where the organizational culture supports the development of belonging.

Organizations foster the development of **competence** by providing youth with structured opportunities to develop skills and construct knowledge in areas that are important to them. In addition to learning from what adults are explicitly teaching, youth are mentored as they practice skills and use knowledge, often alongside adults, in challenging situations that result in personal satisfaction and significant learning.

Youth seek to fulfill their fundamental needs for the development of **agency, belonging, and competence** and will be drawn to social organizations— gangs, teams, schools, community-based organizations, faith-based groups, cliques, families—that satisfy these basic social and psychological needs.

Organizations that foster the development of youth agency, belonging, and competence are places where adults also typically experience profound development of agency, belonging, and competence (Carver, 1998).

EXPERIENTIAL EDUCATION:

Organizations that successfully attract youth affiliation and participation share a pervasive cultural norm of valuing meaningful and personalized education. They provide structures and opportunities for **experiential education** (see Dewey, 1938; Cousins, 2000) as a means of fostering the development of agency, belonging, and competence of both individuals and groups of youth and adults (Carver, 1998).

Experiential education draws on the personal experiences of individuals and groups participating in the educational process. The core content of the curriculum includes both the experiences that people bring with them to an organization, and the experiences that they share with one another through their involvement within the organization. For example, if the organization is a performing arts center, education of a dance troupe may draw on both the improvisational dance that participants perform together and the ways in which individuals expressed aspects of their personal identities through their dancing. In an organization that functions as a youth-run newspaper, a group of the journalists who are living in foster care may draw on their individual living experiences while also learning from the process of writing and editing articles in collaboration with other newspaper staff.

Experiential education prepares people for the future by stimulating them to make connections between what they are learning and how the lessons might apply to different situations that they might face in their daily lives ahead. For youth, seeing the purpose of what is being taught is a critical element to developing an internal motivation to learn. Youth, like children and adults, strive to learn but they seek to learn what they perceive to be valuable.

Service-learning is a type of **experiential education** that tends to be effective at supporting positive youth development because it addresses the common desire of youth to feel more needed (which speaks to their sense of belonging) (Eccles and Gootman, 2002). It also allows them to build agency (by taking initiative and sensing that their efforts make a difference) and competence (by increasing their capacity to help others). The term "**service-learning**" means that significant forms of community service are integrated with meaningful education. In addition to **service-learning** involvement outside an organization, youth may be engaged in leadership roles within an organization and thereby learn from both serving their community and from the experience of taking on responsibilities related to organizational management.

Organizations that incorporate positive aspects of youth culture provide natural environments for spontaneous learning in authentic settings, creative problem solving by ad hoc groups, and youth-directed projects that engage youth and adults in learning.

AUTHENTICITY AND COMPASSION

Organizations that support positive youth development through experiential education demonstrate values of authenticity and compassion. To gain the trust of youth, adults need to demonstrate patience, compassion, respect for the dignity of all people, and appreciation of youth. Actions are at least as important as words. It is essential for adults to "walk their talk." It is not enough for adults to say that they respect youth; they need to show it. Instead of just saying that they value communication, they need to consistently ask for youth to express their thoughts and feelings, listen to what is being shared, ask for clarifications and confirmation to ensure that they understand what youth are expressing, and integrate those ideas into the core business of the organization. Youth need to feel needed, respected, and valued. When they are engaged in decision making, problem solving, and planning activities that have high stakes, their development of agency, belonging, and competence is supported.

If adults are authentic in expressing their value of education, they will learn alongside youth. They will show their joy for learning and how satisfying it can be to achieve educational goals. They adapt to unexpected situations, capitalizing on teachable moments, and work with the strong emotions that youth express about real life situations and community issues.

Challenges, struggles, and problems are all part of life. In an authentic learning environment, they are not minimized or ignored; they are embraced as opportunities for personal and interpersonal development. Where authenticity is valued, people act in accordance with their espoused beliefs. The consistency of behavior and dialogue sets the stage for understanding and negotiating differences in individual values and expectations.

When it comes to discipline in organizations that are effective at supporting positive youth development, adults are self-disciplined enough to respond quickly and clearly when rules are broken. There are very few rules. In fact, "respect each other" may be the only rule. The rules make sense to and are owned by members of the organization. It is not uncommon for a young person who is reprimanded for pushing boundaries to eventually come back to the adult who held him or her accountable and express gratitude for the fact that the adult cared enough to take action.

Compassion is a core value in organizations that blend positive youth culture into their very being. While adults show appreciation of youth culture, people of different ethnic backgrounds are more likely to express their appreciation of each other's cultural assets. The ground is set for appreciating diversity and creating a truly multicultural environment.

Youth are encouraged to treat themselves with compassion, learning to be both kind and disciplined. People care deeply for one another as they work together to meet shared goals and struggle alongside each other for personal growth.

DUAL GOALS

It is critical for organizational leaders to recognize differences among youth rather than treating them as one uniform group. Organizations that are successful at blending youth and organizational culture encourage youth to develop identities that continue to draw heavily on their unique demographic and personality characteristics while also reflecting their association with the organization and acceptance of values that are common among members.

Youth are respected not only as potential adults, but also as full-fledged members of society with expertise, positive energy, and worthwhile ideas to contribute to community endeavors. All youth are treated as "at-promise." They may be viewed as artists, athletes, activists, educators, service providers, or positive role models. They are all viewed as students of life and experts on their own life experiences. At the same time, it is recognized that any one can become at risk of failure to thrive in circumstances that do not provide opportunities to satisfy basic needs. All youth are at-risk and all youth are at-promise. This is an underlying premise of organizational culture that reflects an appreciation for critical dimensions of youth culture. Youth are full of possibility and promise, and at the same time feel fragile and vulnerable. They have an acute sense of change that they experience as part of their every day life. Their identities are ever changing, and feedback regarding their promise and the extent to which they are at risk of failure to achieve their promise has serious implications for this identity formation.

Blending youth and organizational culture implies considering both youth development and organizational goals. There is usually a dual purpose to the key activities in organizations that are effective at supporting positive youth development. On the surface, there is a stated purpose that relates to the mission of the organization. For instance, to train youth as health educators and have them teach community members about effective strategies for addressing a community health problem, or to produce a performance of dance, theater, or music. The focus may be on a sport or art form or type of community service. It can be on any problem-based or at least project-based learning goal. Meanwhile, there are underlying goals of positive youth development such as: youth facing personal challenges and achieving success beyond their initial expectations, youth developing communication, critical thinking and project management skills, youth becoming friends with people from different ethnic backgrounds. In other words, developing agency, competence, and belonging.

There is always room for youth to develop more competence and take on more responsibility in organizations that successfully blend youth and organizational culture. Typically, youth begin to assist adults in leadership roles and then progress to taking the lead while being assisted by adults or youth with more experience at performing the leadership tasks. Again, there is a dual process of providing leadership and supporting the learning of the youth who are participating in the leadership activities. In time, some youth progress to leading on their own and serving as advisors and mentors for youth who are coming up behind them in the course of their leadership development within a specific realm of activity (e.g., competing at a sport or caring for animals). If youth are not rising to independence as leaders, one might do well to question if the youth leadership is authentic and how extensive a blending of youth and organizational culture exists.

ONGOING PROCESS

Youth need to learn responsibility. They, like anyone else, make mistakes. Organizations that value experiential education, authenticity, compassion, community, and youth development function in a manner that is consistent with the recognition of this phenomenon. Rather than being judged or given external penalties for making mistakes, youth are supported in dealing with the situations in which they find themselves and encouraged to learn from these experiences. Once again, youth culture is oriented to a different temporal gauge than adult culture. Youth need to experience success and see the value in their work and interactions within a short time frame for membership in an organization or participation in its activities to appear to be worthwhile to them.

Organizations that are successful at engaging diverse populations of youth often start by working with a small number of youth (e.g., less than 10) and a high staff to youth ratio (e.g., 1:5). Over the course of several years, they grow, welcoming new members who learn from established members about the norms of the organization. Youth themselves often cultivate a collective appreciation for diversity and social justice, communication and systematic approaches to problem solving. They learn how to be effective in supporting one another and how to satisfy their own needs for support as they pursue group and individual goals in the realms of education, health and fitness, community service, identity development, and common areas of specific interest such as a particular art form or sport.

Resources

Carver, R. L. (1996). Theory for practice: A framework for thinking about experiential education. *The Journal of Experiential Education*, 19 (1), 8–13.

———. (1997). Theoretical underpinnings of service learning. *Theory Into Practice*, 36 (3), 145–49.

———. (1998). *Education for all: From experience, through guidance and reflection.* Doctoral dissertation. Stanford, CA: Stanford University Press.

Cousins, E. (Ed.). (2000). *Roots: From outward bound to expeditionary learning.* Dubuque, IA: Kendall/Hunt Publishing Company.

Dewey, J. (1938). *Experience and education.* New York: The MacMillan Company.

Connell, J. P., & Wellborn, J. G. (1991). *Competence, autonomy, and relatedness: A motivational analysis of self-system processes.* In M. R. Gunnar & L. A. Sroufe (Eds.), *Self processes and development: The Minnesota symposia on child development* (pp. 43–77). Hillsdale, NJ: Lawrence Erlbaum Associates.

Enfield, Richard P. (2001). *Connections between 4-H and John Dewey's philosophy of education, FOCUS.* Davis: University of California Press.

Eccles, J., & Gootman, J. A. (Eds.). (2002). *Community programs to promote youth development.* National Research Council and Institute of Medicine. Washington, DC: National Academy Press.

Heath, S. B., & McLaughlin, M. W. (1994). Learning for anything everyday. *Journal of Curriculum Studies*, 26, 471–89.

McLaughlin, M. W., Irby, M. A., & Langman, J. (1994). *Urban sanctuaries: Neighborhood organizations in the lives and futures of inner-city youth.* San Francisco: Jossey-Bass Publishers.

Used to It

George Sanchez

I'm here in my couch
Sitting still, all alone
Thinking of how this world
Is all messed up.
I hear the deadly roar of a gun
And I don't even move,
I don't jump to the floor
Like I used to do before
Because I've gotten used to
Going to sleep with the sound
Of the ambulance's siren
As they come to pick up
Another innocent
Who wanted to be a thug,
Then comes the police
Clearing the streets
And closing the road
Their lights blue and red
Going on and off
And listening to their radio
Is like listening to a soft song.
When I see something wrong
I hardly care anymore
Maybe it's because I have become accustomed to it
Because I see it everywhere
Because lazy cops turn their heads the other way
And right next to them a body is laying dead
Why should I care if nobody else does?
Why should I do something
If when I'm in trouble no one ever shows?
Why should I say something
If the rest of us
Prefer to look up

Rather than speak up
And tell what they saw?
Why should I try to stop it?
If crime is already a synonym for New York,
Can you tell me
Why we choose to be silent
And ignore the fact that it's our fault
That our streets are violent?
If we don't try to stop it now
Crime will not be against the law
It will be as common
As part time jobs.

Section Two

MEDIA CULTURE
AND YOUTH

People All the Same

Crystal Crespo

In this world
everyone looks the same
Pepe, EYCE, Gap
It's all the same.
I want to be different
I want to stand out ...
I walk the streets,
I notice the stares,
I laugh.
The attention,
the attitude,
the way of the world.
I just want to be different;
I'm comfortable the way I am.
Nike, Timberland, New Balance
It's all the same,
I want to be different.
To stand out from all these people
People who don't care.

MTV: KILLING THE RADIO STAR

Joe L. Kincheloe

Within thirty seconds after I first viewed MTV in 1981 I was torn by what I considered competing dimensions of the new medium. My first reaction was that Hollywood had taken over my beloved and sacred rock n' roll—MTV was slick and well produced, the antithesis of what rock represented; my second response was more positive, as I thought of the possibilities of fusing music and video as an innovative art form. I was suspicious but intrigued. The VJs were interesting amalgams of AM and FM radio disc jockeys—a little too hip for their own good, but nonetheless relatively respectful of the rock ethic. I was enthralled by the graphics and the innovative use of the camera—the music riff that accompanied the man on the moon planting the MTV flag, and the various psychedelic colors and patterns of the MTV logo shook my artistic sensibilities. And the Buggles's *Video Killed the Radio Star* was so good. I thought it contained some subliminal dimension informing the world that the moribund 1970s were over and the 1980s were here to extend the renaissance of the 1960s. Of course, I was disappointed—that dimension was stillborn, aborted by the regressive forces sowing their oats in the early Reagan era.

Thus, my perceptions of this phenomenon called MTV. If you are in the 18 to 24 age group—the average age of the contemporary MTV viewer—these insights may seem to you as if they came from another planet. It was a different political time and many of us believed that rock held a special, if not mystical, ability to change the world. Anything that affected rock demanded intense scrutiny on our part—and MTV, to say the least, profoundly affected rock. Most young twenty-first century fans of MTV have little notion of how it developed, where it came from, or its effects on entertainment in general, popular culture, television, cinematography, or the world of music. This essay is designed to provide a few insights into these questions.

> I remember that it really wasn't about the Buggles (whose *Video Killed the Radio Star* was the first video played) and the future of music, but instead the big emphasis was on the "I want my MTV" promo ads. As I remember it, these ads relied on people like Pete Townshend and Mick Jaggar, not the new bands of the late 1970s and early 1980s. Remember Sting's parody of the line in Dire Straits's *Money for Nothing*? Even one of the VJs was older (J.J. Jackson, the *safe* black guy). Then the cultural thing started to happen when the channel caught on—the new bands were more fashionable (and visual) and record companies started "breaking" bands on their visual style as much as their music. This was same thing that happened with Elvis, and especially Ricky Nelson in the first TV revolution. The established bands were then required to have videos so they could get into rotation on MTV to break their new albums. To this day, I hear a tune on the radio that I have only heard on MTV, and it sounds like a different song. This may say something about the visual dominant. The medium is the message.
>
> Phil

Robert Pittman—the father of MTV—had the idea of asking popular music stars to produce short films constructed around their hit songs. Combining innovative visuals with ground-breaking fashion, MTV transformed the music industry and created the cosmos of music videos. Only 27 years old, Pittman ushered in a new generation of TV programmers, producers, and marketers who discarded the old assumptions about video production to appeal to a new TV-weaned generation. Many argue that Pittman in his work on MTV formulated an entire new way to think about and watch television. For those not around in 1981, MTV altered all subsequent music and television.

MTV'S IMPACT ON THE MUSIC AND ENTERTAINMENT INDUSTRY

Within a matter of months MTV became one of the most powerful forces operating in the music and entertainment domain. In only a couple of years MTV took over radio's longstanding role as the medium that moved acts from oblivion to celebrity status. As hot as the surface of the sun, MTV became the center of the popular music solar system. Since videos sold records, music companies began coughing up huge sums of money to make the films hipper and more chic. In 1983, Michael Jackson's fourteen-minute *Thriller* video debuted with production costs of $1,500,000 dollars. The record became the biggest selling album in music history. Artists with

MTV dominates Times Square

visual appeal began to gain a distinct advantage over those "who didn't have it."

I remember the shuttle that landed on the moon, the spaceman coming out and sticking the flag—the Neil Armstrong flag with the MTV logo on it—on the moon, the rotoscoping of neon colors. I recall the

VJs coming on and their talking. There was a 3-D animated video of Dire Straits' *Money for Nothing*. I had to go over to a friend's house because he had cable. The actual music videos were not as important as the VJs. I remember all the promotion for MTV. Black people were not listening to artists like Paul Young, but then I heard a lot a black people singing along to Duran Duran, Sting, Tawny Kataen, White Snake, and other new wave, white music.

Roy

For example, Duran Duran—an unsuccessful British band with substantial visual appeal—was unknown in 1981. In TV markets where MTV was available, the sales of Duran Duran records exploded after the airing of their videos. Of course, the band enjoyed a successful career for the next several years. In its early years MTV promoted the careers of other musical artists who had visual appeal including Madonna, Michael Jackson, Prince, George Michael, Peter Gabriel, and U2. The video promotion of MTV brought the record industry out of a slump, catalyzing the sale of more records in one year that radio could influence in five years. Drawing on the power of MTV's promotion record sales climbed throughout the early and mid-1980s. In 1981 only 23 of the year's Top 100 songs were tied to a video; by 1983, more than 50 had videos aired by MTV.

In 1981, I was only seven but the everlasting image of Madonna draped over a tiger in her *Like a Virgin* video was certainly symbolic of MTV's cultural phenomenon. The whole video was breathtaking, shocking, and controversial! So it goes without saying, MTV and I went hand in hand in the 80s. It brought refuge, drama, and inspiration—especially in my junior high and high school days. Also, I loved watching MTV's postmodern culture musicians—groups like the Cure, the Cult, Depeche Mode, the Smiths (Morrissey), the Sugar Cubes and the P.I.L.—which had tremendous influence over my thinking, sense of style and life!!!

Gulbanu

My earliest memories of MTV involve desperately wanting my Dad to get cable so that I could watch it. Before cable it was a good day if we got five channels. Like all things having to do with pop culture, my father hated it. MTV was a big deal because it was so new. Needless to say, my family didn't get cable until after my father split in 1987. What I do remember from friends' houses was Madonna and Run DMC. It was hot.

Rebecca

MTV not only exerted a major impact on popular music but also on cinematography and other aesthetic forms. MTV-inspired handheld cameras and quick-cut editing soon revolutionized TV and movie making, as subsequent cinematography took on the look of rock videos. From *Miami Vice* to the present, TV displayed the distinct mark of MTV. The music videos on early MTV usually contained footage of the singer or the band in a live concert interspersed with lip-synching and pantomimed guitar, drum, and keyboard playing. Dancing became more and more common, and more complex, and narrative constructs marginally connected to song lyrics were added to the formula. Such a combination of activities was quite unique in the early 1980s and soon MTV videos were being referred to as a new art form. Sometimes the form was brash and controversial, as it addressed edgy sexual, violent, and other touchy themes. Even MTV's "Rock the Vote" helped change the aesthetics of American politics, as when in 1992 Bill Clinton accepted an invitation to appear while his opponent George H. W. Bush refused to go on such a show. Clinton later attributed his electoral victory in part to this TV appearance where he answered questions such as "boxers or briefs?"

Too bad there was no MTV in the 1970s when I was a teenager. There was no easy access to universally disseminated messages under which we could unite and bond as a group—think of the potential power of that! Sure, we had our sometimes fragmented network of friends and favorite radio programs to rely upon for advice and style cues, but where else are you going to get the message, visually-delivered 24/7 and reinforced by the creamy throb of the dance-music beat, that wearing your underwear on the outside is okay?

The thing I love about MTV is the visible underpants element: Let's turn everything inside out, jump around upside-down, and backwards and show each other our undies. It's a good message, and one we all need to hear. For sure we all need to wear better underwear, and even more for sure we all think about getting laid. Come on, admit it: You know you think about it too. Stop denying it and show me your underwear: Tell me what's *really* going on under that surface! Let me smell the real you! Making the invisible visible, pronouncing our innermost desires—this is the great contribution of MTV. That and raising our quality standards for, and appreciation of, undergarments everywhere.

Anne

THE EXPLOSIVE SUCCESS OF MTV

The first words spoken on MTV on August 1, 1981 were by creator John Lack: "Ladies and gentlemen, rock and roll." With this understated beginning, MTV emerged on the American and eventually the world scene. For the next six years MTV aired back-to-back videos—this persistent "flow" differed significantly from the individual programs one watched on other channels. Particular videos were replayed in particular time arrangements designed light, medium, or heavy in relation to the clip's popularity. The typical video—with the exception of special productions such as *Thriller*—lasted three to five minutes. The foundation of the video, of course, was the soundtrack on the record it "surrounded," but as time passed sound effects and introductory dialogue were added to the mix.

This simple formula led to the earliest and biggest success story of cable TV. After far-reaching market research, MTV was founded by Warner Amex Satellite Entertainment Company (WASEC). Central to MTV's initial success was the company's access to record company-produced music videos. In the early days record label executives viewed these clips as advertising for their "products" and thus provided them free of charge to MTV. Reaching fewer that one million cable subscribers in 1981, MTV by the middle of the first decade of the twenty-first century reached over 350 million homes. Always working to change with the times, MTV's history falls into three main phases:

1 1981–1983. The beginning phase characterized by non-stop video clips of rock bands directed at a young U.S. audience.
2 1983–1986. This second phase marked the explosive rise of the network. During this era MTV became available in Manhattan and Los Angeles for the first time.
3 1986–Present. The third phase began with Viacom's purchase of the station from WASEC. At this point Robert Pittman's vision of the network was replaced by an emphasis on variety, as MTV moved into rap, dance music, and heavy metal. The music video was no longer the central attraction of the network, as Viacom executives introduced news, sports, sitcoms, documentaries, cartoons, game shows, and other long-established TV genres. After the Viacom purchase, viewers began to see reruns of old TV shows, the daily airing of *Club MTV*, Cindy Crawford's *House of Style*, *MTV Unplugged*, *Liquid Television*, *Beavis and Butthead*, *The Jon Stewart Show*, *Singled Out*, *Road Rules*, *The Real World*, *The Osbornes*, and so forth.

Honestly, I remember watching Sting and the Police sing "Do do, do, de, da, da, da, that's all I want to say to you" and becoming hooked from then on. I watched whenever I could at the age of eleven. It was a bonding experience between my brother and me. I watched during my homework, before dinner, after dinner, and whenever I could. Once my favorite bands like The Cure and The Smiths started with videos, I latched on even more.

SJ

THE CULTURAL POWER OF MTV

As one can tell from the brief vignettes included in this entry, MTV unleashed an enormous cultural power, complete with the ability to alter lives and ways of seeing the world. The young twenty-something founders of MTV, especially Robert Pittman, believed that their generation processed data and visual input faster than previous generations because of their immense experience with television. Pittman and the others had the prescience to understand that young people would not be confused by rapid, nonlinear TV images, and that they would be massaged by the producers' recognition and signaling of their media and cognitive savvy.

Such insights seem obvious in retrospect from the vantage point of an era of computers, IM, iPods, etc.—but in the early 1980s few people recognized these psychological capacities of a mediated group of young people. Such abilities have expanded in subsequent years with children now being able to multitask. Many of us have watched eight-year-olds do their homework while carrying on multiple IM conversations, talking on the phone, listening to music they've downloaded on their iPods, and watching MTV. The advent of MTV helped inform many of us that young people—and even adults—were far more capable of complex cognitive tasks than traditional psychologists had believed. Based on this understanding dramatic cultural changes are occurring and will continue to take place in the future. So powerful was the impact of MTV on young people coming of age in the 1980s that many commentators referred to this demographic group as the MTV generation. There is no doubt that on numerous levels MTV changed the social, cultural, and political world.

We didn't have cable and neither did most of my friends, but we were always on our sk8s and in the streets anyway. So I never saw it, only heard of it. At that time, cable, to me, seemed like it was for families who had money and big houses. I just remember hearing about one of my friends dropping acid and staying up all night watching videos on MTV. It really had no impact on my life. I don't think they were playing the punk rock I was into anyway, so I wasn't even curious. To me it was just another part of the dominant society's mass-produced, plastic culture of boredom and dis-ease.

Curry

I don't remember MTV until MTV Raps's first one-hour special in the late-eighties—I was working at Tower Records near Lincoln Center at the time. The first video I remember clearly form the show is Eric B and Rakim's *Follow the Leader*. I *do* remember watching Friday Night Videos on NBC (Channel Four in New York City) when I was in high school in the mid-1980s. For whatever reason, the only video I remember clearly was Cindi Lauper's *Girls Just Wanna Have Fun*. I'm not sure why! I also remember *Video Music Box* with Ralph McDaniels on some UHF channel. I don't think my neighborhood was wired for cable (except HBO) until much later.

Greg

Resources

BBC News. MTV's irresistible rise. Retrieved September 18, 2005 from http://news.bbc.co.uk/1/hi/entertainment/music/1456093.stm

Lane, S. World premier of music television (MTV). *ClassBrain.com*. Retrieved September 18, 2005 from http://www.classbrain.com/artholiday/publish/article_363.shtml

MTV through the years. *Milwaukee Journal Sentinel*. Retrieved September 18, 2005 from http://www.jsonlin.com/enter/tvradio/jul01/mtvtime26072501.asp

Museum of Broadcast Television. Music television. Retrieved Septermber 18, 2005 from http://www.museum.tv/archives/etv/m/htmlm/musictelevis/musictelevis.htm

Remembering MTV's original VJs. Retrieved September 18, 2005 from http://www.80music.about.com/library/weekly/aa010801.htm

Thanks to:

S. J. Miller, Rebecca Goldstein, Greg Dimitriadis, Roy Carter, Anne Brownstein, Philip Anderson, Gulbanu Tashkent and Curry Malott for their narratives.

THREE-MINUTE CLIP CULTURE

Birgit Richard

There are different ways to analyze the different kinds of moving technical images that show a lot of common features as well as basic media-structural differences: namely, film and music video. Against the background of the fine arts, both of these pictorial forms are still regarded as trivial and thus, to legitimize their examination, the employed strategies usually contain the proof of references to the avant-garde in art. But how are both medial forms connected with each other? Peter Weibel argues that the music clip's design features are partly derived from the formal language of classical avant-garde, which then also radiates via film. However, his argument has to be relativized. In fact, the interdependencies of both pictorial forms are more complex and not just a matter of moving image and commercial context. Intermediality, as so often self-evidently assumed, does not exist. Cinematic screen and video-monitor show, in the audio-visual run off, principally different space-time relations. And the difference of both gets even more evident in the phenomenon of the picture rhythm. Whereas cinema is dominated by a mechanical pictorial rhythm produced through the projector, the video image appears and disappears via the writing cathode ray. In contrast to the movie image, fixed in the projector, the video signal does not project light but an image from an image. The different medial principles are also obvious as the music video is in each scanning point a pulsation of the image itself. The rhythm turns into a figurative element and is no longer caused by the connection of the figurative difference in picture and beat, instead its pulsation blends with figures of musical vibration.

For Paech counts the medial-structural premise, according to which the electronic image, produced by the cathode ray, is connected to the arts only by a simulation and destruction of avant-garde pictures. Therefore, music videos represent only to a very limited degree a hybrid link between artistic avant-garde forms of expression and mass-culture. The music video is a nonlinear, non-Cartesian, recursive medium, determined by a permanent time axis manipulation. Kittler assumes that the age of the image has ended, in which the human being is the decisive standard. The music video indicates Kittler's future of a mutated human double. Standards of picture criticism are changing: now the artistic technique is in the center of interest. The digitally manipulated picture is the "acrobat" performing unbelievable stunts on the screen on a non-stop basis.

Digital pictures appeared first in music clips not in commercials to which they are often compared because of the similar length. Meanwhile digital technologies play an important part in contemporary movies, too. Here the digital ornament embraces also actors and actresses, like in *Gladiator* (2000) or *MI:2* (2000). But even before that, many films polemcized against traditional picture forms, respectively against terms like "truth" or "reality." The concurrence of the following movies is actually quite scary: *Dark City* by Andy and Larry Wachowski (1998); *The 13th Floor* by Josef Rusnak (1999); *Pleasantville* by Gary Ross (1998); and *The Truman Show* by Peter Weir (1998). The huge impact of digital sequences and invented images stirs a growing mistrust against the traditional. It falls upon the digital in these movies firstly to turn against the analog and secondly to shake the basic belief in images.

Music videos recycle society's pictorial memory, which contains all kinds of pictorial products, ranging from the altarpiece to the press photo. Due to the natural limitation of history's picture and information storage, the magical circularity of technical pictures can get entangled in an eternal circle. Because of the high demand for pictures, the entire world is available as an image data bank. Independent of content, everything in pictorial form is used and can be used. Rhythm and cut merge even the incompatible into a new metamorphosis. Characterizing for this are split screens, simultaneity and a fragmentary narrative, features that can also be found in contemporary films. However, even if they are partly derived from film, in music videos they gain a different quality and are not unavoidable system-immanent means. In movies these features form the basis for a particular way of dealing with images. The roots of this attitude may be traced back to Hitchcock, Godard, Greenaway, and, last not least, Lynch. Currently, though, they become particularly apparent and actual movies are not even thinkable without them, as the continuous variation of *Romeo and Juliet* (by Baz Luhrmann, 1996, and Andrzej Bartkowiak, *Romeo Must Die,* 2000) shows on the one side, and *Lost Highway* by David Lynch (1996) shows on the other side.

Film, as well as video, is primarily pictorial media. Video interpretation concentrated up to this point on the interplay of music and image, on synaesthesia, whereby the image was subordinated to sound. However, in analogy to the technique of film analysis as picture analysis we enter a new field, explicitly dividing the two levels of image and text. In film analysis the presented method concentrates on the film image, however, without ignoring the film text as context. Video, as well as film, produces an iconic surplus, which needs to be traced out with an adequate method. Two approaches have to be differentiated: On the one hand images are "expression-carriers" with particular contents. This perspective is indicated by the rubric "picture sciences." On the other hand images carry also certain attitudes, as implied by the term style-analysis. But this means not to ignore that both levels are continuously overlapping each other and cannot be clearly separated. However, the indicated "Entmischung" separation/de-mixing/un-mixing of two eventually connected elements should be understood as a methodological tool.

MUSIC VIDEO, SHORT MOVIE, OR ANOTHER MEDIUM?

In the case of film, the scenes so rich with images can hardly be elucidated. In the case of short music clips the problem of interpretation is a different one. There is no opportunity to introduce a subject that will determine the plot for quite a duration of time. This does not mean that there is no central theme in music clips. The clip can be seen as a compression of content, therefore it is forced to present striking images or to force their circulation pace respectively.

Directors of music clips are honored with art awards: In 1999 Chris Cunningham was awarded the Golden Nica for the Aphex Twin video "Come to Diddy" at Ars Electronica. Many directors, such as Spike Jonze, are also engaged in movies. The director of *Being John Malkovich* (2000) has previously produced clips for The Beastie Boys (Sabotage). Since 1999 the best German music video is awarded the MuVi at the annual presentation of short movies in Oberhausen. Clips can be regarded as a highly important aesthetic phenomenon; since the 1980s they have also been presented in art exhibitions. The directory of the short movie festival in Oberhausen understands the music video as a medium that goes beyond the pure illustration of a product; it develops instead visual autonomy. Music videos, however, as specific media for young and post-adolescent viewers, are still regarded as a negative sign of the accelerated pace of images in the new digital worlds. The catchword "three-minute-culture" expresses an undifferentiated disapproval to be found particularly in pedagogic literature. In fact, music videos form a part of the possible training fields for the experience of future velocity and the new worlds of perception within the commercial laboratory. Thus they provide a preparation toward the requirements in the new electronic world. Clips contribute to the international expansion of youth culture styles, and they lead to national variants as well as to a homogenizing of scenes. Since the 1950s, film has been the global medium publishing youth culture's style messages—until the start of the first pure music-channel, MTV, in 1981. Meanwhile the number of music-channels on television has grown. In Germany four programs are targeted at different age and style groups: MTV, VH1, VIVA, and VIVA plus.

Music videos are primarily commercials for artists and records, but they also transmit the representation of a style. In the beginning the video clip denies its artificial character and appears as a medial extension of the live performance in concert halls. The medial music-images offer new creative opportunities; however, as they are produced within an economically defined context, the percentage of innovative images remains, similar to film and video art, fairly small.

An interdisciplinary methodology for an analysis of the scene-topology as a whole, including the medial representation of youth cultures, forms the framework of an image-focused analysis of video clips. Richard's concept of the aesthetic field study contains the collection and examination of all of a scene's cultural products, including flyers, magazines, and video clips. In addition to Spradley's social situations, the music video displays an aesthetic situation, integrating actions (dance), objects (dress), and interdependencies with real spaces. The next part of this essay will develop a contextual method of analysis, concentrating on visual elements. Dick Hebdige's interpretation of a style's "secret signs of grace" in medial representation will be of importance for drawing conclusions regarding social and political conditions—even though Hebdige's analysis chiefly neglects the cultural-industrial background of youth cultural production. The basis of the following analysis is formed by a general appreciation of Willis's "grounded aesthetics and profane culture," as well as by the concept of "visual culture" extended by semiotic components and specifically the "pictorial turn" approach. With respect to the analysis of art, the work-immanent analysis of color, form and material of an object concentrates on the vivid character of aesthetic appearances, completed by the consideration of the respective media-structural components. In its entire process of cultural and medial reproduction, and the production of cultural capital and symbolic surplus value, the emerging visual universe can be understood in the sense of a critical style-theory. I will now turn to the analysis of music videos from the hip hop scene, an innovative contemporary youth culture whose character as a classical street-corner society is reflected in the medium.

HIP HOP VIDEOS: REPRESENT! REPRESENT!

Hip hop is not a classical working-class subculture, but a cultural expression of a socially marginalized youth living in the urban spaces of metropolitan centers. The inner differentiation of hip hop is expressed through visual means. Setting and creative means are varying with respect to g (gangsta) funk or p (party) funk. Up to the middle of the 1990s, videos only rarely integrate techniques such as electronic distortions, detailed sections, or hard and quick cuts. Sampling and scratching techniques are not yet transferred to the visual level. Experimental videos accompany an involved rhyme style (leaders of the new school include Busta Rhymes, Pharcyde, Ol' Dirty Bastard). Flashbacks are exclusively used for scenes actually referring to the past, such as film documentaries showing Martin Luther King, Malcolm X, or sequences from the history of black discrimination with references to slavery or intimidation by policemen. The clips follow a narrative structure and are presented in real time. They have a documentary tendency, and appear like live reports on the neighborhood. The pictures form a pendent to what Ice T calls "reality rap." The reduction to black and white pictures produces an authentic touch of the videos and indicates the hard reality on the street. Masking people's faces with black bars and blurred image details are particularly visible in gangsta rap videos. As a "veiling" of violence and guns these techniques are used to dodge censorship, even if the scenes make no secret of what is really going on. To express the respect of the gangster also formally, many videos are recorded in a low camera perspective.

Hip hop videos have recently become more differentiated with an increased use of digital techniques. Good examples are the videos by Missy Elliott and Busta Rhymes, which represent eccentric characters. A typical stylistic means here is the distortion through a fisheye, a 180 degree wide-angle lens.

The work-immanent analysis of hip hop images is demonstrated by Busta Rhymes's video *Get Out*, produced in 2000. *Get Out* is a mixture of typical hip hop video plots. But the video diverges from the common schemes, especially in its critical message against the image world of gangsta rap. It also differs from Busta Rhymes' earlier videos, which centered exclusively on his character as "mad nigga." The aesthetics of "posers" (the term goes back to Isabell Brombach) and posh luxury in the video's beginning is right from the start disturbed by the presence of a small child romping disrespectfully in the white enameled interior of a fake castle. Authenticity is constructed by the gold record visible on the wall in the background, belonging to the rapper. After teasing the child, the singer Busta Rhymes steps out of the door of the white castle and walks down the steps. The camera remains in the perspective at the landing. He is dressed in white clothes, wears a white unfastened denim jacket, showing off his naked skin, and sunglasses. He climbs into a white Ferrari. The color white plays the decisive role in his world of luxury. Standing for cleanness it forms a distinction against other typical representations of gangsta rap. It presents "someone who made it" and who now supports nonprivileged kids. The camera still remains at a respectful, distanced perspective, circulating now around the sports car. The camera accompanies the artist in a driving sequence. With the focus on the car window it records the rapping Busta Rhymes, who underlines his words by gesticulating with his tattooed, muscular arms. The limousine ride ties the whiteness of the world of luxury to the green of the normal neighborhood, which is represented through a fenced basketball field on which Rhymes appears amid playing children, now dressed in anarchy-shirts and bandannas. The change of clothes demonstrates his solidarity with the community. The camera perspective changes to the children's eye-level. Rhymes stoops to adopt the position of the kids. His rap is about prostitution and gambling in the hood, encouraging the kids to fight against these conditions. Signs of gangsterism are represented in a quite neutral and subtle way, for example by gambling men hanging out at the corner and ice-licking "chicks" standing for prostitution. The kids accompany Busta Rhymes and form his posse. The camera again adopts the children's perspective and records how they start to appropriate objects from the adult world, like a monitoring van. The van's content is introduced in a close-up: The door is opened and the zoom focuses a pair of handcuffs. The children start to dress up with sunglasses, moustache, and riot sticks. The following close-up from the cab of the van shows one of the children's riot sticks in action expelling the gamblers. In a parallel sequence showing Busta Rhymes, the riot stick now corresponds to the pointed forefinger. The kids masquerading as adults are then shown in suits with FBI cards, removing criminals from the neighborhood. In a scene showing a raid of a club and a street corner, the kids collar the gangsters and kick out all the prostitutes, drug-dealers, and pimps. On the right side of the picture is a police car shown in front of the club;, the zoom records gesticulating policemen. Then the NYPD car, indicating the setting of the video, drives out of the picture, implicating the police's passivity and corruptness. The signs of unwelcome wealth in the neighborhood are displayed in the club scene showing status symbols such as mobile phones, gold chains, women's expensive designer clothes, bandannas, and reversed baseball caps. These objects, in other videos rather positively connoted, are turned into negative signs that lead to banishment from the scene. The neighborhood supports this operation and intermediary scenes show the entire hood backing up Busta Rhymes.

The video follows a narrative structure, with only a few scenes having an experimental quality: Busta Rhymes appears between the scenes in the gangster club in blue-violet lighting accompanied by dancers dressed in orange. He is additionally shown illumined by black light, which plunges him in a blue tone nearly past recognition. The lighting separates the world of gangsters from the world of luxury, which in contrast offers space for kids and enables them to get rid of the surrounding dangers. Busta Rhymes is the linking figure between these worlds, nearly always shown in front-view. He is constantly approaching the camera, either by walking toward it or by gesticulating extensively with his arms. Vertical movements within the pictorial frame are reserved for the gangsters and their banishment out of the picture. The images in this video are quite traditional with a nearly chronological plot. Sequences from parallel plots structure the video without interrupting its linearity. The tempo in which the images are shown is rather slow. The video has the character of a short movie, visible also in the reduction to a 16:9 format with white beams. However, the single images and the narration, detached from the usual context of the representation scheme in hip hop, appear rather insignificant. For this reason, the work-immanent analysis must be completed by the consideration of the social background.

REPRESENTATIONAL SCHEMES AND A PRIORI INTERPRETATION

The content analysis of a hip hop video is determined by certain preconditions: The fixed perspective of a white critic results in the problem of a different perception of the video. Certain postures and expressions are based on rhetoric strategies such as the "signifying monkey," a generic term for the interplay of rhetoric figures such as distortion of words, repetitions, and subversions. "Playin' the dozens" is a rhetoric form alongside rapping, loud-talking, testifying, marking, and sounding. The entire universe of discourse must be taken into consideration to understand the meaning of certain expressions. Hip hop is not simply a revival of African American tradition (music, oral tradition) but a representation of a second level of medial narrative art. Topics in hip hop are the appropriation of citations from the image world of media such as T.V. shows, sport stars, video games, and designer articles.

On the pictorial level four basic patterns can be distinguished regarding the contents and stereotypes of hip hop videos: gangsterism; luxury and consumerism; the dark side of gangsterism; and the jumping and crazy gesticulating "mad nigga" who lives in an imaginary universe.

Gangsterism is depicted as hanging out with the homies, the homeboys of the (neighbor)hood. The scenes show boredom, assaults, gangbanging, shooting, fighting, drug dealing, gambling, and collective posing with the gang. The scenes are aggressive, showing clenched fists, veiled gangster faces, guns, and fighting dogs. Fire and destruction illuminate the dark and ruined spaces that form the background of the gangsters. Their representation is further subdivided into stereotypes of fighter, kid, and macho.

The second major stereotype is luxury and consumerism. The status of a successful gangsta is displayed in symbols such as a luxurious villa, swimming pool, and cars, preferably European brands such as Mercedes, BMW, Ferrari, or American jumpcars and low riding models. Other popular status symbols are mobile phones, whirlpools, luxurious bath tubs and chic interiors, gambling, expensive cigars, gold, and diamonds, as well as bubbling champagne bottles as a sign for uncountable and excessive orgasms (see the videos by LLCoolJ, Dr. Dre, *Parody* by Aphex Twin Windowlicker). Last, but not least, are the scenes completed by uncountable, sexually willing, and only barely dressed women. Party-scenes, which are often situated in public space, can be divided as parties with the homies on the streets of the neighborhood, at the pool, or at a live concert—often without women—or parties with the entire family, like barbecues in public areas (for example Jazzy Jeff and The Fresh Prince: *Summertime*).

Hip hop videos also include the dark side of gangsterism, often depicted in a stereotypical manner. Death, funerals, prisons, police, homeless kids, and widows (Ice Cube, Nonchalant: *Five o'Clock in the Morning*) show the results of discrimination and unequal opportunity caused by white authority. However, clips warning against the madness of black male youth killing one another are actually rare. The warning words are in most cases expressed by the female rappers who no longer want to suffer in the tragic role of the mourning woman.

Finally, the jumping and crazy gesticulating "mad nigga" who lives in an imaginary, silver-futuristic fairy or comic universe, different from the luxurious world, is a repeating theme in these videos. One of the prime figures is Flavor Flav of Public Enemy. Also a member of the Wu-tang clan, RZA, represents himself as a cartoon figure named Bobby Digital. The scenes in imaginary spaces as well as the costumes of the mad characters are often presented in primary colors.

The first three categories reflect—often slightly distorted—situations from the lives of African Americans, the "afro-diasporic culture" at the margins of a postindustrial urban America. Many hip hop videos attempt to render black discrimination in American society visible or to abolish it at least on an imaginary level.

To a white audience the scenes that present extreme situations, such as gangbanging and exceptions from the daily routine such as parties, appear as rather uncommon living conditions. The visualized situations follow a principle of "living on edge": an existence between danger and pleasure—actually quite familiar to the male, black, lower-class youth. For this demographic, which is usually ignored or reduced to silence in the United States, rap is an instrument to construct the male black body as a location of pleasure and power. As bell hooks has suggested, the young black man presents himself as dangerous and desirable. A permanent feeling of inferiority to the white population causes black men to emphasize their specifically male characteristics: demonstrative sexuality, bodily virility, and aggressive behavior. As McLaren documents, negative connotations like laziness and violence are turned into positive attributes of power and serve to resist white domination. The videos show an excessive consumption of luxury goods. Expensive cars, clothing, and high-tech equipment are status symbols for the ones who made it. In fashion, hip hop begins not incidentally with the overt citation of the elitist signs of haute couture, a world full of striking logos (see the emblems of Gucci or Chanel). Through strategies like the blow up technique, the signs of unreachable wealth and power are carried to extremes. Black hip hop culture appropriates unentitled—in the eyes of the white middle class—wealth. The citation of dream images and their transformation via strategies of hyper-consumption testify that the dreams are in fact unrealizable in the social reality of black communities. According to Tricia Rose, the excessive emphasis on expensive commodities in hip hop is a means to draw attention to class distinctions, social hierarchies, and the conquering of new cultural territory. The representation of consumer power turns into an instrument of cultural expression, manageable also by the means of fakes and illegal practices. But a successful gangster is not only marked by allurement but also by the effects of gangbanging and criminality, ending in the fatal vicious circle of prison and death. The successful rapper—somebody who could escape the ghetto, but who still decorates himself with the respective attributes (such as Ice T, Ice Cube)—presents another figure for identification. Alongside his sexual attractiveness, personality, and commercial success, his self-praise centers on his rhyme artistry. Urban metropolitan spaces form the setting for this: the ruined streets of the Bronx and Brooklyn in the videos of East Coast gangsta rappers (Onyx, Black Sheep, House of Pain). Clean and sunny neighborhoods with nice houses in suburbs like Compton in Los Angeles—no less dangerous, though—are the typical West Coast images in the videos of Ice T and Snoop Doggy Dog. The setting of those daily life scenes is precisely recorded, often indicated by street signs visible in the videos. Abstract regionalism referring to East and West coasts and concrete regionalism (as in the title Straight Outta Compton by NWA, Niggers with Attitude) form several levels of local color. The globality of the style is indicated by graffiti paintings. However, the videos are limited to images of the black communities. White people are only shown as neutral figures in party crowds or as representatives of white power, for example in the role of either the violent or stupid cop. Many of these videos present extreme discrimination against women. Along with cars and other luxurious items, women are presented as a part of men's property. These functionalized women exhibit their bodies in a very proud way. This is, according to bell hooks, because they were educated in a way that gave them no access to intellectual alternatives or roles other than the one of the serving body. Searching for the reasons for the limited number of black female intellectuals, hooks states that African American culture offers only two stereotypes of women: the whore or bitch, and the feeding, caring mammy. To black women, hip hop videos mediate that they have to fit into the role intended for them by the followers of the conservative Nation of Islam under Louis Farrakhan, as well as by the original myth of the fertile mother Isis: this is housewife and mother. The strong sexist tendency of hip hop is criticized by numerous Black cultural critics. Greg Tate regards black male posturing as a culturally necessary basis for black practices such as basketball, jazz, or hip hop and understands them as style attitudes. He criticizes the phallocentric direction of male nationalism for avoiding the real problems, such as daily discrimination. To critics the roots of black men's sexism are white racism. The self-hatred of black people leads to black men's hatred against black women. And this can be understood as an extension of the functioning of white stereotypes. A critique of the thesis of inferiority and self-hatred is put forward by Stanley Crouch, who claims that black Americans' self-hatred is an ethnic variant of a discontent with contemporary beauty standards. Actually, a similar dissatisfaction can be observed among white people, too, whose wish for better bodies turns them into regular clients of plastic surgeons.

With the exception of rappers like Queen Latifah, hip hop assigns women a marginal role without any stylistic creativity. Producer Missy Elliot, with her real and medially impressive body volume, breaks with the principle of a massive, male bodily presence. Although women stigmatized as bitches are only barely dressed, men demonstrate screen-filling volume with ample bodies and voluminous clothing (Big Punisher, Notorious B.I.G.). In street reality, the enlargement of the male body silhouette becomes a threatening gesture (the principle of dread). Here the popular oversize-principle and the shrill colors of the clothes serve to deter possible enemies. The street as concrete social space is occupied by graffiti as a sign of presence as well as by the cultivation of a certain shuffling and space-taking way of walking. In the videos this is reinforced by the rappers' extensive gestures, emphasized again by the fisheye and a low camera perspective, which enlarge the body. The body moves back and forth frontally to the camera, often culminating in extreme close-ups. They are less produced by camera movement or zoom than by the real movement of the figures. The representational images in the clips, together with the street setting arouse the impression of a direct documentary transfer from material into virtual reality, thus producing a permanent reciprocal action between the two surfaces. However, certain stylistic features are less easily transferable, for example the crinkles in baggy pants. The medial aesthetic of hip hop can present voluminous, pseudo-three-dimensional, but nonetheless only smooth surfaces.

A work-immanent analysis of hip hop is ambivalent and difficult, because violent and sexist image-clichés are dominant. It is the question of whether the sexist and often racist words of the rappers so openly directed against women, gay, and Jewish people are repeated because of commercial reasons or because they refer to particular tendencies in the scene itself. Record labels such as Def Jam and black producers such as Dr. Dre or rappers such as LLCoolJ market gangsta attitudes offensively because they sell so well. On the basis of a work-immanent analysis, despite the awareness of a white person's interpretation, this ascertainment cannot be pushed aside. The interpretation of the images in the context of different recipients renders a prohibition of criticism for reasons of political correctness obsolete. Its stereotyping can be explained from the commercial production context.

MUSIC VIDEOS IN THE PERSPECTIVE OF A NEW PICTURE SCIENCE

As the preceding interpretation should make plain, in a precise picture analysis, the relation to the social context of a represented scene can be reconstructed even in the most trivial video. A further task following the presented interpretation, would be to examine the functioning of the pictorial realization of rhetoric strategies: for example if the refined linguistic strategies now fall victim to simple pictorial stereotypes, or if the word plays in raps show similar mechanisms? Entering more intensely than before into the meaning of the pictorial would bring up further levels of content to the analysis of video as well as film.

Such an examination proceeds from the idea that pictures first of all fulfill a specific function, which lies within the film text or story, respectively the video's narrative level. However, after that the quality of the pictures must be taken into consideration, leading to new problems, which can only briefly be referred to here: A film image is not a painting, although in its disposition it must be understood as such and needs to be compared with traditional (pictorial) media. This creates again a new kind of problem, which cannot be mastered in the analysis as there are far too many single pictures in a video and even more so in film. But despite that, a scene, an angle, or a sequence of a video can be compared to traditional pictures. Thereby the film image should be taken as seriously as any other pictorial medium: it has a structure, a composition, figures are arranged more or less dominantly, spaces are created via objects, figures, light, etc. and of course the movement and angle of the camera as the point of view has to be considered, too.

The exemplary analysis of video images has shown how significant the function of images is within this media. Neither film nor video is a sum of their single images; they contain an optical surplus, their openness allows the access via different levels of reception. The creators of these images produce a structure, they prearrange a culture's pictorial archive. A particular "pictorial event" happens, when it comes to an explosion of images in the viewer's mind. This allows a new perception, a new seeing. The work-immanent approach toward pictures enables a conscious process of "inner" seeing, it promises certainty and understanding. Thus we do not talk about images while overlooking them, but instead we follow all the new pictorial universes opening from the images seen.

Resources

Bordwell, D. (1997). *On the History of Film Style*. Cambridge, MA: Harvard University Press.

Decker, J. L. (1994). The state of rap. Time and place in hip hop nationalism. In T. Rose & A. Ross (Eds.), *Microphone fiends: Youth music & youth culture* (pp. 99–121). New York: Routledge.

Hebdige, D. (2002). *Subculture. The meaning of style*. New York: Routledge.

hooks, b. (1992). *Black looks. Race and representation*. Boston: South End Press.

Rose, T. (1994). A style nobody can deal with. In T. Rose & A. Ross (Eds.), *Microphone fiends: Youth music & youth culture* (pp. 71–81). New York: Routledge.

———. (1994). Contracting rap. An interview with Carmen Ashhurst-Watson. In T. Rose & A. Ross (Eds.), *Microphone fiends: Youth music & youth culture* (pp. 122–144). New York: Routledge.

Techno/House, Hip Hop Clubs, and Videos

Birgit Richard and Heinz-Hermann Krüger

This entry deals with the real spheres and imaginary spheres represented in the media—music video clips, to be precise—of two contemporary and innovative youth cultures, the techno/house and hip hop scenes. Choosing the hip hop and techno youth cultures is suitable, because the example of the former can be used to demonstrate remaining elements of the classic street corner society of adolescents. The ephemeral world of the latter, however, and the creative appropriation of spheres by this adolescent scene rather mark the transformation into a cyberspace culture. When analyzing the real spheres, we predominantly focus on studying a socio-ecological segment of the lives of these adolescents, the exterior forms and the appropriation of dance venues by these groups of youth culture. As far as possible, we also try to consider the appropriation of public spheres, quarters and public places by these scenes of youth culture.

Although, when analyzing the real locations and the interactive appropriation of these venues, we can still apply views developed in socio-ecological approaches of youth studies by Baacke or Becker, Eigenbrodt, and May, for an analysis of spheres in the media in contemporary worlds of images, these approaches have to be expanded. Beside the instruments of cultural-sociological and semiotic analyses, we also use approaches of media theory.

Although we are predominantly interested in real spheres–first of all dance venues—of contemporary youth scenes, the interrelations between these spheres and the respective styles of youth culture and the representation of these styles in the imaginary spheres of international media, in front of these analyses we put a concise historical sketch of the transformation of dance venues for adolescents and the world of media for youth cultures since the 1950s, to be able, against this background, to demonstrate the changed quality of contemporary appropriation of spheres by youth cultures and their representation in the media.

AESTHETICS AND APPROPRIATION OF REAL SPHERES

The young people make a habit of dancing, in a way that mocks any sense of decency, in badly aired, small overcrowded cafés and floors.[1]

HISTORICAL PRECURSORS

Autonomous dance venues are of fundamental importance for all styles of youth culture. Putting dance venues at their disposal often follows the massive presence of adolescents on the streets: the 1950s did not know any discotheques or youth centers. Adolescents could only listen to music in cinemas or perhaps in a milk bar with a jukebox. The first dance clubs and dance cafés for youngsters, established by municipal authorities for some kind of prophylactic youth work, developed after the riots by young hooligans in the 1950s.

The 1960s were characterized by beat-clubs with live music, where the youngsters, from today's perspective modestly dressed, sat at rows of tables draped in white or danced in front of the stage. Other opportunities for dancing were found at beat-festivals and at concerts. The first discotheques developed at the end of the 1960s. From the beginning, they were suspected of commercial manipulation and of re-shaping adolescents. However, the alternative venues of the hippies do not impress the pedagogical observer either. The second generation of hippies in the 1970s were found in white-washed disco-dives. At the time, the big discos were greatly improved technically. The supply of technical innovations in lighting and sound became increasingly important. Simple claviluxes and disco bowls were followed by carousels for colors, stroboscopes, black light, carbon dioxide snow, and a computer-directed laser lightshow. The commercial discotheques did also make an effort to become lavishly decorated. They were turned into spaceships or airplanes, with DJ-cockpits resembling flight-decks (film: *Thank God It's Friday*) or they borrowed from films like *Saturday Night Fever* and had the dance floor illuminated from below, enhancing the stage-like character and drawing a distinctive line between dance floor and the surrounding part of the premises. Owing to the structure of the venue, the style of dancing remained down to earth. The lighting contributed to the design of the venue and "brightened it up." It created a pleasant atmosphere for dancing and did not lead to distress among the audience. In disco-culture, stressing the role of the dance floor and illuminating the legs hints at the growing awareness that dancing offers an opportunity to present the body.

Furthermore, the newly developing club culture formed certain rules for access, controlled by the so-called door-policy. Selection was the constant principle in the clubs: After the audience had been selectively chosen, the DJ selected records. The stylistic innovations of punk expanded the range of dance venues. Alongside commercially styled clubs, crumbling and bare spaces in industrial or decaying buildings became venues as well. They symbolize the exchange of the interior for the exterior. The exterior, the street, was brought inside.

New wave, the depressive branch of punk, introduced another variation of the design of dance venues: cold and artificial equipment like neon light, steel, mirrors, and floors of pimpled rubber left behind the comfort of the hippie-disco and the punk-aesthetics of decay.

The 1980s saw the development of cultural centers and multifunctional open-plan discotheques in disused industrial buildings. These premises house the actual dance floor, restaurants, bistros, pubs, coffee bars. Eating, dancing, communication, and drinking are clearly separated from each other. This kind of architectural design anticipated what in the 1990s was to be called "event gastronomy" Dancing is only one of many activities.

The 1990s not only saw the development of venues for large events and cultural centers, where the audience is mixed, but also the introduction of scene-discos and an assigned day of the week for almost every style and age group. On a particular day of the week, only one style's favorite music will be played. The differentiation of the styles is also reflected in the multiple use of existing dance venues. Clubs and cultural centers, following the English example, offer different styles of music on different days of the week, not only on weekends, thereby attracting different kinds of people. The design of the venue, however, is not adapted to the style addressed.

HIP HOP VENUES

For the hip hop culture in New York the street is a training venue for break dance and mobile sound systems to create open-air community centers in the neighborhoods, where no infrastructure for parties and dance could formerly be found. Meanwhile, hip hop clubs have been established here.

In Germany there are hardly any clubs entirely being devoted to hip hop. Straight hip hop nights, if we disregard concerts and jams, are very rare. Hip hop is a street style, not really occupying any other spheres than the street, which might be put at the style's and its followers' disposal. Thus, their chances for an independent shaping of the scene are slim and, owing to the scene's flexibility, perhaps not even necessary. The only thing you need to break dance is a relatively smooth surface, not a specially assigned dance floor. The line between dance spheres and surroundings is drawn by the on-lookers, who group around the break dancer to spur him on and judge his performance. The scene meets in sheltered rooms, like youth centers. In Germany, a lot of male, foreign youngsters have a sense of belonging to the scene. Some symbols of their presence are graffiti and tags on the walls. Just like the early venue of punk, hip hop venues resemble the street environment.

This term, however, does not refer to anonymous, functional places, as they are preferred by punks—public places, railway stations, escalators—but to meeting points in the neighborhoods. They are only points of departure, not places for hanging around. Graffiti bear witness to the youngsters' nomad-like wandering around, and leave traces outside their own quarters. They mark territories and raids through metropolitan areas (e.g., when they appear on underground trains traveling through other parts of town). Hip hop venues are characterized by male activities. In most cases girls are only admitted as observers, not as active participants in contests and jams.

TECHNO AND HOUSE VENUES

When we consider the real spheres of the techno and house scene we see a different picture: It conquers a large part of the commercial and parts of the alternative discotheque spheres and addresses a mass audience from various social strata. We have to differentiate between individual events, rave or event, and frequent techno and house club nights, either with a regular DJ cast (the so-called residents) on different days of the week or additional guest DJs.

The club provides a weekly continuity at a concrete location, while mega raves are selective events. Flyers as an ephemeral medium, only giving the latest information, should be read as reminiscences of the quickly changing locations, often only rented for one night. Techno-discos and temporary mega raves in the 1990s take place in, among other venues, vast factory buildings, thereby borrowing from the English warehouse parties (which were, incidentally, illegal). In Germany, for the big events easily available multifunctional venues are used. To turn the premises into a specific venue for raves, a special design using decorations, lights, and animations is necessary. On weekends, the techno and house scene disappears into these venues, sealed off from ordinary life, for hours on end or even the entire weekend. To make this disappearance perfect, the rooms have to dimmed, so that the "lightning storms" are set off. Computer-generated lighting effects reduced to a particular color-spectrum, a lot of white light, and stroboscopic flashes are dominant features. Space is transformed into an immaterial cosmos, a parallel world, resembling computer-generated virtual realities. The room, mostly box-shaped and rectangular, becomes a screen, a phenomenon created by effects such as stroboscopes, fog, and black light. These elements of design refer to the interior of a screen, virtually turned inside out. The color design of the rooms, reduction of the color spectrum, a lot of white light, follows the principle of color separation; information on the screen is build up by single dots and lines of color.

The dancing body is displayed into a temporary manifestation of light. The momentary existence in space/on screen is only confirmed when the bodies are hit by pencils of light, which is reflected by the special fabric of the clothes. These elements produce fragmented motions, resembling silent films not shown in real time; the other dancers are perceived as if they perform in such a film, artificial creatures in strange motion. By dancing as if on screen, the dancers have both entered an area of the media and cyberspace. They do not face the images and projections, but are part of them. Effects, light, and music, combined with the dancers, create an abstract video clip, projecting nothing but themselves.

Lighting design is not supposed to brighten up the room. Light and projections raise the room into another dimension. The floors are mostly dark, and lighting too shuts off the rooms toward the floor and opens it up toward the above. Room design and clothing suggest a calculated elevation without actually leaving the floor. A good example is the platform shoes, which ensure adhesion to the floor despite weightlessness, an experience similar to the first astronauts'. The stroboscope is not supposed to create an atmospheric room design, but ecstasy and disorientation, the selective suspension of the sense of time and space. The dancers enter a physical-mental sphere, detached from ordinary categories of time and space and determined by abstraction, dissolution of contradictions and of the world of objects. Through the reduction of material objects (e.g. the Berlin techno club Tresor in its founding years), these rooms do not provide a lot of static points for orientation. It is only the other dancers, who, though disappearing again into the room's darkness, confirm the individual dancer's presence. The scene's yearning for physical contact is supposed to provide the assurance that the other person is actually physically present.

Apart from special chill-out lounges, there are no areas for rest. The rooms do not offer facilities for lingering, sitting, or talking, just predominantly dancing. Objects like platforms, which may or may not be found, are intended for go-go dancing, letting individual dancers stand out from the crowd, but not for resting. The evacuation of all objects only permits absolutely necessary infrastructural elements such as the bar and the DJ-desk.

The scene has taken over dark cellars, bunkers or strong rooms, and old power stations. For outsiders, the doorman of the club Tresor seems to open the gate to the seven circles of an inferno, in which damned adolescents compulsively fulfill the Sisyphean task of "meaningless dance excesses": fog and smoke clouds and the regular beat of the bass drum pour out from the door opening. Space, music, and light in combination generate a kind of creative elemental force. The combination of acoustic and visual stimuli represents a certain compulsive quality. The body has to react with the controlled motions of dancing.

Anyone not dancing here is certainly dead.[2]

The Tresor, the former germ cell of the Berlin techno scene, with its lockers and bars, symbolizes the voluntary locking up, the shutting out of the outside world. This isolation does also apply to clubs specializing in house music. However, these rooms have a different design. They overemphasize material and ornaments. The interiors are characterized by golden frames, red plush, baroque bordello-kitsch (often, the clubs are located in former bordellos, e.g. the "Unique" in Düsseldorf's old town), brocade wallpaper, lava lamps, and many accessories that bear witness to a cultivation of the bad and trashy taste of the 1970s combined with "baroque from Gelsenkirchen" (proletarian taste with the pretension of sophistication). House dance venues are retro-rooms dominated by objects. The popularity of "sweet" devotional items can be put down to the transfer of the principle of travesty to the general design. This is the artificial-ecstatic exaggeration of the "feminine," pointing to the existence of a gay culture with its own aesthetics. The personal furnishing of these clubs is a hallmark; even a living room can turn into a party room or its model. The world characterized by designer-chic and celebrations in the ruins of former industrial buildings is counteracted by the frowned upon principle of grandmotherly coziness and a petit bourgeois version of a playful drawing room in rococo design.

After having visited a house club or a techno event as an ecstatic excursion into a virtual future, on early Monday morning, the nightly party nomads reenter ordinary life. Even the illegal parties of the "underground," using anonymous normed and neglected non-locations like tunnels, passage ways, areas beneath motorway bridges, underground garages and building sites, are, in contrast to English raves, not really conspicuous in Germany. These are places of decay, unfinished, of through traffic, uncomfortable places that are not really inviting you to stay. The nightly occupation resembles a racket, the party squatting no longer has anything to do with the appropriation of dwelling space by real squatters. The party nomads are able to find these places everywhere. They do not stick to particular locations.

The parades (Love parade Berlin, Streetparade Zurich, Union Move Munich, Hamburg G-Move) and processions, numerous now, are their symbol of physical presence in the streets. This means the techno and house scenes' selective conquest of the street, which formerly wasn't developed as a dance venue by any other youth culture. It fights for its right to parties and celebrations, which, against the background of the Criminal Justice Bill in England, can be considered a basic right. The occupation of public spheres as a party zone during the day focuses on arterial traffic routes in city centers. The explosive growth of parades and participants, commercialization (MTV Love Parade) and their established role as part of the cities' public relations efforts, however, diminishes the subversive character of these public demonstrations of physical presence to a kind of carnival or funfair.

SPHERES IN THE MEDIA

The media are of great importance for the representation of a style of youth culture. They spread the image of the style internationally and lead to national variants as well as the homogenization and uniformitization of scenes.

FROM CULT FILMS TO MUSIC VIDEO

In the 1950s, film was the first medium to make the messages and music of youth cultures public. Cult films reflect the music and the style of a generation by the visual realization of the music (e.g., *Rock around the Clock*, with Bill Haley). The 1960s saw the first regular music shows on television in which bands performed, such as the "BeatClub" in Germany, alongside music films (*Yellow Submarine*, *Yeah Yeah Yeah* by the Beatles), which should not be confused with film versions of musicals. This kind of TV show derives from *Top of the Pops*, a BBC show about the music charts in England. The 1970s gave us shows like *Disco* with Ilja Richter. One of the films in cinema leaving a mark is the disco film *Saturday Night Fever* in 1978.

In 1981 MTV, a channel entirely devoted to music, started to broadcast in England. The program mostly consisted of music videos, which before only served the purpose of advertising a product, (i.e., band and record). It certainly was not a medium in its own right. This canned material was supposed to be more than just a recording device and offered new opportunities for design. However, in the beginning these opportunities were rarely taken advantage of. The pseudo-documentary presentation of bands underlined the video's role as a promoting product. Performing on video was supposed to show a part of the life of the star or the band. In the beginning, the video clip denied that it was stage managed and was an expansion of the venue of a live concert in the media.

Music videos as a new medium have developed into an ideal means of transport for the representation of a style. The first pop-bands to use the new medium excessively are the English New Romantics or synth-pop bands (Visage, Spandau Ballet, Ultravox . . .). In Germany, the first regular TV show with music videos was *Formel eins* in the early 1980s. Before, we only find sporadic music shows, mostly with "live"-(playback) performances by bands or broadcasting events, such as the *WDR-Rocknacht*. Music films on cinema screens in the 1980s include the punk/new wave film *Breaking Glass* and two hip hop films: *Beat Street*, emphasizing dance and music, and *Wild Style*, showing the style's aesthetics.

In the mid-1990s the number of music channels increased to four: MTV, VH1, VIVA, and VIVA 2, each addressing different age groups and styles. Since 1988 MTV has had its own show for hip hop, *YO MTV Raps*, which in 1996 was renamed *Wordcup*. Later VIVA followed with *Freestyle*. On MTV, techno and house can be found in *Dance* and *Partyzone,*; on VIVA it is *House TV*, formerly *Housefrau*.

HIP HOP VIDEOS

The various styles of music also express their inner variety by different visual means. Thus, hip hop videos show different settings and means of design, depending on whether it is g (gangsta)-funk or p (party)-funk. The videos shown (on VIVA and MTV), which, to be sure, only represent a small selection, are rarely arranged by means of electronic distortion, selectivity or sharp, fast cuttings. Sampling and scratching is not transferred to the visual level (an exception in g-funk is, for example, Public Enemy's first clip "Night of the Living Baseheads"). The misuse of consumer electronics does only take place on the level of music. Experimental videos are rare and in most cases accompany a complex style of rhyming (leaders of the new school include Busta Rhymes, Pharcyde, Ol' Dirty Bastard). Even flashbacks are only used for scenes of the past, such as excerpts from films of Martin Luther King and Malcolm X, or the presentation of black history showing images of repression such as films about slave transports or police officers beating up blacks. The videos are not determined by technical experiments.

Computer animations are rarely to be found. The clips follow narrative patterns and are shown in real time. They seem to be documentary, such as live broadcasts from neighborhoods. The images are supposed to be the counterpart to what Ice-T calls "reality rap." The restriction to black and white images gives the videos authenticity and demonstrates the toughness of street life.

Distortions and superimpositions like black bars or blurred spots predominantly appear in gangsta rap videos, where they hide violent scenes or weapons from the censors, although the scenes do not conceal what it is all about.

Before analyzing hip hop videos, some preconditions should be taken into consideration: the determined viewpoint of the white interpreter, which cannot be left behind, and the problem of a distorted reception of videos by a white, German audience, who directly translate images of Afro-American everyday culture into their own world. Certain postures and expressions are based on rhetorical strategies such as the "signifying monkey," a generic term for all rhetorical figures: word twisting, repetition, and reversal. "Playin' the dozens" is a rhetorical form, in addition to others such as rapping, loud-talking, testifying, marking, and sounding. With many expressions the whole universe of discourse has to be taken into consideration, a difficult undertaking for white listeners.

As Rose writes, hip hop is not simply a revival of African American traditions (music, oral traditions), but represents a second stage of narrative art conveyed by the media. The topics of hip hop are "appropriations" of quotations from the world of images in the media (TV shows, famous athletes, video games, and branded articles). By "using the misuse" of conventional, antiquated technologies, hip hop turns black consumers into producers of music. These technologies are combined with high-tech products such as samplers, which quite early on were creatively used by artists like Grandmaster Flash.

On the level of images three basic patterns of content and stereotypes assigned to them can be ascertained:

1   Gangsterism: hanging around with the homies, the homeboys, mates, in the hood, the neighborhood. Boredom, hold-ups, gangbanging, shootings, fights, drug deals, gambling, and posing with the gang are shown.

2   Luxury and consumer worlds: the successful gangsta presents his pool, cars and low riding, mobile phone, bathtubs, whirlpools, luxurious interiors, gambling, and innumerable women, barely dressed and willing, as attributes of his status. Party scenes, mostly occurring in public spheres, are divided into parties with the homies on the streets of the neighborhood, at the pool or at concerts, where (their own) wives might be missing entirely, and parties with wives and large families, like barbecues in public parks (e.g., Jazzy Jeff and The Fresh Prince: "Summertime").

3   The dark sides of gangsterism: death, funerals, prison, police, orphaned children, widowed wives (Ice Cube, Nonchalant: "Five o'clock in the Morning") are presented as consequences of repression and the lack of chances opposite white authorities; clips warning of the insanity of mutual annihilation by male black youngsters are rarer.

The warning voices are predominantly those of female rappers, who are no longer prepared to accept the tragic role of the mourning wife that was left behind. In general, sections of African American life, the "afro-diasporic culture" (Rose), are distortedly shown to take place on the fringes of postindustrial, urban America. Hip hop videos try to make visible or, imaginarily, do away with the discrimination against black citizens in America. The scenes leave the white viewer with the impression of unordinary events; extreme situations such as gangbanging or exceptions from ordinary life such as parties are shown. The principle of "living on the edge," of a life between danger and joy, a quite ordinary situation for male black youngsters

109

of the lower classes, is visualized. For these youngsters, normally overlooked in the United States or brought to silence, rap develops the male black body into a place of joy and power. As bell hooks has written, rap and dance represent the intensity and joy of life. The black male simultaneously presents himself to be dangerous and desirable. The permanent sense of inferiority to whites has the effect that black men show off very masculine characteristics: a demonstrative sexuality, physical ability, and belligerent behavior. Negative connotations such as laziness and violence are turned into positive attributes of strength and are used to resist white supremacy, as Peter McLaren discusses in his work.

Gangsta rap must be seen in the context of narratives specific to poor, young black male subjects in L.A.[3]

The videos show excessive consumption of luxury items. Expensive cars, clothes, and high-tech gadgets (mobile phones) are status symbols of the achiever. However, the attributes of the successful gangster show not only the allures but also the consequences of gangbanging and crime, the fatal circle of prison and death. The successful rapper who escaped from this ghetto circle and is nevertheless able to show off the same attributes (Ice T, Ice Cube) is the ideal surrogate role-model. His self-appraisal, besides his sexual attractivness, commercial success, and personal merits, predominantly focuses on his linguistic competence and his ability to make up rhymes. He is an icon of hope for male black youngsters, the social group most affected by the crises of restructuring American industrial society into a service economy with low-paid jobs.

Metropolitan space is the action-setting, including the decaying, run-down streets in the New York Bronx or Brooklyn, where the videos of the East Coast gangsta rappers (Onyx, Black Sheep, House of Pain) are set, and the typical images of the West Coast (Ice T, Snoop Doggy Dog), the hoods, at first glance pleasant and sunny, with their detached family houses in suburbs like Compton in Los Angeles, which, however, are no less dangerous. The locations, where these scenes of ordinary life take place at the time of shooting, are meant to be accurately recorded. That is why these videos often show street signs.

The videos are restricted to images from the black communities. Whites only rarely appear as neutral characters; if they do at all, it is in party crowds. In most cases they are representatives of white authority, for example, police officers, either extremely brutal or extremely dumb. We also find massive discrimination against women in the videos broadcast. Often, women are presented as property alongside cars and other luxury items. When the women thus functionalized present their bodies with pride, this, according to bell hooks can be put down to an upbringing that withholds from black women any (mental) alternative to this role as a serving body. hooks is looking for reasons why there are so few female black intellectuals, and finds that in Afro-American culture only two female stereotypes exist: the bitch, or the feeding and caring mammy. The hip hop videos require black women to adapt to the role of housewife and mother, which has been assigned to them by the elemental myths of the fertile first mother, Isis, and also by black men,in particular by followers of the conservative Nation of Islam under Louis Farrakhan. Many rappers are followers of the Nation of Islam or a splinter group, the Five Percenters. Only submitting to the patriarchal welfare principle will turn a woman into a person who can share the luxury in the images they indulge in.

The question is whether the sexist and sometimes racist undertones mentioned above, which openly confront women, gays, and Jews, are only repeated for commercial reasons or rather point to particular currents within the scene. The stereotypes mentioned are not maliciously forced upon them by white producers to confirm clichés. Black businesses, including record companies like Def Jam, are marketing this gangsta attitude offensively, since it sells well.

Black cultural critics criticize the sexist tendency of hip hop. Greg Tate thinks that black male posturing is culturally necessary for basketball, jazz, and hip hop and wants to restrict it to these areas as mere attitudes of the style, which, frankly, is impossible. He criticizes the phallocentric tendency of black nationalism, because it only diverts from the true problems, like the repression experienced every day. For all these black cultural critics the origin of black sexism derives from white racism. The blacks' self-hatred leads to the hatred of black women by black men. There is an extension of white stereotypes. This inferiority—and self-hatred hypothesis is criticized by Stanley Crouch, who says that the black's self-hatred is an ethnical variant on the dissatisfaction with the standards of beauty of the respective eras. A similar desire for physical change among whites would let plastic surgeons flourish.

TECHNO VIDEOS

The abstract techno videos do not require a theoretical background for interpretation. They show surfaces. In most cases these videos do not follow any narrative structure. Their design is essentially based upon the opportunities offered by digital image processing. The computer animations show journeys through virtual space, weightless flights over virtual landscapes and driving through tunnels. A thematic focus is the presentation of technoid worlds, robots, and space stations. Flying and weightlessness are the means of locomation of the characters who are moving in these artificial worlds and are often transformed into a variety of figures by the rather overused digital process of morphing. The desire to rise above ordinary life, in the real world a theme in dancing, can be realized in the media world.

There are only a few static images; figures and objects move or change their appearance. The images are processed and merge, one image replaces the other, no image is allowed to stand out. The videos often do not amount to more than trying out textures put over imaginary creatures and objects, and show abstract, rotating bodies in space, devoid of all content. The virtuosity in dealing with digital technology is the most important feature (an example is the X-mix video series). A lot of the animated characters resemble an infantile physiology: imaginary animals, clowns, animated toys. The clips leave the impression of animated picture books. There is a slight predominance of artificial figures over real human characters. If real persons are shown, they are set in the framework of dance scenes from parties. Scenes from the great parades in Berlin or Zurich are very popular. However, these images are also distorted digitally.

The structural characteristics of the images can be described as abstraction, immateriality, self-referentiality, and light phenomena. They show motion, dynamics, and speed. Everything is flowing. For techno and house production of a video as a medium is only a supplementary element. Videos and projections are additional visual stimuli, supposed to accompany the music. A meaningful image is not really intended. The motifs have an illustrating character and are integrated into artificial spheres. The real experience of the body in real spheres is important, although, paradoxically, at an event the body becomes a medium again.

INTERDEPENDENCIES BETWEEN "REAL" SPHERES AND SPHERES IN THE MEDIA

Looking at the relationship between real presence and representation in the media tells us a lot about the character of the respective style of youth culture. Hip hop and techno/house seem to be outstanding antipodes in both areas. Nevertheless, both styles have their roots in black communities and use similar technological and structural principles and devices: record player, vinyl, sampling, archive, and DJ. Both styles form communities that resemble families: brothers and sisters (hip hop), we are all one family (techno).

The description of real spheres and spheres in the media revealed different focuses. When analysing hip hop we concentrated on spheres in the media, since the real spheres did not offer many opportunities for a detailed description, while techno permitted a closer description of real spheres (venues), the spheres in the media having only a supplementary meaning for this style.

The hip hop videos demonstrate the gap between a national style and a global style conveyed by the media, between black music and white listeners. Russel Simmons of the hip hop record label Def Jam, using the images of the style presented in the media, sells the style to white kids, who like the music but do not really understand the content, and to black kids, who try to imitate it. For white teenagers the "slumming style" is a lower-class or working-class style, provocative and the epitome of coolness. They follow the principle of "dressing down," while the black kids on weekends follow the principle of "dressing up," "smartening up."

In hip hop both real spheres and spheres in the media tend to masculinity. They are regressive spheres, where women in particular do not have a place. The videos of the American gangsta rap plead for turning attention to a male (black) subject of the lower classes, marginalized in other contexts. However, the dangerous slips of an insecure subject, who, like a gangbanger, not knowing how else to deal with it, has to destroy everything around him that seems to threaten him—b****es, rival gangs, police—are no disasters handed down by nature.

According to McLaren, the obvious sexism can be accepted, because the consumer goods pool, cars, horses, and the always available sex are unattainable for both the black and the white average citizen. The full-bosomed string-tanga beauties, always ready for the rapper, are a parody of the representation of the successful black consumer. With Angela Davis we should raise the objection of hip hop's complicity with misogynous practices and its distancing from the resistant roots from which it grew.

Although the aspect of parody cannot be denied, the open sexism cannot be ignored. Thus, the few female rappers (MC Lyte, Queen Latifah, Salt'n'Peppa: She thing) vehemently oppose in particular their degradation to "b****es" by appropriating their own spheres in media, even as female gangstas (Boss).

Is the desire for excessive consumption another regressive trait of hip hop or a parody? In hip hop, disparagement of consumption as a political and artistical sell-out and glorification of their own commercial success do coexist. In Afro-American culture commercial success is regarded as a symbol of artistic competence and independence. Rap might be able to embody a celebrated economic independence from crime. The rapper's own capital is generated to appropriate and develop cultural spheres. Tricia Rose interprets the excessive emphasis on consumer goods in hip hop as a means to downplay class differences and hierarchies and conquer cultural territory. Consumer power becomes a means of cultural expression. Hip hop appropriates the symbols of a consumer society: oversized false gold chains and diamond colliers are worn, oversized emblems and trademarks of fashion companies such as Gucci are printed on T-shirts and trousers.

In hip hop the focus lies on the representation of the style in the media. Spheres in the media release the signs of existence of a different culture, otherwise limited to the neighborhoods. Nevertheless, the images underline the local orientation of hip hop, taking shape in clothes, language, street names, and its posses and crews. These homies and gangs often function as surrogate families. The concrete street sphere in society is occupied by graffiti as symbols of their presence and as a cultivation of a particular kind of walking conquering that space. This cultivation is supported by voluminous clothing. Thus, via their style hip hop gangs demonstrate their claim to territory. A closed system is formed, which requires isolation and a hierarchical organization, based on contests, to be self-sustaining. Life is stage-managed as a perpetual contest and competition; you have to be the strongest, the best dancer, the best painter to be able to survive (contests, jams) and to receive the respect you need.

Hip hop is a clearly defined, hermetic style based upon the exclusion of women and strangers, who have no command of the language and are not prepared to contest other males, but techno and house potentially want to integrate all people. With the latter scene, no explicit verbal message marginalizes or excludes from particular places—on the contrary, metropolitan centers are selectively occupied. The real techno venues promote a democratic style especially because of their artificial character. They do not offer any opportunities for making obvious advances, there is no beer bar for boozing, hanging around, or gawping. The lighting often makes orientation difficult, more so gaping at women.

The isolation and immateriality of the spheres dissolve all separating differences: gender, profession, color of the skin. Techno and house strive for a harmonic synthesis. Since differences and contradictions are not endured, but leveled, the scene is not able to develop social perspectives for the world that would reach beyond the event. As a selective forced synthesis ruled by rhythm, the style does not offer any solutions for ordinary life. Nevertheless, techno can be understood as a sphere for development or a laboratory for new relationships between the sexes and new ways and speeds of perception. A combination of androgynous, homosexual, and infantile physical images on the surface leads to a "detachment from the detachment" usually observed in western culture when physical contact is concerned. Since physical contact no longer has a sexual background, it is permitted. In this experimental area one's own body and different sexual identities can be tested. Thus, at an event or in a club, skirts, hair-slides or platform shoes for men do not astonish anyone, since here men try the "change sex" principle, just as they do on the internet. The female body is masked by a sexually undeveloped, infantile exterior. The infantalization, as a consequence, leads to the inviolability of the child-woman. Although girlies and babes are no direct expression of the "riot girl" mentality, they are, however, an attempt to do away with representative images of feminity characterized by male influences.

An event is training of perception. It launches the dancers into new technological dimensions. The body becomes a medium between the biological existence and an immaterial data spheres. The dance can imaginarily resolve the schizophrenic situation of being citizens of two worlds. Lighting, music, and drugs compensate for backwardness and slowness of the body. To stand still, not to move in the real spheres and the spheres in the media of techno means not to exist. Techno spheres are spheres to relish in the submission to the rhythm (slave to the rhythm) of the dancers own choosing, which, according to Baudrillard, can be interpreted as a symbolic action and therefore as a radical alternative plan to social repression. Techno occupies the night like a vampire. When the sun rises, the pale party nomads disappear. Interiors and the streets are only selectively included into the dance movement. Hip hop, on the other hand, puts some emphasis on the occupation of day-spheres as points of departure. In both youth cultures fixed ties to particular locations are resolved. The loss of this fixed ties points to a certain flightiness and the detachment of youth cultures from fixed and permanent concepts of space. Techno is a global style with a language of images in the media, which can be understood internationally, fictional artificial spheres of images and similar constellations of spheres in real spheres. Hip hop spheres, real and in the media, can only be understood against a particular national background. They cannot be easily transferred to all countries, which is shown by the problematic transfer from the United States to Europe. After all, German rappers are no black ghetto kids.

Techno is looking for a universally comprehensible meta-language in music and images, whereas hip hop maintains an insider-language and continuously develops its own puns. Techno's sphere in the media is iconic, images-orientated, whereas hip hop renders its complex, ritualized language into images, which therefore have to be deciphered like a text. Techno spheres are interfaces to virtuality, which, however, can only be experienced via the whole body and when dancing. They are rather a compensation for incorporeal worlds on the net.

Nevertheless, techno spheres contain references to subcultures on the net in the future, which may be completely immaterial. Hip hop still has the tradition of classic street styles or street corner societies. The style no longer is a working class culture, but the cultural expression of marginalized youngsters in society, who have to look for their cultural roots and often commute between two worlds (white-black, German-foreign). The expansion of the style into spheres in the media serves the purpose of making up for the cultural invisibility in the public, at least a bit.

Notes

1 Quote from the pamphlet of distress issued by the Vereinigung der Saal-besitzer von Hamburg und Umgebung [Association of the ballroom-proprietors of Hamburg and its environs], Hamburg, 1932, quoted by Eichstedt & Polster, 1985, p. 38.

2 Comment of a reporter on a love-parade wagon, *Die Zeit*, July 19, 1996.

3 Mike Rose quoted in McLaren. McLaren, P. "Gansta Pedagogy and Ghettocentricity: The Hip Hop Nation as Counterpublic Sphere." Manuscript. Los Angeles, 1995.

Advertising and German MTV

Klaus Neumann-Braun

The selection of music broadcasters today in the German television market is represented by a rather stable group. Five types of music channels are all presently competing for the patronage of young people: MTV EUROPE/ GERMANY, VH-1, VIVA, VIVA ZWEI, and ONYX. The following entry is devoted to the market leaders MTV and VIVA, and the successful strategies they use to showcase their being the channels for adolescents and young adults. Up to this point in time, what devices have they used to reach their young audiences? How have they solicited their young clientele? The advertising campaigns used up to now by MTV and VIVA serve a double function, each of equal importance: first, the creation and maintenance of a youth oriented image for the channel; and second, direct addressing and stimulating public interests. Precise analyses of their advertising are subsequently conducted in order to determine which ideological patterns of orientation and rhetorical strategies the channels use in order to reach their target audiences. In pictorial hermeneutical analyses, individual campaigns are discussed using exemplary illustrations. These indicate the degree of leeway that has been opened up for fantasy and the presentation of identity for the viewers through the language of imagery in the advertising.

First, however, let us take a look into the history of advertising campaigns between the years of 1994–1997. At the dawn of the 1990's, MTV-GERMANY was confronted with an entirely new situation. The program had long since become well known, not least for the vehement public debates it had sparked concerning the potential changing cultural effects of the new aestheticism involved in music video clips. In the industry, there were rumblings that the foundation of a German-based competitor, VIVA, was imminent and would in fact be completed by the end of 1993. In order to maintain those audiences that had already been won over by the "music for the eyes," MTV began an advertising war with the campaigns *Willkommen Zuhause* or *Welcome Home* in 1994 and *Heiß und fettig* or *Hot and Oily* in 1996. In contradistinction to MTV, VIVA upon its entrance into the market placed its bets on regionalism and produced their programming in the German language rather than in English. As soon became apparent, they did so with success. VIVA soon began to do well in the ratings. As a consequence, the MTV programming was also altered and a German-language spot was integrated into the daily programming. This initiative was then accompanied in 1997 by an advertising campaign called "Made for Germany," the slogan of which was to reflect the obvious efforts on the part of MTV to solicit both German and German-speaking youth. VIVA could then in good conscience, given its success, continue to pursue its strategy of close proximity to the public. In 1997 it launched an unencumbered, physically direct advertising campaign called "Kiss." It was hoped that the comparatively intimate images of couples deep kissing, which were to be photographed in graphic detail, would especially strike a nerve among the younger members of the viewing audience.

The seductive power of this advertising campaign is readily explicable, if one knows how to either decode or decipher the chosen language of images. The first large print-media campaign *Willkommen Zuhause* or *Welcome Home* by MTV-GERMANY was based on the concept of presenting visually a radio-station, which managed to serve as a virtual home for adolescents and young adults. The new self-confidence of the MTV generation was to be "authentically" presented. Instead of professional models, "Kids from the street" were used to speak to their peers. The fliers and posters were all oversized black-and-white photographs on which young people between the ages of seventeen to twenty-four were shot from the waist up, looking directly into the eyes of the viewers. The clothing of the youth related to the aestheticism of the various youth scenes, for example, grunge, rave, and neopunk, etc. On their chests, the emblazoned insignia of the protagonists was shot. In blue letters against a white background framed in black, stigmas are read, such as "Slut," "Pr***," "Egoist," "Little S***," "Head-Banger," and "Spoiled B*****." The photographs were reminiscent of greatly enlarged images of police mug shots, which, as a rule, combined poor quality black-and-white picture aestheticism with the necessary administrative requirement of asking for a delinquent's name and registration number. In the lower right corner, outside of the immediate field of vision, one could read, in small print, "willkommen zuhause" and even smaller "MTV." The type and layout of the presentation prompts the question, "What might all of this be about?" It was then only the initiated who knew what the almost too small to read logo "MTV" stood for and only they were able then to understand the message being sent.

As to the campaign and the images, there are a number of elements that are unusual. For example, the way in which expressions not normally a part of the young people's vocabulary were used was atypical. The youth who are presented and the expressions attached to them, such as "Little S***," along with their negative connotations, are much more typical of the conservative vocabulary from a part of the generation representing the grandparents of the young viewers. Furthermore, the appearance (for example, the pale complexions, dreadlocks, and short hair cuts) as well as the clothing (the simple, austere, partly faded either black or some other dark colored fabrics) of the youth featured pointed at their membership in that generation of young people from the early nineteen nineties which American author Douglas Coupland described in his 1991 book, *Generation X*. According to him, the common denominator of Generation X is the search for a niche in the modern society in order to be able to purposefully but inconspicuously hide out. Another common denominator of these youth is the fact that they, unlike any generation before them, have been exposed to the influence of the modern media, especially television. As images and language of the advertising subject show, the campaign *Willkommen Zuhause* or *Welcome Home* targets those stylized members of Generation X who take-up a niche in society, but want to know relatively little of said niche and prefer instead to be left in peace. For these so-called "Outsiders," MTV offers a virtual home. Or in the words of the aforementioned police bulletin or APB: Wherever you may have hidden, however you all are dressed, no matter what group you belong to, regardless of which behavioral rituals you keep or values you feel obliged to possess, stay right where you are and continue to be who you are, 'cause MTV is coming at you and is offering you any and every media environment and community of like-minded people you may desire twenty-four hours a day. MTV is looking for you, because the established authorities discredit you and you can only be what you want to be with us.

Seduction by the *Welcome Home* advertising campaign tapped into young people's predilection for subversive word games. Here a specifically unobtrusive or hidden form of distancing vis-a-vis the cultural domain of adults can be pursued. Symbolic borrowings from the world of adults are in a way reevaluated via a form of reversal. A frequently cited short example that is often described in the relevant literature as being derived from black English is as follows. When a so-called upstanding white person says to a black person, "He is bad!" the person being spoken to first accepts this stigmatization, in this case meaning the word "bad," but then reinterprets it by inserting a seemingly small change. Namely, by lengthening the vowel in the word "bad," a new evaluation that more precisely is equivalent to the self-appraisal "good" is created. Whoever understands the nuance contained in the sentence "Yes, I'm <ba:d>!" belongs to the circle of the initiated who set themselves apart from conservative adults. In advertising, the hegemonic reign of the common culture of the "straight-laced" conservative is dethroned as a symbolic authority. With the help of newly contextualized inversion made up of symbolic borrowings from the cultural domain of the adult world, specific prizes of identity are the goal. These are based upon the special construction of difference through that which is the converse. Word games and changes in meaning are the fundamental material of the social cement needed for what Goffman terms the "accomplice-driven communication" that represents such a great attraction for this age group. Seen from this light, it then becomes an honor to allow oneself to be called a "Slut," "Pr***," "Egoist," "Little S***," "Head-Banger," or a "Spoiled B****."

The return to semantic reversal and reevaluation in the social competition for symbolic superiority plays an important role in the subsequent campaign by MTV titled *Heiß und fettig* or *Hot and Oily*. The *Hot and Oily* campaign always features the same actor named "Gregor," representing someone who is a part of the grunge scene; approximately twenty to thirty years old, he is like a "cool Drop-out." Just as in the *Welcome Home* campaign, the protagonist here looks directly into the face of the viewer, face-on. At the same time, his gestures and facial expressions are markedly expressive. He moves in an odd manner and strikes "Drop-out" poses. The text reads "Go home, people, there is nothing interesting to see here" or "Landed again on the wrong station, did you?" or "Can you look a little faster?" or "Kiss me, I am a magical television" or "Has anyone ever told you, you have beautiful ears?" To the bottom right of the images, the MTV logo is once again to be found; only this time, the sentence "This is where the music plays" is written across it.

In this advertising campaign, the focus is also the difference between the generations; and once again in this campaign, as well as the other, both the expressions and reprimands made by the authorities (i.e., the police, parents, and teachers) are appropriated and with the help of minor textual changes as well as sardonic gestures and facial expressions they are turned around to mean just the opposite.

In 1997 MTV once again reacted to the now well-established competition coming from VIVA with its own "Made for Germany" campaign. Mostly to be seen in muted, plain colors are photographs of scenes from the everyday life of young people who yet again invert the meaning of classic German values such as the following: made in Germany; good traditional German food; "Gemütlichkeit" (i.e., being comfortable and at ease); time to knock off work; "Stammtisch" (i.e., a favorite table at the local pub where friends and family regularly meet to drink and relax); "Reinheitsgebot" (i.e., the national purity standard for such German staples as beer; Poets, and Thinkers); as well as the feelings associated with home sweet home. On the lower corner of the photo, the viewer finds as usual the MTV logo, as well as the slogan "Made for Germany: in short and in German: new shows, new Vjays, new music. Daily from 2–8 pm."

The goal of the campaign is to show that it was possible in the meantime to be positioned well in the national German market with special German language programs and to thereby show that MTV had learned how to cater to the German taste. The question is only, what in the final analysis *is* "German taste?" The MTV campaign presents the typical elements of everyday German life. Things were raised that Germans consider to be sacred and untranslatable into foreign languages. Included among these are the German concept of comfort, cleanliness, and the local pub, or "Gemütlichkeit," "Reinheitsgebot," and "Stammtisch." These German concepts, being a part of the bastions of bourgeois German culture, are illustrated and sardonically examined with unexpected and surprising images and scenes from the everyday world of youth and young adults. Thus, four skateboards in front of a cement ramp were chosen for the concept of quitting time; a dazzling assembly of tattoos on the various body parts of young people illustrates graphically the notion of "Made in Germany" and shows what the Germans are capable of producing; and a Graffiti-festooned toilet wall stands for the country of poets and thinkers. The motifs were intentionally photographed as if they were done by amateurs. The attraction of the pictures lies in, as stated before, the decoding of the reversed relationship of text and image. The associations that one develops to the primary German vocabulary are counter-illustrated, as it were, through the visual events. The MTV community then has a different idea of "Programm Deutschland" than the concepts called up in their traditional meaning. The tense relationship between the text and the image brings clarity. Being at home is new; it is the rewarding alternative to that life that exists beyond the conservative and traditional concepts. "Willkommen Zuhause/ Welcome Home" at MTV—Come together!

Whereas in the MTV "Made for Germany" campaign the youth engaged in harmless petting during the comfortable gathering, VIVA ventured much closer to the most important issue of young people: love or sex. The advertisement "Kiss," beginning in 1997, presented a close-up of a young couple sharing an intimate kiss. In a corner of the picture, placed on a white background, the text "Dani and Sascha (or Vera and Martin, Gordana and Yacob, or Anna and Markus) love VIVA" can be read. Next to that the VIVA logo is pictured. What is especially noticeable and for many viewers, both male and female, perhaps a little shocking is the untouched close-up of an intimate scene. Almost the entire surface of the picture is taken up by faces, most of which are only to be seen in a cut of the lower lip to the eyebrows. The skin of those people shown looks oily and unclean and shines under the lighting. In three pictures, one can look into the mouth of one of the featured people; in two, one can discover moist red tongues.

The heading for the photomontage reads: "VIVA is now getting even closer!" The untouched close-ups seem more realistic and authentic than the pictures of the competing "Made for Germany" campaign. The issues of love and sexuality hit straight in the heart of the "real-life" desires, needs, and concerns of younger people. The kissing couples in the VIVA campaign stand for the worries and the desires of young people; they arose the curiosity and signal that VIVA can also present a forum where emotions and interests can be openly talked about.

Obviously, for their different target audiences, the two competitors have different marketing strategies, which are tailored to the various physical and psycho-social needs and constellation of the interests involved. VIVA is primarily geared toward those younger cohorts, especially kids and teenagers. By contrast, MTV speaks to older adolescents and young adults. VIVA focuses on living life with one another from the point of reference of peer groups and friendships. With that, a central developmental task of youth is approached; namely, the relativization of the significance of the parental home and school, which are symbolized in the images of physical union with a partner outside of the family. MTV, instead, places its emphasis on the dynamic involved in individualization, which the older youth are concerned with and which are to be found in the forced interest in distinctions. This distancing from the others, whether it be from those who are older such as parents, or those who are of the same age (i.e., those people in the other youth scenes), is of immanent importance here. The *Welcome Home* campaign shows, correspondingly, a series of symbolic representatives of varying musical styles and from diverse subgroups found in the cultural domain of young people. As explained earlier, MTV offers to serve as place where the community of the different can share a common roof. The purpose of the MTV home is to transmit identity as alterity. This is made evident in the practices involved in programming. They have mainstream and trendy, alternative programs. This makes it difficult to find a balance between the mainstream programming and specials, which in turn leads to the problem of offering a palatable diet of trends. The image campaigns are, however, unencumbered by such concrete problems in program design. There the point is simply to create an attractive project space in which the addressees enjoy moving around.

What remains undecided for the MTV campaigns is whether the main emphasis will be placed upon radicalizing or ideological hoodwinking of the viewers. Hoodwinking would be the case, if the individual campaigns more or less clearly exploited the myth found in rock music that pretends to subvert youth. The enticement of this myth for young people is the promotion of the idea that there could be an independent, pure life; one that is separable from the world of the conservative and the world of consumption, where only dependence and corruption rule. While watching TV, this is however not easy! In the mug-shot photos featured in the first MTV campaign, individual special young people are turned into just one among many others who listen to music and are caught up by consumerism whether they want to be or not. There is no rock or pop music without the cultural industry.

At the same time, the campaigns also "play" ironically with the myth of subversion. As play, the cultural model of subversion becomes a "knowing" form of code critique through which paradoxical elements of that myth become clearer. The second and third campaigns are more devoted than the first to this distancing; or, more precisely, the "knowing" relationship with the world of "expressions" and ideologies.

However, does not the entirety also represent a picture of vexation that counters the young people themselves and their tendency toward authenticity and subversion? In the "Gregor" campaign, a de-mystification and mockery of the culture of youth and their posturing is to be seen. And the "Made for Germany" campaign could even be understood as a certain retroactive ironic incorporation of the rebellious youth into typical German tradition or custom: Even skateboarders call it quits at the end of a hard day's work; and youth also ensure that there is more left behind them, albeit at the local pub; and it is also very important for the lovers of tattoos in the time of AIDS that there is the concept of German reliability (and hygiene). Once again the interaction between the picture and the text has been called upon. The words are not only commented upon by the pictures;

the pictures are also in turn framed by the words. With that the irony exposed becomes an ingenious, tongue-in-cheek self-criticism. The contents and the style may change, but the central values and principles that are depicted here using fundamental German expressions do not change. No one can escape from either society or the market!

Resources

Adorno, T. W. (1967). Résumé über Kulturindustrie. In *ders.: Ohne Leitbild* (pp. 60–69). Frankfurt: Suhrkamp.

Frith, S., Goodwin, A., & Grossberg, L. (Eds.). (1993). *Sound and vision.* London: Routledge.

Neumann-Braun, K. (Ed.). (1999). *VIVA MTV! Popmusik im Fernsehen* (VIVA MTV! Pop Music on Television). Frankfurt: Suhrkamp Verlag.

Theodor W. A., & Horkheimer, M. (1993). The culture industry: enlightenment as mass deception. In S. During (Ed.). *The cultural studies reader* (pp. 29–43). London: Routledge

AGEISM, STEREOTYPES, TELEVISION

Myrna Hant

It is estimated that most people spend about 33 percent of their free time watching television. Because so many people are engaging in this activity it is critical to analyze what messages are promoted and what the effects of these messages are. Prime time television shows for more than fifty years have presented a typically consistent portrayal of older people, especially older women, as ridiculous, interfering, obsessed with the family, and incapable of functioning outside the home. These portrayals are one form of ageism which permeates our society. What is ageism and where did it come from? Do our perceptions of older people really make a difference as to how we think about older people and how we subsequently behave towards them? Perhaps most importantly of all, why does any of this matter to a young person? By looking at particularly popular TV shows that young adults are still watching such as *Bewitched, All in the Family, The Golden Girls,* and the more recent *The Simpsons, Everybody Loves Raymond, The Sopranos,* and *The Simple Life,* it becomes obvious that older people are mainly stereotyped as undesirables in our culture, people to avoid.

AGEISM

The word "ageism" is a relatively new term, coined by Dr. Robert Butler in 1975. It is similar to sexism and racism in that it is a form of discrimination, in this case based solely on a person's age. The discrimination comes when you see an older person and immediately connect him or her with stereotypical classifications such as senile, old-fashioned, calcified in their thinking, unable to learn new skills, and always talking about the past. It's an automatic reaction and it becomes incumbent on the older person to change your mind. Often, we don't care enough to have our minds changed so we see an older person in a certain way regardless of how he or she behaves.

What are the roots of ageism, particularly in highly developed Western societies? In preindustrial societies, no distinctions were made between adulthood and old age. For those who lived long enough, the roles of parenting and worker were intertwined throughout a lifetime. The children grew up and stayed nearby or in the same house and no one experienced a formalized retirement. But as younger men, particularly, began leaving the house for employment, those remaining began to take on very specified functions specifically related to age. So, you started seeing mothers and grandmothers taking on more of the household functions such as cooking, cleaning, and caring for children. Gradually, certain work in the household became age-based and slowly there became less for older people to do. As they did fewer chores around the house, older people became less important in the running of a household.

According to Erving Goffman the tainting of the image of older people had already begun to appear in the United States in popular literature at the end of the nineteenth century as America was becoming more industrialized. Another thing began to happen as well. People no longer believed that the elderly were somehow more closely connected to the eternal. As people began to lose their fears about the afterlife and death became less integrated into their lives, they no longer worried that somehow the elderly could and would be revengeful. In other words, if you believe that a person, after he dies, will somehow come back to wreck havoc on your life because you treated him/her so poorly, you'd try to treat this person better in this life.

Besides the enormous effect of industrialization and increasing mobility of families as they sought urban environments, ageism crept into society's perspectives for other reasons as well. Medical technology in the twentieth (and, of course, the twenty-first) century, along with an increased life expectancy, meant an increase in the older population. Other factors feeding the ageist mentality were the momentum of the technology revolution and the "cult of youth" being so deeply embedded into people's psyches. Many would argue that the negative stereotype is different for older men and older women. A woman no longer has her maternal role and her youth and consequently, in a patriarchal world, she loses her femininity as well. In looking at TV shows, the portrayals of older women are far more negative than those of older men.

TELEVISION AND AGEISM

One of the 1960s shows that is still popular is *Bewitched* (1964–1972). Samantha, the main character, is a desirable role model for women. She knows, through witchcraft, how to manipulate the man in her life, Darrin, as well as how to eliminate many of the domestic drudgeries and chores typically assigned to women. She is attractive and focused happily on her home and later on her daughter. Even though Endora, her mother, has equal powers and is a co-conspirator with Samantha, as an older woman she is portrayed rather grotesquely. There is something witchlike in her appearance, an unappealing crone who has bright red hair, very long eyelashes, and heavy eyeliner. She is not exactly attractive to men, nor is her appearance something women would want to emulate.

Unquestionably Endora offers a form of liberation for women in her unwillingness to placate men and in her honest and sometimes blunt expressions of her opinions. She gets to say what she wants to say without the consequences that haunt a younger woman's foray into assertiveness. Since Endora is older, she is just an aging woman who is naturally cantankerous and out of control.

Endora's ex-husband, Maurice, is portrayed as a pathetic older man chasing after younger women. In "Samantha's Good News" (*Bewitched*, April 10, 1969) Maurice becomes involved with his very young secretary. Endora decides to turn the woman into an old lady because she's angry at him. Alas, Endora cannot escape the ravages of getting older and being denied her position as a powerful young woman. Her solution to the problem is to make the beautiful secretary the most awful thing imaginable, an old woman. The lessons are clear: old people try to be young and while doing so make themselves look foolish.

Another extremely popular series beginning in the 1970s, *All in the Family* (1971–1980) features a likeable, but dippy, older mother, Edith Bunker and her irascible husband, Archie. Archie calls her "dingbat" because she appears to be clueless about what's happening around her. When Archie, in discussing Disney World, tells Edith they "got an all bear band," Edith's retort is "They got a naked band at Disney World?" Or when Archie's socks are missing, Edith asks, "Did you look in the top drawer?" And as Archie declares, "Certainly I looked in the top drawer," Edith demurs, "Well, they ain't there." Edith cannot seem to fathom that her daughter Gloria and Mike have a sexual relationship. Archie asks, "How long have them two been up there?" Edith replies, "an hour and a half." Archie, knowing they're having sex, retorts, "and in the afternoon." And Edith, trying to figure out what's happening and never really able to proclaims, "Seems like an awfully long time to be showing her his grades" (*All in the Family*, 1971).

The message is that older women, although lovable, are incapable of rational thinking. She is a sexless, dowdy middle-aged woman with few interests outside of the family. Yes, she displays likable qualities but only those proscribed for her gender and her age. While laughing at her ridiculous antics, we are also imbued with messages that reiterate her place within an ageist society.

She does act as a buffer for Archie's rantings about Mike and "coons," "spics," "Jews," and "Chinks." When Archie says, "There's a black guy who works down at the building with me. He's got a bumper sticker on his car that says 'Black is Beautiful.' So what's the matter with calling them Black Beauties?" Edith proudly asserts, "It's nicer than when he called them coons" (*All in the Family*, 1971). So Archie represents the bigoted buffoon who remembers fondly how things used to be, loudly singing "Those were the days" as his theme song.

Sophia Petrillo in *Golden Girls* (1985–1992) is the wise-cracking, smart-mouthed senior member of the quadrangle of "golden" women. In her demeanor and dialogue she epitomizes how surveyed audiences consistently describe older people on television: frail, confused, laughable, superficial, and degraded. Older male characters, who play minor roles, are often pathetic as well.

When Sophia is not sniping at her three roommates, she is talking about illness (her cataract and laser surgery) and loss or how life isn't as good as it was. She laments, "People think you should just be glad to be alive. You need a reason to get up in the morning. Life can turn around and spit in your face." (*Golden Girls*, September 19, 1987). When dialogue occurs regarding her sexuality it is mainly used as a device to ridicule her. When Rose asks Sophia why she's in such a bad mood, Sophia replies, "Excuse me Rose, I haven't had sex in fifteen years, and it's starting to get on my nerves." Or when Dorothy asks her mother where she is going, Sophia sarcastically answers, "To the boardwalk. I like to watch the old guys rearrange themselves when they come out of the water."(*Golden Girls*, 1985) These attempts to "sexualize" Sophia are devices to make her look ridiculous. Even when there are wedding possibilities for Max, a widowed friend, and Sophia, both get sick and the dream of a new life together is over. Their adventures into sexuality are pictured as disgusting. Thus, older people cannot and should not be sexual and have dreams for the future.

Although Marie Barone in *Everybody Loves Raymond* (1996-2005) is an Italian matriarch, she could be any of the stereotypical Jewish mothers so prevalent on television for the last fifty years. They are women who are constantly nagging and demanding with unfilled expectations from their children. Always competing for Raymond's attention, Marie wants her son to admit that his mother is more important to him than his wife. The episode in which Raymond receives an honorary doctorate degree makes it clear that young women and old women are antagonists fighting for the attention of the son. In accepting his degree Raymond gives a thank you speech specifically recognizing his mother. A petulant Debra reminds Raymond that she was not mentioned in the speech. Raymond, to make amends, writes in his sports column how "full of gratitude and feelings that were so overwhelming" he has for his wife. Marie is incensed with this public validation of Raymond's wife and admonishes, "Debra gets all the credit in front of 850,000 readers while mine were perfunctory." The episode ends with Raymond's double entendre, "Sweet Mama, without your pushing I'd still be in your womb." (*Everybody Loves Raymond*, October 5, 1998) The father, Frank Barone, is depicted as a somewhat senile, defeated old man who cannot escape the clutches of his wife, Marie. Neither the portrait of the long-suffering Frank nor the argumentative Marie are very desirable representatives of older people.

Another Italian mama, the unforgettable Livia (mother of Tony, Barbara, and Janice) in *The Sopranos* (1999–present) is a blueprint for the worst qualities of the stereotypical Jewish mother combined with a sadistic woman's desire to literally and figuratively devour her offspring. Although Tony tries to be a devoted son, Livia makes it very clear to Tony that he's a terrible son. While talking to his psychiatrist, Dr. Melfi, he reveals that he cannot do anything for his mother without feeling guilty. It's difficult to find any redeeming qualities in this bigoted ("Blacks steal") and anti-Semitic miserable mother who is so angry with her son that she wants to have him killed. Even after her death, Tony will be burdened psychologically with his mother for the rest of his life.

Ageist and sexist ideologies are replete in the episodes featuring Livia. She not only complains constantly about her health but she presents herself as an elderly unattractive woman whose idea of fashion is a cardigan sweater or a bathrobe. Her hair is appropriate for this demeanor—no style at all. She focuses on the past, a past that never existed, and she uses her "dementia" to manipulate the family. Her elderly brother-in-law, Uncle Junior, although vicious, is still portrayed as a person who has all his marbles and is quite capable of maintaining an active life.

Even when looking at popular shows like *The Simpsons* (1989–present) and *The Simple Life* (2004–present) that feature older people as tangential to the main characters, mature characters are portrayed stereotypically, which means usually negatively. In "The Front" episode of *The Simpsons*, Grandpa Simpson, living in the Springfield Retirement Castle, can't remember his first name and needs to check his underwear to figure it out. When Lisa and Bart pretend that Grandpa Abraham wrote an "Itchy and Scratchy" cartoon episode, the producer of the show is amazed to find such an old man writing comedy. And while Homer fantasizes about putting his dad in the nut house, Grandpa is busy writing to the President that we need to eliminate three states in the United States because there are too many. Even when a character appears periodically such as Rabbi Hyman Krustofsky, father of Krusty the Clown, ("Like Father, Like Clown") the rabbi is presented as so stubborn that for twenty-five years he wouldn't accept his son because of his profession. In *The Simple Life,* when Paris Hilton and Nicole Richie are visiting the Skinner family in Mississippi, Grandma is a dumpy, no-hairstyle frump who gives the prayer before meals. When they visit the Click ranch, Paris and Nicole have to teach their elder, Bob, the ex-marine, how to be romantic with his very heavy-set and basically dowdy wife, Gayle. And in Texas with the Bahm family, Nicole and Paris do a makeover on an "older" woman so she will look younger and attract her aging boy-friend. Again, older people are depicted as senile, invisible, stubborn, or needing to learn from younger people.

HOW DOES AGEISM AFFECT YOU?

Why does it matter that ageism is so prevalent on TV shows? If you believe that the only way to be beautiful and handsome is to be young you may be spending a great deal of time and money on denying your age. It is not just older women and men who have internalized the self-loathing so frequently promoted in the ageist stereotype but many young people as well.

According to Naomi Wolf, magazines largely ignore older women and if they do feature an older woman she is air-brushed to look ten or fifteen years younger than she actually is. Rarely do you see older women in magazines anyhow, but rather computer-enhanced and retouched images of the perfect woman: white, skinny, perfect skin, and no older than in her twenties. What happens to you, then, as you get older? Do you become increasingly ashamed about your looks?

Millions of women (and now men) are convinced that if they just try hard enough and buy enough they will not age and be "junked" by society. Billions of dollars are spent to become "visible" in our society. A society that is to be eternally young. We can "pass" as young if we buy the right cosmetics and clothes, have the right friends, and do the right activities. It is not coincidental that we see politicians like John Kerry skiing and wind-surfing and George Bush chopping wood. We're all supposed to be young and the opposite is too abhorrent to contemplate. Our culture has convinced us that in order to lead a happy and fulfilled life we must remain young or at least pretend to be young.

Aging is a particularly difficult problem for women. Letty Pogrebin talks about a Rutgers University study in which being attractive turns up as the most important concern for girls from age ten on and girls as young as age twelve are seriously depressed because of a poor body image. Horror stories of anorexic and bulimic college students abound in the literature.

Because patriarchal values are so prevalent throughout the culture, both young and older women have adopted the "young as worthwhile" mythos. And this, inevitably, pits younger women against older women. Faced with a barrage of media indoctrination that aging is ugly, younger women are not going to ally themselves with something that is considered repulsive.

Consequently, younger women will not seek advice or counsel from older women who have been portrayed by the media as worthless. It is not by chance that young women feel they have so little to learn from older women and the connection between female generations is systematically and deliberately denigrated. In an insidious fashion, women young and old are programmed to distrust each other. The youth culture ethos is not as toxic for young men as for young women as body image and beauty have traditionally been greater problems for women than men. There are indications, though, that anorexia and bulimia rates for young men are increasing as well as male cosmetic surgery to maintain and/or regain youth.

It is incumbent on all of us to become "media literate" and aware of the constant bombardment of largely negative images about older people as helpless, fragile and aimless. If we become aware of how we're being manipulated by television maybe we can consciously reverse in our minds the images that we're supposed to accept. If we continue to fear aging we'll be willing followers of the advertisers who try to convince us it's possible to defeat the human condition. We know that's a myth and hopefully we can educate ourselves to overcome these falsehoods.

Resources

Antler, J. (Ed.). (1998). *Talking back: Images of Jewish women in American popular culture*. Hanover, MA: Brandeis University Press.

Browne, C. (1998). *Women, feminism and aging*. New York: Springer Publishing Co.

Cohen, H. L. (2002). Developing media literacy skills to challenge television's portrayal of older women. *Educational Gerontology, 28*, 599–620.

Douglas, S. (1994). *Where the girls are: Growing up female with the mass media*. New York: Random House.

Dow, B. (1996). *Prime time feminism: Television, media culture, and the women's movement since 1970*. Philadelphia: University of Pennsylvania Press.

Featherstone, M. (Ed.). (1995). *Images of aging: Cultural representations of later life*. London: Routledge.

Friedan, B. (1993). *The fountain of age*. New York: Simon and Schuster.

Healey, T., & Ross, K. (2002). Growing older invisibly: Older viewers talk television. *Media Culture and Society, 24*, 105–120.

Kaler, A. (1990). Golden girls: Feminine archetypal patterns of the complete Woman. *Journal of Popular Culture, 2* (3), 49–60.

Memorable quotes from *All in the Family*. (1971). Retrieved July, 2004 from http://www.us.imdb.com/title/tt0066626/quotes

Memorable quotes from *The Golden Girls*. (1985). Retrieved July, 2004 from http://www.amazon.com/exec/obidos/tg/detail/

Miller, T. (Ed). (2002). *Television studies*. London: British Film Institute.

Pogrebin, L. C. (1996). *Getting over getting older*. Boston: Little Brown and Co.

Richmond, R. (2002). *TV moms: An illustrated guide*. New York: TV Books.

Rucker, A. (2000). *The Sopranos: A family history*. New York: New American Library.

Wolf, N. (1991). *The beauty myth: How images of beauty are used against women*. New York: Doubleday.

Yacowar, M. (2002). *The Sopranos on the couch: Analyzing television's greatest series*. New York: Continuum International Publishing Group.

RAISING WORLD CITIZENS: NEWS PROGRAMMING FOR YOUTH IN THE UNITED STATES AND THE LOST LANGUAGE OF DEMOCRACY

Carl Bybee

The big news about news in the United States is that fewer and fewer people, young and old, are following the mainstream news, whether it is delivered in print or by video, and they are more likely to be piecing together their own "news" from traditional sources as well as a wild array of Internet sites, blogs, late night talk shows, and other entertainment venues. The traditional model of press practice is in a state of crisis, and the future of democratic journalism is at risk of being dramatically undermined. According to "The State of the News Media," a new annual report compiled by the Project for Excellence in Journalism Institute affiliated with Columbia University and funded by the Pew Charitable Trusts:

> The traditional notion that people go primarily to a handful of types of news outlets for their information appears to be less and less accurate.

> Americans are now news grazers sampling, through the course of the day, a varied media buffet. Categorizing people by education, region, or income or trying to imagine them as primarily newspaper readers, or consumers mostly of local TV news, is increasingly futile. . . . In a sense, news consumption today should probably be viewed in the way diet is viewed in this age of plentiful, fast and often processed

American food. The array of offerings is so vast and varied, being concerned mainly with what is offered seems futile; the proper concern may involve educating consumers about what they should imbibe.

The real crisis may be news obesity, consuming too little that can nourish citizens and too much that can bloat them.

However, this report misses two central issues. The first is that "traditional news" in now for the most part corporate news, corporate news that has aggressively joined in the media spectacle of entertainment, sensationalism, and trivialization that dominates the multitude of media channels and sources that create a 24/7 cultural environment surrounding young and old alike at home, at the office, in their cars, and even on their skateboards. The second issue is that this report fails to take up the particular focus on how this crisis is affecting youth and their understanding of themselves and their relationship to their communities and the world.

This entry explores the range, structure, and content of news programming in the United States produced for children and youth and places these findings in relationship to what is being called a "crisis of citizenship," marked by political apathy, declining trust in politics and political institutions, and rising political cynicism.

I also take into consideration the decreasing public financing for both public affairs information and public education. Given these decreases, it details how corporations are increasingly becoming the primary source of children's news programming, but with little or no oversight from the public. This leads to the central question of this essay: When we look at the growing presence in U.S. youth's everyday life of corporate media culture, what effect is this likely to have, not on their physical or mental health, but on their civic health, their civic identity and their sense of themselves as world citizens?

The entry examines the lack of debate in U.S. society, and particularly in youth media, over the competing world models of democracy—from market-based to participatory. Of particular interest is the extent to which the neo-liberal model of democracy, based on the idea that market capitalism is a superior system for managing money and people as contrasted to every other form of governance or distribution model, first widely established during the presidency of Ronald Reagan, has now emerged as the taken-for-granted or hegemonic definition of democracy for vast numbers of U.S. citizens and particularly for youth.

And yet, like the dark Lord Voldemort in the Harry Potter media spectacle, neo-liberalism is the face of evil "who must not be named." The results of this transformation in the meaning of U.S. democracy in the last fifty years, from pluralism to neo-liberalism, is considered in relationship to the range and structure of public affairs programming and public affairs media for youth. These structural outcomes set the stage for an examination of

Scholastic Inc., the largest distributor of printed "current events" materials for schools with an extensive news Web site and "CNN Student News," a daily video newscast also with an extensive news Web site and a subsidiary of CNN, which is, in turn, a subsidiary of mega-media giant Time Warner. The focus of this analysis will be on the construction of the mean-ings of "democracy" for read-ers and viewers of Scholastic Inc.'s "Scholastic News" Web site and "CNN Student News" viewers and readers and read-ers and viewers of the "CNN Student News" Web site.

Home viewing of dvds and videos is popular all over the world

Taken together this analysis indicates, on the one hand, a growing media spectacle organized around an increasingly empty idea of "democracy" and a shrinking vocabulary of democratic words, images and conceptual categories being offered to U.S. youth to think beyond a neo-liberal worldview. On the other hand, particularly in the less accessible and less widely used "CNN Student News" resources, what is found is a willingness to occasionally consider critical views of current U.S. visions of democracy, but without providing an adequate critical vocabulary or historical context for understanding the weakness of the "U.S. = Democracy" myth of the U.S. political, economic, and social system.

NEWS FOR YOUTH

The first thing one notices when an adult starts looking for sources of news for kids is that these sources are for the most part invisible.

There may or may not be a youth news section in your local paper. There are no youth news magazines, unless you want to count *Teen People*, on newsstands in bookstores and on the magazine racks in grocery stores. A dedicated search of cable channels and listings might help one find the list-ings for three video news programs targeted at youth: *Teen Kids News*, jointly produced by Weekly Reader, a subsidiary of WRC Media Inc. and formerly owned by mega-media giant Primedia; and a group called Kids News, *Nick News with Linda Ellerbee*, produced by Nickelodeon, a subsidiary of the MTV Network, which is in turn a subsidiary of the mega-media giant Viacom; and

CNN Student News, produced by CNN, a subsidiary of the mega-media giant Time Warner.

Teen Kids News was created to syndicate to stations trying to scramble to meet new, more demanding standards set by the FCC for carrying "educational" programming. In fact, the promotion to stations for purchasing the product heavily stresses the fact that it meets this FCC standard. For most stations the once-a-week program is considered to be a write-off buried in marginal airtimes but with the one redeeming feature that it at least provides another marketing salvo aimed to hit the very difficult to reach "tween" audience.

The once-a-week *Nick News with Linda Ellerbee* is also dumped in marginal time slots, currently 6:00 AM Wednesday mornings, although the show's occasional specials such as *Kids Pick a President* and *Safari So Good* may be aired during prime time on Sunday evenings. In contrast to *Teen Kids News*, which hosts only a bare bones Web site, *Nick News* hosts a full-blown Web site in which news and news resources play a fairly small role. The site is primarily an advertising venue for Nickelodeon programs, features, and products. Its key object appears to keep the user inside the "My Nick" world of youth entertainment media culture.

CNN Student News is the most comprehensive of the youth news sources an adult might find outside of a school setting. *CNN Student News* is a ten-minute news program aired five times at week at 3:12 AM ET (that's correct, 3:12 AM) designed specially for classroom use. Teachers are expected to record the program and bring it in to the classroom for viewing. *Student News* hosts a comprehensive news oriented Web site where one can watch each day's episode via video streaming. In addition transcripts of previous programs, teachers' guides, and other news related educational news resources are provided. The site also runs banner ads and has been known to air as mini-documentaries on its newscasts, portions of television advertisements produced for CNN customers like Nokia.

Where *Teen Kid News* and *Nick News with Linda Ellerbee* can be viewed primarily as either image management strategies or FCC compliance efforts on the parts of the cable channels and networks carrying these programs, *CNN Student News* can be viewed as a more serious corporate mainstream journalistic effort to reach youth, even though it can certainly be argued it keeps the CNN brand name for news products in front of an audience just coming of age in determining its news brand preference.

For the most part, then, these video news programs, stretching our definition a bit to include the 3:00 AM airing of *CNN Student News*, ironically produced by for-profit corporations constitute the "public" face of youth news sources—examples an interested adult might turn to for a look at what passes for commercial journalistic civic education for youth.

The primary reason the mostly widely used, viewed, and read youth news sources remain invisible to adults is that they are delivered in a school setting. Three media giants dominate in school delivered news: *The*

Weekly Reader, which reaches preschool through high school age youth with a range of age targeted products; *Scholastic News*, which reaches the same age groups with a similar range of products and the 800 pound gorilla of school-based news, Channel One's daily twelve-minute video newscast, which claims to reach 40 percent of middle and high schools across the United States. Channel One is currently a subsidiary of Primedia.

There is also a fourth private player in the for-profit school business, Newspapers in Education (NIE). However, what makes the NIE program different than Weekly Reader Corporation, Scholastic, Inc., and Channel One is that it is an association and not a single corporation and that it is not engaged in direct marketing in the schools—although this is changing too, as newspapers see the opportunity to offer selected sponsors the opportunity to have their corporate name brought into the classroom. For instance, *The Detroit Free Press* and *The Detroit News* have created a program called Michigan K.I.D.S. (Knowledge and Information Delivered to Students) that solicits corporate sponsors to underwrite the distribution of their newspapers into classrooms. Current major corporate sponsors include the Ford Motor Company, Compuware, Toyota, Comerica, General Motors, AAA Michigan, Kmart Corporation, Big Boy Restaurants, Blue Cross Blue Shield of Michigan, and the Detroit Auto Dealers Association.

Historically, the use of newspapers in the schools had been encouraged and supported by a number of individual news organizations throughout the 1930s and 1940s both as a civic contribution to the community and as a training ground for raising new generations of newspaper readers. In the aftermath of World War II, the beginning of the Cold War, and the Commission on the Freedom of the Press' 1947 report "A Free and Responsible Press," these concerns, and particularly the idea of the democratic responsibility of the press, were taken as a serious concern. Given these different origins and currently low level marketing aggressiveness compared with the other in-school news providers, the NIE will not be taken up as a major focus of our current discussion, although the group is more thoroughly discussed elsewhere.

All of these youth news sources delivered in schools are private for-profit corporate ventures. *The Weekly Reader* and its related products have been around for nearly a century. *Scholastic News* and its related products have been around for nearly as long. Channel One was launched in 1989 dramatically changing the dynamics of the in-school news business game.

THE ECONOMICS OF NEWS FOR YOUTH

The early efforts of the Weekly Reader Corporation (WRC), Scholastic, Inc. (SI), and the Newspaper In Education (NIE) programs were, at best, low to invisible efforts on the part of corporations to bring news to young people. Even while the efforts of WRC and SI. became more aggressive and diversified throughout the 1980s and the NIE stepped up their efforts to stop the hemorrhaging of the youth news audience, overall they had done outstanding jobs of maintaining their brand identities as primarily small-time, educational do-gooders.

In 1989 Chris Whittle blew the top off this corporate news game in the schools with the launch of his ambitious daily in-school video news program *Channel One*, and this led the way for a corporate invasion of public classrooms that has continued to accelerate every year. Over fifteen years later, after waxing and waning controversy, *Channel One* is still going and claims to reach 40 percent of all middle school and high schools across the United States and eight million teenagers. Most parents, most adults, have never heard of the program. Most high school and college students have, particularly those from low-income areas where minimal education funding has been more likely to drive schools into contracts with *Channel One* in order to obtain access to the media technology *Channel One* provides as a key component of their contract with schools.

In 1989 Chris Whittle, realizing the rise of neo-liberalism, laid the groundwork for a new business plan directed toward public schools. Schools had been under neo-liberal attack for nearly a decade, endlessly described as inefficient, wasteful bureaucratic dinosaurs harboring lazy, do-nothing, unaccountable public employees. At the same time the combination of tax cuts for corporations and for the wealthy and a historically unprecedented peacetime military buildup had coalesced into the "starve government" neo-liberal politics of the 1980s forcing cutbacks in social programs making up the nation's "safety net" and decreasing tax revenues for schools and all levels of government. The Reagan administration preached fiscal austerity and tripled the national deficit.

At the same, the new industrialization of information—computer technology was exploding—with its attendant ideology that whatever the problem was, technology, not equitable public policy, smaller class sizes, or social justice, was the answer. Media deregulation was in full swing. The call for privatization of all things public was also being pushed with increasing stridency by the newly founded collection of neo-liberal think tanks, from the Heritage Foundation to the Enterprise Institute. At the same time, corporations were just beginning to appreciate the dazzlingly successful "cradle to consumer" marketing strategies of the McDonald's and Disney corporations. And their own research divisions were just beginning to crunch the numbers on how quickly the purchasing power of children and their ability to influence family purchases were growing. Youth between the ages of twelve and nineteen spent $155 billion of their own money in 2001 and influenced family purchases of nearly $200 billion dollars.

Chris Whittle, who had founded Whittle Communications in 1970, had already discovered the growing importance of niche marketing—finding those small but enticing advertising-free zones overlooked by the major media, but increasingly lucrative. Lucrative, first, because they were untapped advertising territory, and, second, because they had the potential to offer high quality viewer demographics—for instance, producing specialty magazines at no charge for physicians' offices, in order sell advertising space, and advertising posed as editorial content to bored patients.

In the case of *Channel One*, Whittle also had the extremely successful print prototypes offered by Scholastic, Inc. and WRC Inc.—getting one's marketing foot in the door with what appeared to be an obviously positive educational product: the news. Why not offer cash-strapped schools a free daily video newscast, produced specifically for the middle and high school market? And to make it a deal that most poor schools literally could not refuse—provide all of the technology, the television sets for every classroom, the video-recorders for every classroom, the satellite receiving stations for free. Principals were merely required to sign contracts committing their schools to air the twelve-minute program at least 90 percent of the regular school days, to 90 percent of the classes. A school, for allowing twelve-minutes of what was promoted as high-quality, kid friendly news (but which study after study has found to be primarily 80 percent advertising hype and 20 percent infotainment) to be piped into their school could receive, on loan, as much as $50,000 worth of perhaps otherwise unaffordable video equipment. The only catch was that each daily newscast would contain two minutes of television commercials that the Whittle Corporation could sell to advertisers desperate to address this precious but notoriously difficult to reach demographic group.

As Ed Winters, one of the co-founders of *Channel One* with Whittle, put it in 1997, "Marketers have come to realize that all roads eventually lead to the schools." Whittle would be there waiting for them when they showed up.

By the 1980s and into the 1990s and the twenty-first century WRC Inc. and SI had adopted and adapted the *Channel One* model, aggressively using their decades of brand name goodwill to use their student news delivery system as the tactical entry point for a wide array of marketing strategies and product sales. Other corporations, which didn't have the positive news image to help them gain entry into the schools, soon found that the growing educational funding crisis across the nation as the neoliberal anti-tax movement gained more and more ground, encouraged schools to throw open their doors to business/education "partnerships."

WHOSE "DEMOCRACY"?

On February 9, 2004, *CNN Student News* ran the story "Teaching Democracy in Iraq." The story was focused on the conduct of U.S. sponsored seminars in Iraq which have "drawn anywhere from 50 to 1500 people eager to discuss the meaning of democracy and the form it should take in the new Iraq." On the *Student News* Web site was a "learning activity" promising students that they would "learn about the development of democracy in various countries, and compare these countries with Iraq as it aspires to develop its own democratic system." Although the United States was not included in the list of countries to be studied for its contributions to the development of democracy, the activity page explained that completing this exercise would help students developing competencies in the National Social Studies Standards, specifically in:

- Standard VI: Power, Authority and Governance: Students will understand the historical development of structures of power, authority and governance and their evolving functions in contemporary U.S. society as well as other parts of the world.
- Students will develop an understanding of how groups and nations attempt to resolve conflicts and seek to establish order and security.
- Standard IX: Global Connections: Students will examine global connections and interdependence.
- Students will analyze the interactions among states and nations and their cultural complexities as they respond to global events and changes.
- Students will address personal, national and global decisions, interactions and consequences, including critical issues such as peace, human rights, trade and global ecology.

Various Web resources were provided for students to conduct their research and a set of key words to be learned was included: Iraq, democracy, direct democracy, representative democracy, direct election, caucus, and impasse.

The critical question of the value of the *Student News* story and its subsequent guided learning activity in promoting a deeper, more critical understanding of democratic culture, and engagement rests with both an analysis of the story itself, "U.S. as "teacher," as well as the ideology built into the "learning activity." Although a critical ideological analysis of the National Social Studies Standards is beyond the scope of this essay, a brief look at the work of the Center for Civic Education and their development of the National Standards for Civics and Government can shed light on the political and ideological stakes involved in this kind of meta-theoretical standards setting. Both sets of standards have been referenced as compatible reference guides for "Making Civics Real" by the joint Annenberg Foundation/ Corporation for Public Broadcasting initiative on Excellence in Teaching.

Richard Merelman reviewed the CIVITAS curriculum that was developed to achieve the National Standards for Civics and Government. Within the curriculum purporting to offer up a unified vision of democracy and civic education he identified what he viewed as *four* competing models of citizenship.

The first model he called the hegemonic model of civics education, which is a form of socialization to existing government and political values where the primary goal is to reinforce the rule of existing elites. A second model, which he labeled the critical model of civics, is committed to communicating the realities of political power, developing an under-standing of "the existence of conflict, the importance of self-interest, the failures of public policies and political institutions to achieve given polit-ical objectives, and the inequalities in the distribution of political power."

The third model Merelman labeled the transformative model of civics education. It combines elements of the critical and hegemonic models stressing, and here he quotes the work of Charles Merriam, a "struggle . . . in the development of civic training: between the older system of tradi-tional indoctrination, and one in which much greater stress is laid upon the element of invention, adaptability, and adjustment in a changing world."

Finally, he outlines a fourth model that he argued recognizes that any model of civics education may be more influential on educational policy-makers than students. In this sense it is a "ritual of political nostalgia, creat-ing for policymakers the illusion that genuine progress in political education has at long last begun." Merelman labeled this the symbolic model of civic education, attuned to reassuring political elites that "'some-thing is being done' to meet the 'crisis' of citizenship."

Armed with these four models Merelman returned to the Center for Civic Education's CIVITAS curriculum and found national civics standards that "emphasize shared political values over political participation; over-simplify the relationships between American political values; assert a highly contestable function (cohesion) for shared values; and rely mainly upon elite statements to identify these political values."

Initially what Merelman found in the CIVITAS curriculum fit most closely with the hegemonic model of civics education. His analysis found that:

> . . . it is the powerful who would benefit most from the paucity of criti-cism and political participation which the proposed standards encour-age; from the rhetorical silences about the actual extent of value sharing, the assumed consistency of values, and the cohesive function of shared values; from the heavy reliance on seminal public documents to define values; and from the implicit exclusion of those who do not espouse these values from being, in some sense, 'American.'

Merelman found this tone well illustrated in its handling of the concept of "diversity." First, it was never defined. Second, students were expected to be able to "explain the importance of adhering to constitutional values and principles in managing conflicts over diversity," indicating that diversity was represented as being primarily about conflict and that when diver-sity gets in the way, it must yield to the timeless values of the Constitution.

Merelman also recognized that the CIVITAS standards did not entirely exclude the critical model of civics. Criticism is simply downplayed or understood as taking place within a normative position.

Ultimately Merelman concluded that beyond the hegemonic specifics of the proposed standards and their ambivalent attention to critique, the overall commitment to providing the necessary resources to implement them either in federal funding or in classroom time were substantially lacking. This led to his final conclusion that in the end, this early 1990s national flurry of concern over citizenship would serve primarily a symbolic function—serving mainly as "a symbolic ritual masked as an educational policy for reinforcing cultural hegemony."

For our purposes Merelman's review of the CIVITAS standards and curriculum makes clear, at the general level, that if we are going to examine the job of kids' news in teaching the lessons of citizenship, we will need to carefully locate both our examination of the meaning of citizenship and democracy within the larger debates over competing models of democracy. At a more specific level it provides some insights into how we might begin to organize our understanding of the various ways democracy could be conceptualized, and tips us off to the likely linkage we will find between the neo-liberal model of democracy and a legalistic definition of citizenship contained within the National Social Studies Standards which youth news like "CNN Student News" has aligned itself.

"DEMOCRACY" AS SPECTACLE: EMPTY WORDS AND THE TERROR OF NEO-LIBERALISM

During the last five years in the United States there have been numerous spectacular opportunities for the meaning of "democracy" today to be thoughtfully examined. The historic spectacle of the 2000 presidential election when the outcome was fought over for nearly six weeks before an ambiguous and contested decision by The Supreme Court allowed George W. Bush to occupy the White House, the 2001 9/11 attacks on the United States, the 2004 historic takeover of both houses of Congress and the presidency by the Republican party, the declaration of the "War on Terrorism" and the rise of the Department of Homeland Security, and the revised explanation for the U.S. war against Iraq from the legally questionable doctrine of "pre-emptive strike" based on the absolute claims that Iraq had or was near to possessing weapons of mass destruction to the justification for the continuing war being the liberation of the people of Iraq through the institution of democracy. Not to mention the January 30, 2005 first-time elections in Iraq.

However, throughout these five years there has been little sustained examination of the meaning of democracy in the United States even while the number of times the word "democracy" or its increasingly preferred synonym "freedom" have been invoked by political and civic leaders at a rate that might make even the French social theorist Jean Baudrillard, creator of the term "hyperreality," blush. And not only has the word "democracy" been uttered and written across every imaginable landscape, but its iconic representations, from linguistic referents like "patriotism" and "support our troops" to its visual representations such as the U.S. flag, whether draped over half-naked fashion models (see the Guess ad series) or printed on cardboard and displayed in car windows to the magnetic "Support our troops" yellow ribbons visible everywhere.

Throughout the last five years and even the last twenty-five years the single word "democracy" has sufficed to stand for a breathtaking transformation of the actual "on the ground" character of democratic culture in the United States. As Susan George put it,

> In 1945 or 1950, if you had seriously proposed any of the ideas and policies in today's standard neo-liberal toolkit, you would have been laughed off the stage or sent off to the insane asylum. At least in the Western countries, at that time, everyone was a Keynesian, a social democrat or a social-Christian democrat or some shade of Marxist. The idea that the market should be allowed to make major social and political decisions; the idea that the State should voluntarily reduce its role in the economy, or that corporations should be given total freedom, that trade unions should be curbed and citizens given much less rather than more social protection—such ideas were utterly foreign to the spirit of the time. Even if someone actually agreed with these ideas, he or she would have hesitated to take such a position in public and would have had a hard time finding an audience.

There has been a revolution in the U.S. idea of what constitutes "democracy," followed by the current ongoing policy revolution to bring into material reality this new vision of democracy. U.S. citizens have witnessed dramatic changes in their economic security, standards of living, access to health care and education, growing rates of poverty and homelessness, and increased racism. Yet, they have not been able, for the most part, to bear witness to the these transformations in a big picture kind of way—in large part because the changes have been all carried out under the increasingly vacuous and ambiguous banner called "democracy" or increasingly called "freedom" or "individual enterprise" or the "free market" or "individual choice."

And along with this revolution there has come a growing acceptance, particularly among youth, that old values anchored in democratic culture are no longer significant or meaningful. So successful has this revolution been that in a recent massive 2004 survey of high school students titled "The Future of the First Amendment" and commissioned by the James L. Knight Foundation found a significant ambivalence among these students regarding the First Amendment. Half the students believed that government could censor the Internet. More than a third of the students thought that the First Amendment "goes too far in the rights it guarantees."

If one mentions the word "neo-liberalism" to a fellow citizens, for the most part all one will encounter is a set of blank stares, and it doesn't seem to make much difference if you are talking to people in a teacher's lunchroom, a construction worksite, a secretarial pool, or even a college faculty lounge. And yet the term "neo-liberalism" is probably the most adequate and critically sophisticated label for categorizing the range of trends, ideologies, and policy transformations that have changed the face and heart of what we call democracy in the last three decades. It is a kind of anti-democratic vision of democracy, setting the stage for what educator/activist Henry Giroux calls the "eclipse of democracy."

So what do we mean here when we describe neo-liberalism? How would we know it if we saw it? What is at stake in terms of the material, social, and political well being of our children's lives, their lives as individuals and as citizens?

Media scholar Mark Hudson provides us with a working definition of neo-liberalism:

> Neo-liberalism can be defined as the belief that the unregulated free market is the essential precondition for the fair distribution of wealth and for political democracy. Thus, neo-liberals oppose just about any policy or activity that might interfere with the untrammeled operation of market forces, whether it be higher taxes on the wealthy and corporations, better social welfare programs, stronger environmental regulations, or laws that make it easier for workers to organize and join labor unions.

When confronted with the adverse consequences of their market-friendly policies, they usually respond by calling for patience, to give the policies more time to work their wealth-creating magic so that the benefits can "trickle down" to the rest of the population. Then, when the promised good life fails to materialize, they fall back on their ultimate defense and claim that, imperfect as the status quo may be, there is, unfortunately, no viable alternative. They point to the failed "socialist" societies of the twentieth century and warn ominously that, no matter how bad things get, any attempt to remedy the situation by forthrightly interfering with the market and the prerogatives of multinational corporations can only lead to state-bureaucratic authoritarianism.

Neo-liberal ideas are as old as capitalism itself, but in recent decades they have seen a tremendous resurgence and have displaced the state-interventionist economic theories of the interwar and post-World War II periods to become the reigning ideology of our time.

Hudson goes on to describe the contemporary landscape of neo-liberalism:

> In the 1990s, neo-liberal hegemony over our politics and culture has become so overwhelming that it is becoming difficult to even rationally discuss what neo-liberalism is; indeed, as Robert McChesney

notes, the term "neo-liberalism" is hardly known to the U.S. public outside of academia and the business community.

The corporate stranglehold on our information and communications media gives neo-liberal ideologues a virtually unchallenged platform from which to blast their pro-market messages into every corner of our common culture.

Several authors have described this "stranglehold" and discussed how we got here and what we need to do to challenge and move on from neo-liberalism's grip on our political, economic and social culture. This essay is committed to doing its own small part in this enterprise by attempting to shed some light to how neo-liberalism operates in the sphere of corporate news for youth in a school setting or as Raymond Williams put it, paying "closer attention to the complex ways in which individuals are formed by the institutions to which they belong, and in which, by reaction, the institutions [take] on the color of individuals thus formed."

The stakes are high. As Henry Giroux reminds us,

> Within the discourse of neo-liberalism that has taken hold of the public imagination, there is no way of talking about what is fundamental to civic life, critical citizenship, and a substantive democracy. Neo-liberalism offers no critical vocabulary for speaking about political or social transformation as a democratic project. Nor is there a language for either the ideal of public commitment or the notion of a social agency capable of challenging the basic assumptions of corporate ideology as well as its social consequences. In its dubious appeals to universal laws, neutrality, and selective scientific research, neo-liberalism "eliminates the very possibility of critical thinking, without which democratic debate becomes impossible" (Buck-Morss 2003, 65-66). This shift in rhetoric makes it possible for advocates of neo-liberalism to implement the most ruthless economic and political policies without having to open up such actions to public debate and dialogue.

At the same time it is crucial that we are reminded that there is a history of a critical and emancipatory democracy as well as a continuously developing vision of democracy in the service of social justice, fundamental human rights, and democratically arrived at social values and policy. This vision of democracy has gone by many names including Benjamin Barber's title of "strong democracy," David Held's concept of "democratic autonomy," and Carole Patemen's title of "deliberative democracy" or "participatory democracy."

The vision of democracy these models share is an attempt to reconceptualize civil society as a place not just founded on private and community values, but as a truly public space between government and the market. Barber usefully summarizes this view:

> The strong democratic perspective on civil society distinguishes our civic lives both from our private lives as individual producers and consumers and from our public lives as voters and rights-claimants.

This is a space that historically existed for only a small group of democratic elites. It is also a space that, even for those elites, was squeezed between a growing governmental bureaucracy and increasingly expansive and intrusive market forces. This is the space that Barber and others fighting to reclaim a democratic culture from neo-liberalism believes must be recovered and enlarged. According to Barber, strong or participatory democracy:

1 Shares with the communitarians the view that we are first and foremost social beings. Our identities are formed, sustained and dependent on our social lives.
2 At the same time, it views the identities prescribed for us only by our belonging to traditional communities and through family bonds as not providing the opportunities people need to create their own lives. Civil society through its voluntary character (which is like the private sector) and through its openness and democratic character (which is like the government/state sector) offers these opportunities.
3 The truth of politics cannot simply be found in decontextualized facts. Political truth, as well as truth in general, is the outcome of debate and discussion of all to be affected by the consequences of a decision.
4 Civic life is not just a means to an end, it is an end in itself: the creation and promotion of public good.
5 The free market sets an example of the positive virtue of free-choice, but its selfish orientation and narrow focus on material objects undermines the values and community it needs to survive.
6 Civic society must be strong to mediate between the tribalizing tendencies of radical communitarianism and the privatizing and morally corrosive force of markets. Democracy creates the conditions for capitalism. Capitalism, uncontrolled, has a tendency to undermine those same conditions.

For these democratic theorists, civil society is the critical space in a truly democratic society. It is the space in which individuals have the opportunity to develop responsible freedom, freedom to consciously create themselves and their values, but in constant relationship to the rights of others to do the same. Civil society is also the space in which a moral value critical to democracy is produced: Public good. Public good is the social and material embodiment of a democratic recognition that we are each other. It is also a recognition that democracy is not simply a technical system for managing a form of government. It is both a process and an end in itself. It is a recognition of the fundamentally social character of human existence.

These authors also see the "myth of the market" as our "most insidious myth" concerning democracy, because as Barber writes "not just because so many people believe it, but because the market's invisible bonds slip on so easily and feel so much like freedom." But the market, he argues, is not democracy.

BACK TO CNN STUDENT NEWS: DEFINING DEMOCRACY

The first thing one notices in watching an episode of *CNN Student News* is that in structure, format, and content it is primarily a mini-version of the adult *CNN Headline News* as well as the other mainstream network evening newscasts. The fast-paced high-tech graphics and camera shot cuts, the standard high-tech looking anchor desk and video screen backdrop, the celebrity-groomed youth anchor, the flawless diction, the "professional" intonations of adult anchors, and the same selection of pack-journalism stories that dominate the adult news shows and newspaper front pages. It is a ten-minute kiddie version of corporate network and cable news with a bit less explicit violence and sex and the same amount of age appropriate sensationalism and trivial news.

There is no possible way a sensible, intelligent, engaged teenager could develop any meaningful understanding of current events, much less crucial current events that may impinge on his or her life, much less in a context that gives them meaning and coherence. In fact, in its superficial treatment of stories, its lack of context, its fragmented and video-bite approach to "news" the program would tend to undermine rather than enhance or develop any form of critical thinking skills.

Nevertheless, *CNN Student News* is the most often recommended alternative to teachers and parents over the hard-sell, hard-marketing, advertising-carrying alternative of *Channel One*. The fundamental reason for these endorsements from mainstream educators and civic educators rests on primarily on a single criterion—the CNN student news product carries no direct advertising. It is clearly loaded with ideology, but an ideology as invisible to most citizens who have accepted the democratic vision of neo-liberalism as the adult evening news programs.

However, so far we are talking about the ten-minute student headline news service itself. The program is linked to its own Web site, and here our analysis becomes more complex.

This Time Warner subsidiary offers a sleek, graphically attractive invitation to enhance one's learning from the news show of the day and from archived programs and specials. Across the top of the page we are reminded that *CNN Student News* is "the most trusted name in news for the classroom." Beneath that slogan a large banner ad runs prominently across the top of the page rotating through a variety of products targeted to a teen market: cell phones, credit card opportunities, and DVD rental services, etc.

However we also see a "teach from the show" section that offers teaching plans, discussion questions, and Internet-based resources to probe more deeply into the news of that particular day. We also find an archive section that allows one to track down past stories, transcripts of those stories, and additional teaching resources and lesson plans where they exist. A menu bar below the banner ad will take you to "archives," "education news," and "CNN.com." In fact both the "education" button and the "CNN.com" buttons take the browser back to the main CNN Web site.

Also featured is a monthly special section, such as "Women's History Month" or "Black History Month," and a "CNN Presents Classroom Edition" that includes features such as "The Mystery of Jesus," "Meeting Point: Tracking the Global Warming Threat," and "CNN 25: Business Newsmakers." *CNN Presents* are occasional hour-long CNN documentaries produced for *CNN Student News* and aired between 4:00 and 5:00 AM to be recorded by teachers and brought into the classroom. They include, like the monthly special section, educator guides, activities and additional Internet-based resources.

What is particularly interesting about the *CNN Student News* site is that it provides a wide range of additional in-depth material regarding featured stories, monthly specials, and the "Classroom Presents" documentaries. A motivated teacher, with time and energy, could construct lessons that put the news of the day into a much more meaningful context than is offered by the program's daily newscast. For instance, "Women's History Month" has the traditional mind deadening, anti-intellectual depoliticizing material most youth have come to associate with "news." Liberal if not apolitical presentations such as time lines that celebrate women's political activity as a thing of the past, as a progressive narrative of women's rights fought for and achieved, is typical. Sojourner Truth is mentioned, as are Elizabeth Cady Stanton and Susan B. Anthony, and the triumph for women of winning the right to vote under the Nineteenth Amendment.

However, the closer we come to current events, the less political the events mentioned in the time line. It is noted that 350,000 women fought in World War II, Title IX (not the brand name) is passed granting women equal funding with men for sports in school (an issue of still considerable controversy but listed as an uncontested moment of success in women's empowerment), Sandra Day O'Connor is appointed the first woman Supreme Court Justice, Sally Ride becomes the first female astronaut, Alicia Keys takes "home five Grammy Awards in 2002, and four more in 2005," and Condoleezza Rice "becomes the second woman to serve as Secretary of State." No mention is made of Madeline Albright being the *first* woman to serve in that role.

A related feature for the month, "Profiles," keeps political and activist women safely contained in historical profiles far removed from contemporary politics or gender activism. In the "Women's Words of Wisdom: Thoughts Over Time," let's know that Annie Oakley once said "I can truthfully say I know of no other recreation that will do so much toward keeping a women in good health and perfect figure than a few hours spent occasionally at trap shooting." The most recent woman featured is Rachel Carson, considered by many to have helped launch the modern environmental movement with her book *Silent Spring,* which detailed not only the destructive effects of the use of industrial pesticides on the environment, but revealed that the lies told by the chemical industry were being routinely accepted by public officials charged with environmental regulation. Her significantly depoliticized quote is "Those who dwell, as scientists or laymen, among the beauties and mysteries of the earth are never alone or weary of life."

At the same time the major thrust of the lesson plan, resource guide, and activities stands as an expected example of, in Merelman's terms, the "hegemonic model" of civic education, it is possible in scouring the site to find a Web link pointing to "Women's Speeches from Around the World," where with more expert searching one might find a speech given by recent Nobel Peace Prize winner Wangari Maathai, organizer and leader of the Kenyan Green Belt Movement. In the speech listed at this site "Presented on the Occasion of the 4th UN World Women's Conference in Beijing, China, 1995," Maathai has much to say about neo-liberalism, or what she calls the "liberalized free market and capital flow." Maathai states,

> Market forces, especially the liberalized free market and capital flow, both of which are very competitive, legitimatize the marginalization of local initiatives which cannot compete with the giant Transnational corporations, foreign capital and attractive conditions which are created to enable foreign investors.

> Further, indebtness of African states is making it difficult for the state to protect its citizen from being overwhelmed by international organizations on whose behalf IMF, World Bank and other donors demand liberalization and free markets. Small local initiatives with comparatively little capital do not stand a chance against the onslaught.

Perhaps the most important point here is that even in the mainstream corporate-produced *CNN Student News* and its supporting Web site, the fact that one might find, after rigorous analysis, one or two sophisticated critiques of the neo-liberal ideology at hand does not move the news source out of the category of hegemonic reproduction and into Merelman's second or third categories of civic education committed to communicating the realities of political power, developing an understanding of

145

"the existence of conflict, the importance of self-interest, the failures of public policies and political institutions to achieve given political objectives, and the inequalities in the distribution of political power" or encouraging the effort to find a transformative between systems of ideological indoctrination and those committed to "invention, adaptability, and adjustment in a changing world" to the principles of social justice and democratic accountability.

So let us turn briefly back to our original example from *CNN Student News*, "Teaching Democracy in Iraq."

DEMOCRACY IN CRISIS AND A POLITICS OF HOPE

The so-called youth crisis of citizenship can be viewed in terms of the rise of neo-liberalism and its war against youth, families, and democratic culture. Giroux's *The Terror of Neo-liberalism*, Piven's *The War at Home: The Cost of Bush's Militarism*, and an updated reinterpretation of Habermas's and Bourdieu's ideas of legitimation crisis are good references. These ideas must be put into an interpretive framework that recognizes that at the same time as youth are offered, through news produced for them, a picture of the world that is less and less related to their own experience (increasing child poverty and homelessness, lack of access to health care, overcrowded classrooms and declining funding for education, as well as declining future job prospects). Their lack of political trust and cynicism may be read as indicators of what Jurgen Habermas and Pierre Bourdieu have called a key threat to the advanced capitalist state: A legitimation crisis of significant proportions. But in this case it is the hegemony of neo-liberalism that is threatened from within as well as internationally

Although it is clear that youth as well as adult pedagogy has shifted from traditional formal sites, schools, news media, and so forth to what Douglas Kellner calls the "infotainment environment," or what Henry Giroux sees as the serious political work of popular culture in all of its forms, youth news still forms an integral portion of the complex hegemonic work at hand and deserves its share of attention.

YOUTH AND PARTICIPATORY DEMOCRACY

What is being "read" as political apathy by mainstream political commentators, as voting rates fall and textbook civic knowledge declines, may be failing to register the significance of the rise in non-formal organized political action such as protests, demonstrations, and individual acts of political action such as computer hacking, copyright violation, and other forms of transgressive social behavior. Clearly, corporate media culture has been working very hard to contain youth frustration and rebellion within the consumer sphere. However, youth's withdrawal from the formal political sphere has many mainstream U.S. political and economic leaders worried. The simultaneous rise of a growing international youth information network and activism suggest a rising youth consciousness of a participatory, democratic world citizenship.

In these terms, the news crisis and the youth citizenship crisis must be read more as a crisis of neo-liberalism/corporate democracy as the world community increasingly rejects the unilateralism of the "U.S. = Democracy" model and the growing economic deficits of neo-liberalism erode the U.S. economy.

Resources
Books

Barber, B. (1998). *A place for us.* New York: Hill and Wang.

Brock, D. (2004). *The Republican noise machine: Right-wing media and how it corrupts democracy.* New York: Crown Publishers.

Bybee, C. (2006). Bad news for kids: Where schools get their news for kids. In S. Steinberg & J. Kincheloe (Eds.). *What you don't know about schools.* New York: Palgrave.

Fox, R. F. (2000). *Harvesting minds: How TV commercials control kids.* New York: Greenwood/Praeger.

Giroux, H. (2004). *The terror of neo-liberalism: Authoritarianism and the eclipse of democracy.* London: Paradigm Publishers.

Held, D. (1996). *Models of democracy.* Palo Alto, CA: Stanford University Press.

Pateman, C. (1970). *Participation and democratic theory.* London: Cambridge University Press.

Articles

Bybee, C., Fogle, A., & Quail, C. (2004). Neo-liberal news for kids: Citizenship lessons from Channel One. *Studies in Media & Information Literacy Education,* 4 (1). Retrieved from http://www.utpjournals.com/jour.ihtml?lp=simile/issue13/issue13toc.html

George, S. (1999). A short history of neo-liberalism: Twenty years of elite economics and emerging opportunities for structural change. Conference on Economic Sovereignty in a Globalising World. 24–26 March. Bangkok: [online]. Retrieved from http://www.globalexchange.org/campaigns/econ101/neoliberalism.html.pf

Giroux, H. A. (2005, Winter). The terror of neoliberalism: Rethinking the significance of cultural politics. *College Literature.*

Hoynes, W. (1997). News for a captive audience: An analysis of Channel One. *Extra!* May/June.

Web Sites

ChannelOne.com. Retrieved from http://www.channelone.com/

CNN Student News. Retrieved from http://cnnstudentnews.cnn.com/fyi/index.html

National Council for the Social Studies. Curriculum standards for social studies. Retrieved from http://www.socialstudies.org/standards/

Nick News with Linda Ellerbee. Retrieved from http://www.nick.com/
    all_nick/tv_supersites/nick_news/?_requestid=261634
State of the news media 2005. Project for Excellence in Journalism.
    Retrieved from http://www.stateofthenewsmedia.org/2005/
    narrative_overview_audience.asp?cat=3&media=1
Teaching democracy in Iraq. (2004, February 9). CNN Student News.
    Retrieved from http://cnnstudentnews.cnn.com/2004/fyi/news/02/
    08/learning.iraq.democracy/
Teen kid news. Retrieved from http://www.weeklyreader.com/kidsnews/

Steal This Article

Peter Dachille Jr.

Technology has brought us more advances in the past fifty years than in the previous thousand. It has expanded our ability to see not only within ourselves on a microscopic level, but to see the planet and galaxy around us. It has also doubled the average life expectancy, given a better quality to that life, and, on a more personal level, brought advances in the ease and entertainment we want in our lives.

With radio, movies, television, and computers, those landmarks have landed in our homes, and become part of our everyday routine. More recently the rise of the Internet has given an unprecedented ease to buyers and consumerism in general, literally bringing it to them. The popularity of the Internet and cable television, and how they help to bring movies and music to us, helps to spike interest in them and place their role and purpose into everyday life as well. They are accepted no matter the price; availability and convenience are seen as enough to justify the costs.

However, as large corporations are making millions of dollars every year, dollars that the average consumer spends record-breaking amounts of with relative ease, and this breeds resentment in those same buyers. When the time or opportunity comes that third parties offer those products or services at a more appealing price, even when the legality or morality of it is in question, it will not deter buyers; rather the lower-cost alternatives will be exploited just as much, as the resentment grows into a justification to do so. If products are available at a low cost or even free, through those same technological advances, people will use them as much as they possibly can.

Stealing from corporations therefore is not seen as stealing at all. Rationalizing that companies will not notice if one person gets their product for free is the main rationale for these activities. The companies affected by this way of thinking, however, are defiant in their belief that no one should get their product for free, or without their consent, and have tried methods to help prevent it. As they drew their line in the sand, individuals and even other companies have worked just as hard to crack through those methods. The piracy battle is fought on many fronts, among them movies, cable television, and music.

TOOLS OF THE TRADE

What are some of the tools of the trade, so to speak, of piracy? It started with blank cassettes and videotapes, and has evolved into blank CDs and DVDs and bytes on hard drives. Even though the media are more advanced and easier to access, it's just as simple and cheap to copy things, and with that technology comes the ability to make those copies identical to the original.

The potential of cassettes was that one could copy songs from LPs and other cassettes, making a full identical copy or mixing songs together. The layman's justification was that records and tapes eventually break down, and that it is completely legal to make a "backup" copy. The General Agreement on Tariffs and Trade, signed in 1994, was aimed to be a formal declaration that this layman's rule was now not only labeled a federal offense, thereby solidifying the stance in lieu of individual state rules, but also covered the importing of bootlegs as well. However, its announcement went ignored and was not enforced. By this time, the average person was so used to doing it, that just about every person who listened to music had a copy or mix tape in their collection or had made one for someone else. Dual cassette holders became standard on any mid-sized and mid-priced stereo systems. This further confused those who heard it was illegal and gave credence to the ones who claimed it was perfectly fine to make copies.

The same is true with VHS tapes. The first purpose of blank videotapes could have been to tape movies off of cable or favorite shows off of regular television, but illegal uses of the machine followed quickly. Devoted fans of shows would tape every episode of a sitcom, edit out the commercials, and when finished with a season, label it and watch it at another time or even sell it to other collectors. With a simple connecting wire and two VCRs stacked on one another, a tape can be easily duplicated many times over. Even more recently, dual-tape VCRs have been made, and even a single DVD/VCR deck is becoming mainstream and easily affordable, with the purpose of both being to make copies.

Computer software is another example. Knowing that floppy disks and CDs are easily broken and can get scratched or marred justifies making copies of them. Having several computers in a house or buying a new one every few years are also reasons for using the same software programs for multiple computers.

This is the first instance where active steps are being taken to try and deter copying. An increasing number of programs, utilities, and even games have registration codes that are mandatory and must be registered online. Once the code is used it is blocked from being used again. Many software companies, including Microsoft, address this issue on a corporate level, selling the license to businesses that are then allowed to install programs such as Microsoft Office and Windows upgrades on an unlimited number of computers being used by that business, as the number of computers in the company will always vary as the business grows and new computers are added. The license is, not surprisingly, also used by employees at home for installation on their computers, whether they do their work at home or not.

Dell computers now offers CD burner drives as a standard feature with its desktop computers. CD-Rs (recordables on which material can be placed only once) and CD-RWs (on which files and programs can be burned and deleted as often as needed) are fairly priced, at about a dollar each, and even lower in packs of 50 or 100. The very tools needed for copying, which has been labeled stealing, are placed in the hands of every person who orders a computer. At this time, nearly every computer is sold standard with a CD writeable drive, and recordable CDs are cheaply and widely distributed. Even the software for copying files and making songs from a CD into individual MP3 files is preinstalled on the computer, and it is all legally allowed, although most use of it is illegal. The software that comes with iPods can copy tracks onto a computer's hard drive within moments, and then on to the handheld set.

The ability for anyone to download, install, and navigate a music ripping program has become very easy for someone with moderate computer experience. Shawn Fanning is a community college dropout who wrote the code for Napster in one night. A search on any popular search engines on the Internet for "rippers" (programs that convert CD music tracks to MP3 files) will net many results, as the programs are easy to put together. File sharing programs are just as easy to find and create, with numerous ones coming and going depending on their popularity, ease of use, security, and, more frequently, until they are hit with lawsuits.

COPYING TAPES/FILMING MOVIES

As stated before, the ability to "stack" two VCRs and simply connect them with a cable gave people the ability to make a copy (or many copies) of whatever is on that tape. Due to the cost of VCRs in the beginning, it was a rare sight for someone to have two in their home, but as time passed, and machines became commonplace, they are now available at a very reasonable price.

Before the idea of putting entire seasons of a television show on video-tape (and later DVD), tape trading—with friends or even through mail order advertised in trade publications and newsletters—was very popular, as these kinds of anthologies were not available anywhere else at the time. In this scenario, selling and trading shows without the consent of the television or movie studio is not only illegal, but doing so by mail is a federal offense as well. Considering that the going rate for particular shows is low ($10–20 for a six-hour tape), the business is brisk, no matter the risk.

A popular method of illegally obtaining a movie is to actually film it with a camera while attending the film in the theater. This type of bootleg-ging is increasing in popularity in urban areas. The quality of these movies is at best average. Consider first the fact that when recording, the move-ment of the film is slowed down due to the way television and movie screens record frames per second when being recorded by a second camera. Therefore characters and scenes do not move smoothly. If the angle is off because the camera needs to be better hidden, the camera itself is of poor quality, or the person taping the movie is not far back enough in the theater, then the picture may be lopsided and the sound might come from one side. If people nearby laugh, cough, eat food, or stand up, it is also included. If one was looking to have that "in the movie feel" then this type of copy would be perfect. For the full effect of the movie itself though, it is far from what one would choose to see.

The advancement of DVDs, and their higher-quality features, helped bootleggers give the illusion that if they copied the movies onto DVDs instead of regular VHS tapes, the quality would be better. However it is not so.

In order to get the best quality bootleg of a movie, sometimes a movie's "master tape" is stolen or copied without the studio's or owner's knowl-edge. These can lead to better quality movies as they are taken from the original source. However this is not always the case, and hardly ever done, as access to that copy is strictly limited. The best example of this would be with the release of "Star Wars Episode 1: The Phantom Menace", a movie that was shot entirely on digital film. Only certain theaters had the capabilities to accommodate such equipment and so the ones that could had to account not only for the number of movies they had at their theater, but the con-stant whereabouts of the equipment as well. Crude bootlegs were quickly on the streets. The more technological (and therefore better quality) copies did eventually follow, but not as quickly.

Sometimes when an early copy of a movie is taken and copied the results can have interesting results. In one memorable copy of "Casper," released in 1995, the master tape was taken, copied, and released on the streets. How-ever, the movie was not yet finished. A movie that includes computer graphics or CGI has to be done in two steps, the first step being the live characters filming their scenes, the second being that the animated graphics are added afterward. This particular tape was taken somewhere in between. Therefore there are scenes where the live characters are interacting with animated ones who have not yet been added! Questions go unanswered, conversations are one-sided, and gestures are made to . . . no one! Its value would not lie in the quality of the movie, but for the fact that this version is rare, if not nonexistent, and fans of the movie and the characters would be the main market for a movie like that.

STEALING CABLE

For as long as cable has been around, the desire and ability to get the signal, or certain channels, without subscribing, has also existed. In the beginning of cable theft, the main way that one would get channels illegally would be to simply (or not so simply) hint, or outright ask, the person who installs your cable to program in extra channels without the cable company knowing, for an under-the-table fee that they would then pocket. Asking would be incredibly risky, as the employee might report the person, but if that person worked in the neighborhood and was known to hook others up illegally, word of mouth would pass quietly between neighbors. It was this sort of modus operandi that inspired an episode of the The Simpsons and the 1993 dark comedy "Cable Guy." In both of those cases however, the "cable guy" had no scruples in giving free cable, but was also a shady or emotionally disturbed person, who continued to invade the subscriber's life and home.

It has come to the point now that cable descramblers are being sold, quite boldly in fact, first by a third party or "someone who someone else knows," and now, in magazine and newspaper ads. They are labeled as "testers" and claim to be legal. The directions that come with the testers are also a disclaimer, freeing the company from lawsuits or prosecution. They give step-by-step directions for installing the device, hooking up and relaying the cables from the box into the unit so as to act as a "middle man." The last step in some companies' directions are to unhook the device, restore the cables back into the original cable box, and to put the "tester" back into the box it was shipped in, and not use it until you need to test your box again. In other companies, they inform you that each and every time you use the descrambler, you are required by law to notify the cable company that you are going to be accessing the signals. It would be safe to say that very few, if any, people actually follow those rules; taking the signal without anyone knowing is the basis for ordering the package in the first place. The theory is that they have directed people to not abuse the potential of getting free cable, but cannot and will not be held responsible if they do, and furthermore should not be held accountable if they do. They are merely offering a product that makes sure that the box a customer has could receive the channels that the cable companies offer, if they were to choose to subscribe in the future.

Cable companies work swiftly to track and shut down such companies, and though they have a fair amount of success, other companies offering the exact product take their place. It is not only the goal of cable companies to confiscate the cable boxes and descramblers; the lists of names and addresses of people who ordered descramblers are also sought. It is a crime not only against the cable company, but, again, it is a federal issue, since the descramblers are delivered by U.S. mail. The lure of free cable, however, is more than tempting enough to have people do it in large numbers.

Cable companies call attention to several important points when describing cable theft. First, and most simply, they point to cable thieves as the main reason that subscription prices are high in the first place. However by pointing out the amount that is estimated to be stolen each year, the amount of revenue generated by cable is also revealed, and the average consumer does not sympathize with the company when seeing that particular number.

Second, they say, by having a "hot box," the signal to the boxes of legitimate subscribers is weakened or may have more periods of being blocked out. If a person knows that a neighbor has an illegal box, the thought that other people are enjoying uninterrupted cable while the channels that they paid for are having problems or not showing at times might put the fleeting thought of reporting the theft to the cable company.

Finally, they claim that since the signal is illegitimate, there is a chance that the signal can interfere with commercial airwave transmissions as well. This might put the thought that the signal from stolen cable might distort something important, such as radio contact between police or ambulance vehicles and their bases, or even airplanes and the flight controllers, with potentially fatal results.

However, even with the rules and advice that cable companies put out, they do not have the absolute power or ability to do much about cable theft, even when discovered. Even with signals called "silver bullets" that are able to detect if a box is receiving a signal or channel that it is not subscribed to (some versions are coded to display the phrase "you are receiving this channel illegally"), cable companies would have to physically see the box being used illegally and see that the subscriber is fully aware of what they are doing, in order to even being the process of confiscating and prosecuting the offenders.

The current task of cable companies is a low, slow, and expensive process. Simply put, they go through various subscription areas and inform subscribers that new boxes are being installed. The new boxes operate under different frequencies, which render the previous inoperable. The machines or testers used previously will no longer work, and though companies who manufacture the illegal descramblers will soon carry a compatible "hot box," the cost of them upgrading, along with the price consumers will have to pay for a new one is done to help dissuade the practice of doing so.

153

STEALING MUSIC

On the surface, many bands do not mind when their songs are downloaded off of the Internet or traded among friends or through programs. In fact, for many new and upcoming musicians, distributing a sample, or even the entire song, is a good way of self-promotion. Tapes and CDs are pressed and passed out at concerts featuring similar bands. Now, with the Internet, it's easier and cheaper to release the music to fans, and the range of exposure is many times over what would be at a concert or music store. Even with a Web site, many new bands encourage fans to download their music, send it to friends, and to support them by seeing them live or purchasing the full album when it is released. At first thought, the logic that fans will buy what they could download for free seems flawed. As one band proved, that is not always true

By 2001, The Offspring had already sold over 4 million copies of 1998's *Americana* alone. Their next step was to offer a new single, followed by the entire forthcoming album *Conspiracy of One* as MP3s on the Internet. Their own label tried to block them from releasing it, but after negotiations, the album was released free of charge on the Internet. The band then offered a million-dollar prize, paid out by the band members and not the record company, to a fan that subscribed to their mailing list.

The Smashing Pumpkins released their final original album, *Machina II*, on the Internet free of charge. Australian trio Single Gun Theory, seeing as they had not released an album since 1994 and that distribution of their albums was scant, were prepared to release their entire discography on the Internet for free as well, until their label, Nettwerk, pulled their CDs from shelves, then rereleased them with extra and unreleased tracks from singles. System of a Down released an album simply titled *Steal This Album* with no liner notes, artwork, or description of any kind; the title scrawled on a disk with a marker looks much like one would see in bootlegs or copies passed between friends.

Pearl Jam released the entire seventy-two-stop world tour promoting their 2000 release *Binaural*, on CDs. Although most fans wouldn't even think about buying all seventy-two performances, the appeal for this set of releases is wide for many reasons. First, each performance is different. The playlists varied at each city and performance, from the slight difference in song order, to the extreme, with new songs, emphasis on songs from certain albums, and even impromptu jams, solos, and covers. Fans could pick a concert that contains their favorites. Some concerts have songs that the band rarely performs, or is not known to have recorded on to an album, so the appeal to those who collect rare performances and recordings is now available. Finally, for those who attended the concerts, they can now not only get a copy of the show they went to, they can get it at a cheaper price and know that the recording will be of good quality.

Dave Matthews Band is another band that sits on the fence regarding their music. It is well known that the band gives full permission to fans to record their live performances, and fans exploit this permission fully. As soon as shows start, so do the tape recorders. However, though they permit fans to copy their music, they do not allow those fans to copy, distribute, or sell their recordings to others. Several cease and desist orders have been placed on music stores, mainly independently owned chains, that carry these CDs, leaving both fans and store owners wondering exactly what the stance is, both from the band, and the legal point of view.

Of course the most infamous step taken against music piracy occurred when Lars Ulrich, the drummer for Metallica, one of the most renowned heavy metal bands in the genre, discovered that songs by his band were being traded freely, and for free, on the Internet. Backed up by several other big names in the music business and the RIAA, they filed suit against Napster. Music fans and downloaders were upset to say the very least, especially when Lars and company set their sights not only on Napster, but on them as well, including their fan base. Many cried foul, immediately recounting that when Metallica was an unknown, and unsigned band in the early 1980s, they encouraged fans to copy their music and distribute it as a "word of mouth," a practice that is, again, still a major promotional tactic for bands. For the majority of the fan base, which had already become critical of Metallica's commercial exposure and a new sound to their music, saw this as the final straw to the band becoming corporate "sell-outs." Though Napster is now a legally run business which sells MP3s, many other clones of the original program have stepped into their place undermining not only CD sales at this stage, but the revenue generated by selling MP3s as well.

A surprising and aggressive move against MP3 downloading was through a hoax by a musician. Copies of songs from Madonna's release *American Life* were reportedly "ripped" and put on the Internet for free. Those who downloaded them found a surprise during the music. In the middle of each song, the Material Girl overdubbed a section of music with her speaking voice, asking "What the f*** do you think you're doing?" Apparently the advance copies were done by her company and placed like worms on a hook for music downloaders, who quickly took the bait. The repercussion by fans and computer users was swift but not permanent; Madonna's Web site was hacked into and temporarily brought down, the home page displaying the message "This is what the f*** we think we are doing."

The recording industry spent an undisclosed amount of time and money creating a code onto a CD that was programmed to not be able to copy. After all of the money, effort, and publicity, along with listing the first releases to include the block, it was only one day before the code was cracked, and the report, containing the specific directions was spread over the media airwaves, in print, and online. Quite simply, all one had to do was hold down the 'shift' key on the keyboard when inserting a CD into the CD-ROM drive for the first time. The secret behind the software was also discovered quickly. Before the first track of the CD, there was a block of scrambled data, and if a copy program was run, it would attempt to read the data before any music, and be stalled. This copy protection was quickly bypassed as well by running a black marker over the outermost rim of the CD. There was an additional problem with the blocking program; some regular CD players and walkman units would try to read that empty data block as well, and hence the CD would not run at all, and many Mac users reported that attempting to just play the CD on their computer would cause a full system crash.

As technology has advanced over the last 100 and even 50 years, we see an ease and sense of convenience in our lives. Some conveniences are with our health, lifestyle, or making everyday tasks easier. Even more, we develop new and more advanced forms of entertainment. Technology, for all that it gives us, also makes all of the above methods for stealing incredibly easy. It will not be law that curtails this, rather ethics and self-control that will prove to be the deciding factors.

Resources

The Cable Descrambler - Consequences of Descrambling Cable TV. Retrieved April 8, 2005 from http://www.expertlaw.com/library/pubarticles/Consumer_Protection/cable_descrambler.html

The Dave Matthews Band—Tape But Don't Sell. Retrieved April 8, 2005 from http://old.valleyadvocate.com/articles/bootleg4.html

The Federal Anti-Piracy and Bootleg FAQ. http://www.grayzone.com/faqindex.htm

Frequently asked questions about Cable TV Descrambler/Converters (Decoders). Retrieved April 8, 2005 from http://www.cableboxoutlet.com/faq.htm

Madonna site hacked in file-trading controversy. Retrieved April 18, 2005 from http://news.zdnet.co.uk/hardware/emergingtech/0,39020357,2133749,00.htm

RIAA—Issues: CD/CD-R Piracy. http://www.riaa.com/issues/piracy/cdcdr.asp

Sony's 'copy-proof' CD fails to silence hackers. Retrieved April 8, 2005 from http://www.usatoday.com/money/tech/2002-05-20-copyproof-cd.htm

Time Warner Cable—Policies and Procedures: Cable Theft is a Crime. Retrieved April 8, 2005 from http://www.twckc.com/help/policies/cabletheft.asp

DORAMA: JAPANESE TV

Serena Parris Larrain

Dorama are Japanese television shows, drama, or soap operas. Dorama is the spelling in the Japanese alphabet known as *katakana* for the American word "drama." Popular with teenagers are the dorama starring teenage celebrities. The serialized, seasonally aired shows evolved from original *manga* (popular Japanese comic books) and *Japanimation* (Japanese animated cartoons and movies or anime, already dear to Japanese teens). The dorama are the most recent technologized version of manga and anime and a natural progression for entertaining a story-hungry youth. Manga and anime are experiencing growing appreciation around the world, including the United States, as evidenced by membership on worldwide sites and creation and maintenance of their own fanzines, Web sites, and Web-rings. Youthful fans are technologically savvy and critical, yet faithful to the authors, artists, and characters they adopt.

Trendy and infused with high drama, teen-centered doramas air on Japanese television, usually during the prime time hours of 9:00 PM to 11:00 PM, the most popular hours for teen viewing in Japan, according to "J-Fan Drama" (www.J-Fan.com). Although the story lines often originate from manga comics series, they gain new life in the television medium. Television actors and actresses take on more complicated human emotions than can be fully appreciated in the comic or animated media, therefore, teens can identify more readily with them.

Much like teen-targeted television programming in the United States, dorama is filled with the everyday dramas of the twenty-first-century teen, as well as age-old themes. Dorama covers as many topics as teenagers have issues. This is as important to the teens in Japan, as teen series are to U.S. viewers in North America. Think of some early U.S. television shows first targeted at U.S. teens of recent decades: *90210*, a popularity and relationship drama (Fox TV, 1990–2000); *Dark Angel*, a science-fiction based drama (Cameron/Eglee Productions, Inc., 2000–2002); *The Gilmore Girls*; about friends, family, and sexual coming of age (Cameron/Eglee Productions, Inc., 2000); *One Tree Hill*, about students (Warner Bros. Entertainment, 2004–present); and one of the latest popular series, *Veronica Mars*, which features a teenage female private detective (Warner Bros. Entertainment, 2004–present). These U.S. shows help one to begin to understand dorama in comparison to teen television in the United States. The difference is located in the Japanese dorama's connection to preexisting and already popularized manga and anime plots and characters. Even in U.S. teen-targeted television we are seeing the old *Superman* plots come to life, in the series *Smallville*, starring

157

characters named Lois, Clark, and Lex. Clark possesses extraordinary powers, and familiar language from *Superman* comics and cartoons abound. Consider an early 2005 episode called "Krypto" involving the kidnapping of Lois, the weakening of Clark by exposure to "kryptonite," and a laboratory for evildoing owned by the corporation, "LutherCorp." (Warner Bros. Entertainment, Inc., 2005).

Similarly, then, issues addressed by the dorama include close examination of familial relationships, friendship, loyalty, the desire for superhuman powers in times of emotional or physical distress, the need to fit in or be popular in school, issues with teachers and authority, and emerging sexual identity or gender affiliations (homosocial and homosexual), as well as sexual abuse, revolution, anarchy, crime, justice, and science fiction-based adventures. Beginning with manga and anime, Japanese authors and artists have a long history of dealing frankly, and even controversially, with teen issues through the media, and these issues extend naturally into the medium of television through dorama, just as we see their stretching into U.S. television programming through a few of the examples mentioned.

Popular doramas are discussed enthusiastically and critically by member fans on the www.J-fan.com Internet Web site. Many dorama reviews are available at the Web site, but doramas aired the past winter season on Japanese TV include *gokusen*, (Morimoto and NTV/The Television/Junon, 2002) and *H2 kimi to ita hibi*, (TBS, 2005); as well as a new series, called *24*, a 24-hour emergency room story (fugi TV, 2005). *Gokusen* is a school-based drama about a seemingly fragile first-year female teacher and her assigned class of "thugs." Unbeknownst to her constant challengers, she possesses skills she learned as a member of a family of Yakuzo, or a group that in the United States would parallel the mafia or "family." Knowledge of these ties by those in authority would threaten her teaching position, but the protagonist's own character's parents have died, and she resides with another family who has taken her in.

The twenty-three-year-old first-year teacher slowly reveals herself as a paragon of strength, wisdom, and determination, as well as defender of the weak and needy among her all-male troublemaking homeroom class at an all-male school. The teacher is played by one of the most popular female actresses in Japan, who has an established record of success in many popular doramas. The series features numerous male teen stars.

Taking a twist away from the female protagonistic line is *H2 ~kimi to ita hibi,* a sports-based (baseball) dorama, centered around two male friends who get involved with an underdog baseball team. There are female love interests, which make this series popular with male and female viewers. The struggles are typical.

Most fans relate new material to animated or manga versions already known to them. One of the earliest examples of a beloved and favorite early series, is the 1963 Fuji TV animated television series *Astro Boy*, which began as a form of *shonen* (boy) manga in 1951, known as *Captain Atom*, which was published originally in *Shonen Magazine*. Anyone familiar with the story of "Pinnochio" will recognize signs in this old story or "ehon," as well as some resemblance to *Superman*, a 1930s comic success created by illustrator Joe Shuster and writer Jerry Siegel. There are more than 4,000 manga and anime creations covered thoroughly in *The Anime Encyclopedia, A Guide to Japanese Animation since 1917.*

Besides numerous Web sites dedicated to individual manga and anime stories and characters, and dorama fans, there are the more professionally produced and established membership sites such as J-fan (http://www.j-fan.com/drama). Technologically savvy teenagers participate in Web-rings, review sites, and blogs, listen to or download their favorite J-Pop or Japanese music, preview anime, games, and manga, and catch up on all the news in the industry. Everything in Japanese entertainment that appeals to youth culture can be found on this site. This site and those that continue to be constructed as the medium gains momentum, including individual fan-developed sites, provide a cyberspace connection for dorama, manga, and anime fans to communicate about their interests.

Commercially, the marketing of entertainment to teens in Japan ties in products from clothing to music, posters, accessories, games, magazines, and just about anything teens in the United States would also find appealing. The teen entertainment industries in Japan and the United States are closely paralleled. In the United States we have only to think of *Superman* (Younis, 2005; http://www.supermanhomepage.com/news.php), *G.I. Joe* (Hasbro, 2005), the *Transformers*, (Cartoon Network, 2004), and the *Teenage Mutant Ninja Turtles* (Mirage Studios, Inc., 2005) to get an idea of the commercial appeal that takes the comic character into the home and the hands of children in the form of the action figure, clothing, school supplies, games, videos, and comics. Japanese commerce caters as efficiently to the teen market as do the American commercial success of the comics, movies, and series mentioned. There is no way to include all of the contributors to the rich American and Japanese markets for the numerous characters, stories, artists, and writers of popular teen entertainment.

Resources

Clements, J., & McCarthy, H. (2001). *The anime encyclopedia: A guide to Japanese animation since 1917.* Berkeley, CA: Stone Bridge Press.

Jones, G. (2004). *Men of tomorrow: Geeks, gangsters, and the birth of the comic book.* New York: Basic Books.

As I Walk

Jonathan Pryce

As I walked into this store
I kind of got a feeling
That as my feet touched their floor
Eyes were watching me almost like from the ceiling
When I took more steps and looked around
I noticed someone following me
Thinking they knew what was going down
But then I thought to myself, "why would you follow me
and not Billy who's standing by the door?"
Is it because I'm black or is it something more?
After 15 minutes of this, I finally realize, "you know
what? That's prejudice even though the owners of that
store were the same color as the skin on my wrist."

YOUTH CULTURE AND VIDEO GAMES

Roymieco A. Carter

When we observe the technology that impacts our daily lives, it is often reflected upon as a "new," punctuated advancement. This is far from what happens when there are changes in technology. It is a slow and iterative process of development and testing. We, as the operators, only witness the by-product of a complex systems thinking. The market research and the expensive product development cycle all but fade from view when the new product is positioned for popular consumption. The video game industry is an energetic culmination of creative, technical, and commercial practices. The economy struggles to find its foothold, but the gaming industry is gaining momentum. It is becoming a viable career option for our new high school graduates. The newly evolving artist/designers, business professionals, and programmers are moving into a career field that has surpassed the financial gains of the movie industry's box office sales. Cinema under went a great deal of criticism when it became popular, the gaming industry has positioned itself as the "new cinema," consequently receiving similar criticism and suspicion. It has genres, a visual language, classics, and celebrities. The one time childish fancy has evolved into a diverse fuel for entertainment, education, instruction, and promotion.

NEW TOOL OF PERSUASION

The video game is designed to be an all-consuming experience produced from extensive research by many of our leading technology developers and scientists. The increased processing power of the gaming console makes it possible for video gamers to experience uncanny visual effects. Realistic light field mapping, 3D objects, and environmental textured surfaces are mathematical configurations that also set the stage for this experience. These elements paired with a cinematic narrative and user-driven interaction spiral into a painstaking mixture of reality and fantasy. It is easy to see why education and training facilities, Hollywood, and the government have all taken notice. Educational software companies are attempting to create games that "make learning fun." The corporate and specialty service sector (engineers, police, and airplane pilots) see the interactive training tool as an inexpensive alternative. Hollywood has jumped in with both feet, diversifying the market by creating crossover promotional media. Blockbuster films are launched with an ever-expansive marketing package, including a sound track with current popular artists, action figures, clothing and merchandise, and its own scenario-driven video game. The audience is targeted through an onslaught of different media. Video games are the latest addition to the marketing package targeting a captive young audience. *America's Army* is an ongoing attempt to recruit North America's best and brightest young people. They are encouraged to go online and download a "free" video game to test their skills in a "real life" military experience.

The freely downloadable, action genre, first-person shooter created by the United States's army is, in their own words, a part of the army's communication strategy. The combat-based game, whose intended audience is as young as thirteen, is designed to give the new recruit a first hand look at the challenges facing the U.S. army soldier. Developing insight into the life of a soldier is one of the stated benefits/goals of the game. *America's Army* presents the player with "realistic" virtual experiences of an American soldier during military training and vivid simulation of realistic military combat operations. When the recruit completes his or her training, the fresh military mind is encouraged to participate in online missions for the 82nd Airborne Division. Although *America's Army* is positioned in the commercial market alongside titles such as *Full Spectrum Warrior*, *Ghost Recon*, *Operation Flashpoint*, and *Delta Force: Black Hawk Down*, it remains fundamentally different from the others. First of all we should beware of anything that is said to be free. Interactive 3D games are quite time consuming and expensive to build. So, who is paying? Second, the other action games are violent, sensationalized, and present many vignettes of combat. *America's Army* claims to frown on the glorification of combat. Teamwork, value, and responsibility are factors of their online game experience. The developers for *America's Army* establish practicing responsibility and value by defining "rules of engagement" during online play. The game's technical support staff enforces these rules. Violators of the rules suffer punishments during online game play. Placing the violator in a virtual prison punishes behaviors, such as team killings. Parents are also able to change the game settings to match the individual's values. The parent can alter game filters to limit the player's exposure to language, blood, and advanced marksmen levels. These preferences or settings are present in most action genre games and can be manipulated to suit the young or adult player. The inherent contradiction within *America's Army* is that the beginning levels of the game, which are a prerequisite to gaining membership into the 82nd Airborne Division, train the soldier to use weapons and execute combat tactics. As stated previously, the U.S. army is marketing *America's Army* as a game that rewards life, not combat or violence.

IMPRESSION AND PROGRESSION

The action game genre is diverse, yet it has some consistent factors that help to define its structure. The game encompasses a specific series of constructed events arranged to resonate with an intended audience. The action genre emphasizes hand-to-eye reflexes, speed, and physical response. This is appropriate because the game should not bore, puzzle, or allow the player of the game to be easily distracted from the pre-defined game objective. The dominant elements in action game design are first person character perspective, carrying a large arsenal of weapons, and destroying all objects of opposition on the dimly lit screen. This genre has much more to offer the young gamer. Remember chess and backgammon? They are military style games that stress the gamers' strategic abilities. The current military action games attempt to blend the action and strategic genres. Games similar to *America's Army* are flooding the store shelves introducing military visualizations and strategies that pale in comparison to the challenging game of chess or backgammon. It is not enough to shrug one's shoulders and say, "Hey, these types of games have always existed." This dismissive attitude lacks the understanding that the first-person perspective amplifies the gamer's role in the action sequence. Game participation is a direct action, playing as one character instead of playing with multiple game pieces as in the board games named above. The visual effects, such as the popular rag-doll effect (the animation of gravity affecting a virtual human body), give a new level of violence, reward, and accomplishment in the game. The implications of the game's agenda extend over time with the realization that the young person is avidly playing this game for at least five years before he or she is even eligible for military service. The motivation for creating the game comes from the research and popularity of computer games in contemporary American youth culture. *America's Army* currently advertises it has over two million registered online players. These players form communities, sharing strategies and tactics to facilitate the completion of challenging missions. These players, of differing ages, genders, and ethnicities are aware that they freely engage in simulations of combat. However it is when a player becomes immersed in this gaming experience that a displacement of emotion, physical activity, and values occur. Real world experiences will conflict with the heroic personas the gamer creates in the virtual world.

The experience is similar to a naïve person standing before a color field painting by Mark Rothko and boldly declaring to everyone in the gallery, "I can do that." The complexity of the painting is not quick to reveal itself. It is, however, layers of paint understood by the master artist and applied with an adept hand. The naïve individual reduces the experience to fit their level of comprehension. The painting and the game are similar in that they are both approachable experiences with a great deal of visual stimulation and appeal. Just as the artist chooses every brush stroke for a painting, a team of creative individuals constructs the content, seductive commercials, and cover art for the video game. The gamer however is engaged in the experience and unable to think of the act of gaming in the critical framework necessary to determine the potential effect of millions of individuals all advancing blindly through the game levels.

READING VIDEO GAMES AS EXPERIENCE

The otherwise apathetic postmodern young mind sits only inches from the radiant glow of the television screen. There is a whirling hum in the ear while the mind races with possibility. Will I be the hero or the villain? What is my weapon of choice? Do I go in using stealth tactics or do I pull a page from the Wild West by kicking in the front door and letting lead fly? Before the mind gets a chance to fully embrace the new reality, the humming stops, the screen now flickers, and the looping audio serenades the new gamer. Excitement and anticipation are the fuel of attraction for the young gamer. This moment is the culmination of hours of game development and promotion. Everything counts when the video game experience is placed under the proverbial microscope. Accepting the play of video games as experience is an acknowledgment of the game as a construction. The knowable and reproducible elements of the game construction offer insight into the agendas, methods, and manipulations at work. A common argument by gamers and developers is that the video game industry does not create the rules of engagement for violence, language, social roles, sexuality, and aggression. They claim no responsibility; consequently as a defense, they present games as only a surreal reflection of pre-existing social patterns. The video game, by their definition, is only a funhouse mirror of contemporary culture. However, the gaming industry in the United States alone grosses over 6.9 billion dollars a year (according to the Interactive Digital Software Association). The gaming industry will capitalize on their success for as long as possible. In analyzing games and culture it is important to note one thing first and foremost, "where there are large amounts of money there are powerful people and agendas." In order to engage in the critical analysis and understanding of video games and youth, as knowable and reproducible experiences, the critique needs to reserve its initial judgment. The desire to describe a game as "good" or "bad" is relative to the conventions and expectations placed on the physical, emotional, technical, psychological, and aesthetic properties of the game. The video gamers of the 1980s knew something that today's academic and business fields are now beginning to recognize, mainly that video games had staying power and reflected the individualistic or isolationist tendencies of the "me" generation. Video games, like the young, are struggling to define their purpose in a world that constantly changes its rules. Youth culture and video games are intertwined because each is dependent on the other. Contemporary youth use video games as an escape, a site of fantasy and experimentation. They can live out defining moments as their favorite sports heroes or push the limits of dexterity, strategy, and fear with games utilizing complex narrative structures. The video gaming industry continuously looks to the young for direction and acceptance.

THE NEW LITERACY

A practical approach for youth to actively analyze video games is to first define the boundaries or parameters of the game. Determine the set of qualities that make the experience distinctive. Use what is known about the narrative or story of the game in order to uncover the meaning of the experience. There are distinctive visual elements in each game that code the experience. What does the game world and the modeled characters descriptively look like and why? Are these representations consistent with the player expectations or do they challenge established real-world roles? The digital narrative of the video game relies on the gamers' perception of pacing and completion. All video games use narrative techniques to convince the player that the game is appropriate in content as well as form. How does the game begin? The young gamer quickly distinguishes if the game contains the necessary or desired elements to start and sustain the gaming experience. Engaging the gamer and maintaining his or her attention in the game is of prime importance to the industry, as they well understand the variable preferences of youth. Change comes rapidly and without warning.

Second, what is the duration of engagement, often referred to as the "game play"? As a result of short attention spans and the diverse multi-tasking abilities of today's young person, it is easy for a game to challenge youth's continued level of involvement. Fortunately game functions allow the gamer to pause play, save, and resume the experience as they see fit. Another property closely related to this one is the ability of the game experience to exceed the physical or emotional capacity of the young gamer. One thing is for sure, the ability to wrestle with complex content while dividing their attention and energy is commonplace. Failing to realize youth can play at various levels of engagement and failing to provide multiple places in the game experience to save the game will often times result in the gamer's disinterest and premature conclusion of the experience.

Finally, what are the requirements for completion? Depending on the appeal and acceptance of a game, the concept or storyline may be continued in sequels or related games. These attempts to extend the experience not only generate money and stability in a rapidly changing industry, but also create a culture, as an extension of the game, bearing its privatized language, customs, values, and borders. It isn't surprising that the gaming industry promotes sequels, as it procures big business, yet it is significant to note that each follow-up game in the series will have its own objectives and distinctive storyline in the greater gaming experience. Although it may seem efficient to pass blind judgment on video games and the young people who play them, it is imperative to engage in extensive, continued, thoughtful dialogues on both youth culture and their experiences with video games.

Resources
Books
Dewey, J. (1972). *Art and experience.* New York: Perigee Trade Books.
McCloud, S. (2003). *Rules of play: Game design fundamentals.* Cambridge,
    MA: MIT Press.
Web Site
The Official U.S. Army Game. Retrieved September 17, 2005 from http: \ \
    www.americasarmy.com

JAPANESE ELECTRONIC GAME
CULTURE

Machiko Kusahara

The Japanese electronic game culture is quite different from that of Europe or North America. In the Western world games are still often associated mostly with kids or adolescents. This is not the case in Japan. Reflecting the status of the hugely popular comic books (manga), enjoying video games or arcade games is a common pastime among adults as well, particularly those under the age of thirty-five or so. Students are naturally avid gamers, and young office workers regularly visit game centers too, often enjoying a relaxing gaming session with their colleagues after work, before having a meal and a drink and probably finishing the evening together in a "karaoke box." Others might continue the typically Japanese tradition of entering night after night one of the countless, hugely popular Pachinko game parlors. These people, mostly men, stare at the balls bouncing wildly on the screen of the machine (kind of a Japanese version of pinball) for hours, obviously totally ignorant of the hellish noise and heavy smell of cigarettes filling the air. Recently one has witnessed the emergence of another form of game play, again reminding one about the consumption patterns around manga. It has been well known that Japanese businessmen (i.e., not only students or kids) read manga during their lengthy daily train rides. Nowadays we don't see many of them. Instead, they play games on their "ketai," or mobile phones—women and young girls as well.

Why are games so popular in Japan? Why have they become such an integral part of the Japanese culture? Why are some Japanese games, such as Tamagotchi or Pokemon, so different in nature from games we have known previously, such as card games, board games, or fighting games? Why do so many talented Japanese students dream about having a job at a game company such as Namco or Nintendo? Why have important electronics companies such as Sony established large divisions dedicated to games and gaming? Why have games become the key application on mobile phones? There are many questions to ask. It will not be possible to answer them all in this essay, but some preliminary analyses and reflections can be provided. My basic argument is that all these issues are closely related to the nature of the Japanese culture in general, including its long history.

GAME AS CULTURAL ACTIVITY

It may not be well known outside Japan that the world famous video game manufacturer Nintendo was originally a publisher of playing cards. It was founded in Kyoto in the Meiji era in 1889. For years, the name of the company was familiar in practically every household, particularly during the New Year's festivities. Playing a certain type of card game was a New Year's tradition among many families, and Nintendo was (and still is) the largest publisher of such cards.[1] The idea of the game is to make matches among one hundred old Japanese poems from the seventh century to the beginning of the thirteenth century. The cards consist of two sets of a hundred cards, one set for a reader and the other for the players. The players try to find the right card from the floor as quickly as possible while the reader recites each poem. Thanks to this game, even children memorized old poems, although they did not understand their meanings.[2] However, this probably made sense, as according to the old Japanese literary tradition remembering texts was the first step to learning.[3]

When the Portuguese brought the playing cards to Japan in the sixteenth century, the Japanese adopted the idea of using pieces of hard paper for card games. The idea met the already existing Japanese technique for producing strong, high quality paper. Paper cards with calligraphy and beautiful illustrations representing poems thus replaced the old habit of using seashells for the traditional "poem match." "Hyakunin Isshu," which means one poem by each of one hundred poets, thus became the part of Japanese cultural entertainment. Hand painting was later replaced with colored wood block printing—Japan was the first country in which color printing for mass entertainment, such as ukiyo-e (Japanese woodblock prints) and illustrated stories, was realized and flourished. Well-known artist-illustrators such as Hokusai also contributed to poem cards. Because of these historical reasons we still call text-based playing cards "karuta," derived from "carta" in Portuguese.[4]

FROM TABLE GAME TO A TV MONITOR

Remembering Nintendo's long-term involvement with entertainment, it is quite logical that their main production line eventually shifted from elegant poem cards and Hanafuda (another type of playing cards with beautiful graphics but without texts) to video game consoles and game software. The success of Nintendo's Famicom (short for "Family Computer"), launched in 1983, certainly changed the world of traditional family entertainments. By that time, watching TV after dinner (more precisely, continuing watching TV, as watching TV during dinner was already a common experience in Japan) had become the new tradition of family entertainment, replacing the old "round the table" type of amusement.

Such a shift can be regarded as a part of the general social change that became visible in Japan in the 1980s. By that time, the face-to-face communication model lost its place among families, partly because the TV set became the center of family life, often physically influencing where family members sit at the dinner table (as no one wants to sit down against the TV monitor).[5] The film director Yoshimitsu Morita caricaturized such a situation in his film *The Family Game* (1983), in which all the family members take seats on only one side of the dinner table. The power struggle for TV channels among family members—or the seizing of the TV remote controller by kids—was often discussed in relation to the fall of the father's power within contemporary Japanese family; the main issue is the absence of the father, as Japanese office workers often devote their life to the company and spare-time activities outside the home.

When Famicon appeared it replaced the content one sees on the familiar TV screen with game figures and situations, adding another element to the after dinner power struggle. Often young children are told to play video games before dinner, but naturally they frequently want to continue after the meal. This is particularly a problem in Japan with teenagers, because many children over ten years or so typically come home late as the result of school and after school activities, and it is only after dinner or even later at night that they have time to enjoy video games.[6] A solution to this problem was to buy another TV set, helped by the economic growth of the era. Later, pocket computer game platforms such as Nintendo's Game Boy (1989) that provided much more sophisticated playing options than earlier pocket game platforms such as Nintendo's Game&Watch would provide another solution. Traditional card games are still played among family members during the New Year period, but *Donkey Kong* (Nintendo, 1981) or Mario (the protagonist of Nintendo's phenomenally successful *Super Mario Bros*) became the major figures of family entertainment, followed by scores of other video game stars.

Video games not only changed the manner of family entertainment and communication within the family, they also changed the modes of communication among friends. In general, Japanese are known for being shy in communicating with others. Being talkative or insisting on one's own idea was almost never considered a virtue in Japanese culture. It is a different value compared to that in many Western countries such as the United States or France. The value is at least partly related to the social structures that had developed on the basis of much less mobility in the society. The stable power structure and the closure of Japan's borders that continued for nearly 250 years had helped developing social protocols that are mainly valid among people who know each other and do not want to cause trouble among them. In a community where everyone knows each other, means of introducing oneself to others would not develop fully. Of course, such protocols are not sufficient in today's urban life, where most people live in big cities and are from different parts of the country.

GAMES AS COMMUNICATION MEDIA

Public entertainment such as playing or watching sports, theater plays, music, cinema, and so forth have always been used as tools of communication in the West. Therefore it is not a surprise that games and gaming became a major tool of communication in Japan, where playing outdoor sports with friends or inviting friends to one's home is still a luxury among common people because of the lack of space. *Space Invaders* (1978, Taito, Japan) became a smash hit in Japan after a table-top version was released only a month after the release of the first stand-type model for game arcades. But why did a situation like "practically all coffee shops installed the game" become possible?[7] Ordinary coffee shops in residential neighborhoods would not have adopted such machines if games and gaming had been considered as a part of a "low" culture, or mere unintellectual pastime for teenagers. Because playing games in general had been embraced with a positive attitude in Japan, *Space Invaders* could openly invade and occupy coffee tables all over Japan. Although games such as Pachinko and slot machines are still regarded as rather low cultural pastimes because of their association with gambling and the somehow suspect atmosphere of the Pachinko parlors, the clean looking electronic games with colorful figures and funny sounds won widespread popularity among a wide range of Japanese people.

The early 1980s was a time when Japanese gaming culture went through a drastic change. Game&Watch (Nintendo) came out in 1980, providing the first commercially successful model of personal video games to Japanese kids; meanwhile arcade games such as *Pacman* (NAMCO, 1980) became international hits. Nintendo's Famicom appeared on the market in 1983, at the time when game arcades were practically seized by teenage boys who might spend time playing games instead of going to high schools. Younger kids who would come to the arcades drawn by their interest in such sort of new games became sometimes victims of older boys who would take money from kids by threatening them. Patrolling game arcades often became the duty of mothers, requested by the PTA (Parents and Teachers Association) at each elementary school. As the result of such situation, many parents welcomed the arrival of home video games because they would keep the kids away from the problematic game arcades. Even more importantly, home video game consoles helped children to play with other kids, offering topics to talk about, and giving them a reason to visit each other after school. As number of children in a family had drastically dropped (to the average of less than two) by then, they needed games or friends to play with in the absence of brothers and sisters.

Game arcades made a conscious effort to make their spaces safer, cleaner, brighter and more accessible for anyone, in order to bring the customers back. Legal control on their manner of operation and their opening hours was also strengthened in mid-1980s. Game arcades would not have a future if they continued to be occupied by problematic teens and game OTAKU. As a part of the "cleaning-up operation," YAKUZA (the Japanese equivalent of mafia), who often controlled the teenage dropouts and used game arcades for their business, were kicked out. Game arcades made a serious effort to change into amusement centers that ordinary people would enter without being scared. The underlying motive was clear: Their market was threatened by home video games.

At the same time, these games reflect the changing role of TV/video screens in today's culture. TV screens, which used to be showing what was happening in another space, usually performed by celebrities that the viewers would never collaborate in the real life, were personalized with home video and video games. The interaction with virtual characters on the screen of DDR gives a simulation of becoming a selected ambitious amateur dancer who performs at a dance competition on TV. Even professional "celebrities" in Japan today are often young "talents" in their early teens who look like anyone from the neighborhood. The entertainment business is closer to everyday life than ever. Arcade games with high-resolution large screens and physical interfaces offer the simulated feeling of being almost inside the TV studio.

SIMULATING A WORLD

Japanese video games have developed on a similar basis as comics and animation. In fact, comics, animation, and games are closely related to each other both in terms of content and the manner of visual representation. A popular manga can be transformed into a video game (as in the case of *Dragon Ball*) or vice versa (as in the case of *Pokemon*). But it is similar to the relationship between Hollywood films, animation, comics, and games. More interesting similarity is observed in the way games are conceived and played. Role-playing games such as *Dragon Quest*, *Zelda*, or *Final Fantasy*, are played by a wide range of users. Besides the beautiful graphics and subtle interaction, literature-like story lines—large scale fantasy with complex stories of love, hatred, humanity, and so forth—is the key element of these games, in which each player is supposed to feel like a character who lives the story, living in the fantasy world. To create a sophisticated and complex story with many episodes that branch according to the action of the player, the virtual world—that is, the background of the story—should be planned and designed to every detail. The world view, or in Japanese "sekai-kan," which originally was conceived for the needs of game designing, has become an indispensable element for the consumers of Japanese role-playing games. Players expect to feel the atmosphere of the virtual world, try to discover the way the world is built through its imaginary history, and hope to find the system on which the world functions. The idea is close to creating and offering a simulated world, within which stories and adventures take place for each player.

The importance of the world view was first recognized by the game designers of *Xevious* (NAMCO, 1982), the first Japanese game with complex storytelling and a spatial notion. It also became the first game made with 3D computer graphics.[8] Although it was basically a shooting game, the quality of the graphics and the richness of the background story were outstanding compared to other games of the time. As the game became very popular, the concept attracted attention and became known among users as well. "World view" became a keyword among game designers and game freaks. Today almost any role-playing game is built on such a worldview, and often the worldview itself becomes a sales point.

It is not a coincidence that *Xevious* was made in such manner. The game designer Masanobu Endo (who was the first to be titled "game designer" in Japan) had a clear idea on his virtual kingdom. *Xevious* realized an idea of a three-dimensional virtual world with the stories of its own (which makes a difference from flight simulator games) that a player will live in and explore, which is quite different from the worlds of *Super Mario Brothers* or of *Pacman*. It might be related to the fact that NAMCO started as a company building physical entertainment facilities for children's playgrounds on the roofs of department stores. Founded in 1955 with two wooden rocking horses for children as its asset, NAMCO has developed its operation with the respect to the real world and the human factors within.[9] The company's interest toward building realistic virtual world with artistic quality seems to continue until now.[10]

Simulation games provide more personalized experiences, because playing them takes more time and requires continuous activity. In July 1999 a shocking incident happened on an ANA (All Nippon Airlines) domestic flight. A man hijacked the plane, killed the captain, and almost managed to crash the plane. At the last moment the co-pilot snatched the hijacker and saved the plane and the passengers. The motive of the hijacker was at least seemingly, simple: He had been immersed in hours and hours of flight simulator games and wanted to have the experience of piloting an actual aircraft. This is an exceptional case, of course. Yet it shows the power such games can have on the minds of hardcore players, and there are many of them in Japan. At the time of writing, the most popular simulator games in Japan are the train simulators, which are available both for arcades and for home computers, as well as on ketai (mobile phones). In Japan, spending hours on crowded trains is the daily reality for many men, who may still remember their childhood dream of becoming an engine driver. The train simulator games fulfill the past dreams of these men, while helping them to combat the frustrations of the present (from being mere passengers they are put in command). Besides, they can use their daily experience—one can choose from many different lines from one's own region and from other part of the country. In fact, the realistic landscape is based on video images. Imagine a Japanese salaryman driving a train on his mobile phone screen, while he himself is on a train!

GROWING ANIMALS, GROWING HUMANS

Another very important form of simulation games is the so-called "growing game" ("ikusei gemu," or often "sodate-ge" in an abbreviated colloquial form, as the word "game" is already a part of Japanese vocabulary). This genre, which can be regarded as originated in Japan, represents certain unique features that relate to Japanese culture. Although there might be a point of view that such form of simulation/entertainment should not be called a game if "game" means something one would win or lose, we already have established simulation/entertainment content, such as *SimCity*, which can be regarded as games in the sense that one can be either successful or unsuccessful, and that the fictional world is established upon rules. The Japanese notion of "game" clearly includes such games as we observe the way the term is used in our daily life.

Since the virtual fish tank simulator *Aquazone* was released in 1993 (for Macintosh only; later for other platforms, now on ketai as well) all kinds of games to grow birds, insects, pets, racing horse, and other virtual life forms have been developed.[11] However, the early classic and big hit is *Princess Maker* (for PC and other platforms), which was released in 1991 by Gainax Co., a leading animation studio. The story behind the game is as follows; the player takes the role of a brave warrior who adopts an orphan girl. Her dream is to get married to a prince when she grows up. So the player should carefully "grow," train, and educate her so that she can be an ideal girl.[12] However, in reality this seems to be only an excuse. Most of the users are young males and the character design of the girl reflects typical girl characters in comics that the users are familiar with. The virtual girl grows up to be a very sexy looking young woman with the typical comic- or anime-style face and body.

The basic concept of *Princess Maker* differs from another classic game with virtual characters, the *Little Computer People* developed by David Crane in the UK in 1985. The user of *Little Computer People* enjoys the game (that some people regard as a screen saver) by merely observing the virtual characters living on the user's desktop. A character will ask from time to time to do something for the user, or make a phone call to the person, or try to please the person by petting him or her. The person inside the computer basically seems to have an independent life.

On the contrary, with *Princess Maker*, the user in a way owns the virtual girl, educating and training her with a goal in mind. The goal is, of course, to help her find her prince (i.e., the user himself, in psychological sense), rather than to help her develop an independent personality or achieve something for herself, instead of waiting for the prince. One might even find a reflection of the Japanese old value that the parents—especially the father—"own" the children.[13] Of course it is also problematic from the gender perspective. Although a version for girl users was released much later, the idea of raising a virtual boy did not get much popularity. In any case, there has been very little discussion in Japan about the gender issues raised by such games, virtual characters, and comic characters.

Interestingly enough, *Princess Maker*, which has already become a classic, is usually categorized as a "growing" game. It means that the game package can be found on the same shelf as games to grow fish, birds, hamsters, or horses for racing—a popular genre for male users, with online competitions and mobile phone versions. The underlying culture has similarities with that surrounding the popular "virtual idols" on the Web. *Princess Maker* and its popularity can be regarded as an example how Japanese comic, animation, and games are related within the traditional social paradigm, including the gender issues.

Such cultural correlation can be also observed between role-playing games and comics and animations, and in the way these are related to other game genres. One can find an interesting similarity between *Princess Maker* and *Xevious*. Like the world view gave depth to the shooting game *Xevious*, a similar background story is given to Princess Maker as the introduction to the game. Although the user's main goal of growing an ideal girl might be realized without such a background story, it is needed to add atmosphere to the game and to offer a guideline for the user. One may remember that "wrapping" is an important part of Japanese culture. By wrapping a game with a larger world or a story, a shooting game or a growing game can achieve a sense of sophistication. In Japanese, "having no case nor a cover" means "expressing one's intention directly without a delicacy." Games needto be wrapped to be a part of the culture. The wrapping can be seen from a different approach as well. Needless to say, role-playing games (RPG) have a strong tradition in Japanese games with well-known titles such as *Dragon Quest* (Enix, 1986), *Legend of Zelda* (Nintendo, 1986), and *Final Fantasy* (Square, 1987). At the same time, the idea of RPG can be used in combination with other types of games, such as shooting, fighting, growing, or other simulation games. In case of *Princes Maker*, for example, an RPG-like situation is used as a background of the game, almost like a mat background painting at a SFX studio. In a sense it is a simulated RPG within another game. Users don't need to go (and can't go) inside the world view, but achieve a feeling that the game is part of an imaginary world with its own history.

SENSE OF REALITY IN GROWING GAMES

Tamagotchi (1996) came out from the growing games tradition, but eventually changed the nature of the genre with much controversy inside and outside Japan. Producers of Tamagotchi conceived and designed the game based on what they learned from other growing games such as *Aquazone*. Some features were inherited from existing games, but new ideas they added made Tamagotchi a mega-hit. Here we can analyze Aquazone in more detail, since it became a model for bringing success to growing games as personal entertainment. *Aquazone* (1993, 9003 Inc.) is a virtual fish tank simulator. Another fish-growing simulator from the United States was marketed around the same time, but it focused on breeding virtual fish to create a new pattern. *Aquazone* took more realistic, down-to-earth approach, simulating the ecosystem with visually realistic representation. Neon tetra, angelfish, and other tropical fish with plants, air pump, heater, and so forth are the items. In addition to "real" fish, robotic fish were introduced later.

A user would purchase a basic set and add other fish species or fish tank accessories. If the tank is taken well care of, the virtual tropical fishes will lay eggs. Baby fish will be born and grow as the user feeds them and maintains the temperature and water condition. One can check the conditions, such as the pH value of the water, and also the health of each fish. The fish swim according to the autonomous behavior, which users found amazingly realistic despite the computational limitation of the time. The fish react when the user clicks on the tank, as in case of real fish. With the original version the image was designed to accommodate the limited number of colors (256 colors) and the screen resolution of the early 1990s. It looked like a video image of a fish tank rather than of a real one, but was still realistic enough to become popular. The quality of visual realism was outstanding compared to any other computer games at the time. The developers and designers of the game took time in observing and studying real fish. When I visited the company's small office/studio soon after the software was released, I found real fish tanks in almost every corner of every room.

An important decision they made in designing the game was that a user should give a name to every fish when it is released into the tank or is born from an egg. Technically speaking each fish should be identified to keep a record and save changes. However, this naming procedure had a significant psychological effect on users. By giving names, a user not only identifies each fish (the name of the fish appears on the screen as the user points to it with the mouse) but also grows a personal tie to each fish. Thus *Aquazone* simulated not only the virtual ecosystem in a fish tank but also human psychology to a certain extent—the way we feel toward pets, the required thrills in playing games, the pride of being an expert in growing and breeding animals, and so forth. Many users felt that the virtual fish gave a sense of life—even the robot fish seemed to have certain sense of a life of their own. Considering the fact that the images and the real-time animation at that time had certain limitations, such attachment the "owners" (rather than the "users") had to their virtual fishes was evoked at least partly from psychological reasons.

However, the game was not meant to give a sensational experience. Rather, it was meant to be a simulation, a quiet pastime for professional users with curiosity (such as designers who used Macintosh computers) who might want to relax at home but would hesitate to have real animals. (It was not really a screen saver for most people, because the volume of hard disk and memory was too limited in those days to run the program safely along with other applications.) While *Aquazone* was not meant for the general public or kids, it was well-known among professionals in the field and was influential. Its success paved the road for the popularity of growing games in Japan.

TAMAGOTCHI AND ITS TRAUMATIC DEATH

During the years from 1996–1998, many children in Japan carried the egg-like shaped mini-console. It was so popular that new models with different colors or features were often extremely hard to get.[14] Tamagotchi, which means something like "Eggie," as a nickname for an egg as a friend, became the first alife-based commercially successful entertainment for anyone. Tamagotchi broke the boundary of growing games and gave a shape to the new genre of entertainment, by removing visual and behavioral realism from the growing simulation and focusing on psychological impact. The manga-like imagery of the character combined with "kawaii" (lovely, cute) design and the smallness of the machine to appeal to a greater public—children in particular.[15]

Tamagotchi was released from Bandai Co. in November 1996 and sold more than 10 million machines in Japan in less than a year. It was also marketed abroad starting in July 1997 and became a huge success, selling 400 million machines worldwide (including Japan) by May 1998, while raising great controversy both in Japan and abroad. Versions for the PC and for the Game Boy were also released later.

A user raises a virtual creature on a pocket machine with a small display, which would hatch from an egg and starts growing, depending on the way it is taken care of. The main interaction a user would take is as follows: feed, clean the toilet, play with or ignore, praise or scold, let it go to sleep or wake up, and give medicine when it's sick.[16] As it grows it metamorphoses into different forms during its lifetime, according to the way it was taken care of (probably combined with some random parameters). If it is happy and healthy it will turn into a nice-looking form, but if it is not treated well the form can be an ugly one. The metamorphosis continues as it grows, changing form every time. The variety of Tamagotchi forms was amazingly rich although the display consisted of only 16x32 dots. Children (and adults) would show what they got on the screens to each other, exchange information, and try to grow interesting or rare forms. However, a Tamagotchi would easily become sick and die while the metamorphosis was still at an early stage. Keeping Tamagotchi alive as long as possible was important for the virtual collection of forms.

Although some children focused on achieving different forms as a sort of new collecting hobby, others were more enchanted by the "life-like-ness" of the virtual pet realized by its autonomous behavior, which was a new experience for them. In fact, some of the interaction was designed cleverly, simulating the trade-offs in the way humans or pets are raised. For example, one can either give normal food, or cakes and candies. Tamagotchi will be happy if it is given cakes, but giving too many sweets will make it sick. Likewise, when Tamagotchi is unhappy and crying, one can either scold it or give it candies to make it happier. Discipline or happiness—the game contained an educational feature, which was a reason why some parents thought it could be a nice toy for their children. Some children grow up without having younger brothers or sisters or elderly people in the family to be taken care of. In big cities keeping real pets is usually forbidden in apartments. These were the main reasons why they thought growing Tamagotchi could be a substitute to real experiences in real life. Many teachers also thought of Tamagotchi as an opportunity for teaching ethics.

However, because a Tamagotchi would make a highly audible beep whenever it required some urgent care, it became a problem at elementary schools. Some teachers banned the game in the classroom. Children had to ask their mothers to take care of them during the daytime, if bringing them to the classroom was not allowed. As a result, mothers often became addicted to the game, and some of them started having problems with the sudden and unreasonable deaths of the virtual creatures. By checking numerous still existing Web sites on Tamagotchi, we can see there were many, many adult users, and they took Tamagotchi seriously.

In fact, the most striking feature of the game was that the virtual creatures would die easily. To kill a Tamagotchi was easy. Just forget to feed it for one day, or miss cleaning the toilet for a few hours—it would become seriously ill and even die if not given medicine. The average lifetime of Tamagotchi was said to be two to three weeks. A user was supposed to use the reset button to start the game from the beginning, with a new egg.

The death of a Tamagotchi was to be discovered by the user in the following manner. When it dies it turns into a Japanese-style ghost and flies sadly around a Western-style tombstone. In Japanese traditional imagination, someone who was killed would stay in this world as a ghost, half transparent and feet invisible, and hang around the guilty person to show hatred. The image of such terrifying ghosts is familiar to children through TV programs and traditional "haunted mansion" kind of entertainment. What happened on the small screen after a death of Tamagotchi was exactly such a case. Some children were seriously disturbed and others started pushing the reset button immediately, to reset the tragic experience. Traumatic death of Tamagotchi became a social issue. Soon some children became accustomed to resetting the virtual life—they would use the reset button whenever they discovered their virtual creatures were turning into something ugly or too normal, "boring" forms. At this point, controversy on Tamagotchi was reported from abroad as well. Although Tamagotchi just disappeared from the screen with the export version, since the Japanese style-ghost would not work, the use of the reset button to achieve another life raised psychological issues for some children as for grown-ups who thought the game was ethically problematic.

What would be the appropriate way to erase a virtual creature from the screen if the creature is not well taken care of? Should it die to punish the lazy user? What kind of experience should the user have to stay with the game? Although Tamagotchi proved the possibilities and existing demand for a life-based growing game, it also raised questions that the game industry had to solve. Actually, Sega had marketed a digital pocketbook for young girls in 1996, with a virtual cat that lived on it. A user would take care of the virtual kitten and let it grow. If she did not take care of it well enough, the cat would leave home and disappear, as a real cat might do. In the process of development they discussed what would be the best solution if the user did not take care of the cat. They decided to let the cat leave, because the death of a virtual pet would be too cruel. The product attracted attention in the industry, but apparently the market was not ready for such a sophisticated game for girls in their early teens.

It was reported that the developers of Bandai had discussed the same issue, but they decided to bring death into the game to obtain the sense of reality. Definitely it proved to be very effective—otherwise Tamagotchi would not have become such a social phenomenon. It was a shock to the general concept of harmless, non-real computer games.

AFTER TAMAGOTCHI: WHAT CAN BE THE SOLUTION?

Because the unhappy death of the artificial creature and the shock it brought to kids or even adults had become such a big social issue, Bandai opened a virtual cemetery on the Internet, while releasing other models of Tamagotchi to solve the problem. For example, with Angel's Tamagotchi (1998), one hatches an egg of an angel, which is the soul of a dead Tamagotchi. If it is well taken care of, it turns into an angel and flies away to the Heaven. If it is not well taken care of, the demon will attract the possible angel and bring it to Hell. It was not marketed abroad because the idea would be too strange in the Western culture.[17]

Another version, marketed in 1998, was the one with "sex"—with two different types, which were called "Osucchi" (male) and "Mesucchi" (female). When they are grown up, two machines can be connected to make them "mate." They make a "quite noisy racket" on both of the screens, according to what a user reports, and then lay eggs. The idea was to give a feeling of continuity and at the same time to profit from the already observed "culture" that children communicate each other on their Tamagotchi. Because the form of the newborn Tamagotchi depends on the combination of its parents, it also added a new feature to the collection-oriented interest in raising the virtual creature.

Now looking back, the interaction a user could have with Tamagotchi was not a happy or entertaining one at all. It was in fact a game, because users tried it over and over again (if not too shocked by the death) to obtain all possible forms of metamorphosis. In a sense it was another form of collecting trading cards—but not in a material form. The process of change and variety was made possible with digital technology. The success and problems of Tamagotchi had left lessons for other game developers in Japan. The biggest lesson was that users should be able to *enjoy* virtual characters. There was little sense of humor in Tamagotchi, after all.

SEAMAN: COMMUNICATION OR DISCOMMUNICATION WITH A VIRTUAL PERSONALITY

"Seaman" (Vivarium/Sega, 1999) is a unique life-based entertainment, which is available on Sony's PlayStation 2 today.[18] Originally released for Dreamcast in 1999, it sold 550 thousand copies in Japan by August 2001. Yutaka Saito of Vivarium designed the game. The story behind is as follows: A researcher named Dr. Gazet explores a southern island and discovers a fish that has a human face. Users are invited to his island and become involved in raising and growing the fish. The fish understands human language and can make a conversation based on an Eliza-like pseudo-AI program. A microphone for Dreamcast was attached to every package of Seaman software. Besides enjoying a chat with Seaman, the user is responsible for maintaining the fish tank in an appropriate condition and feeding the fish.

Well, it sounds quite amusing. However, Sega (now ASCII is the distributor for the PS2 version) achieved such a great success by advertising the product as "the most disgusting pet in the game history" or "Seaman, the forbidden pet." The idea was to make a parody of both "kawaii" (lovely) and realistic virtual pets. Saito, the game designer, had realized that there was an emerging need for a wider range of growing games as the genre had been well established. He also recognized that there were users (and would-be users) who were not satisfied with the too-simplistic ideas seen with most conventional games, including Tamagotchi.

The Seaman and its environment are realistically rendered in 3D computer graphics to every detail, such as the golden scales of his carp-like body, quite ahead of its time. The photorealistic quality of the image is amazing considering that the fish swims and reacts in real time on the game console. But of course such a fish with a man's face does not exist in reality. (The idea apparently came from a then widespread rumor of a man-faced fish that lives in rural Japan.) Moreover, he almost always has a tired or bored look on his face. Certainly it is not a happy kind of pet. It has its own personality—a weird one.

The sound recognition system works very well. If the user says to him something like, "How are you? I hope you are doing all right," the Seaman might answer something like, "Well, why do you think I'm doing all right? Don't think others are doing all right because you are doing fine!" The well-known Eliza type of program is modified to give a more sarcastic impression. Certainly it is not a pet with an admirable character. Growing a Seaman is another thing. Since it's favorite food is a pink-and-green worm, one has to also run a farm for the grotesque-looking virtual animals. Some-times a big spider, the predator, appears to eat the worms. The user should fight back against the spider. Despite these "unpleasant" features, users love the game and it has survived on the game market. Many of the users are said to be young women, and they regard this software as a "healing game." In short, Seaman represents a more private, personal communication space at the edge of the real and unreal. The photorealistic quality of the image works as the key to combine the virtuality and the sense of reality.[19]

POSTPET: WHY DO WE COMMUNICATE?

So-net, one of the Japan's largest Internet providers, owned by Sony Communication Network (SCN), has been visually identified with PostPet. When So-net is introduced in magazines or newspapers it is often written "So-net, which is famous for PostPet . . . ." The pink teddy bear Momo, the major character of PostPet, has been in fact the most successful virtual char-acter one sees in advertisements, followed by Toro of Dokodemo Issyo, which is also developed and published by SCN.

PostPet is playful email software with a digital pet who lives on the user's desktop and delivers email to his or her friends. It is a combination of a growing game and a telecommunication tool. One can choose from dif-ferent characters, such as the pink teddy bear, cat, dog, turtle, penguin, hamster, etc., which are all designed in 3D computer graphics and have kawaii looks. The pet has its own life, moods, and temperament that varies according to the species it belongs to. For example, a cat is more egoistic than a dog. The pet lives in a room or in a house (with the latest version, V3, everything is in 3D and the pet now owns a house, which the user can move to his or her favorite neighborhood). A user would chat with the vir-tual pet (on text basis), caress, play with it, give it food or presents, and arrange furniture in the room, while using the software for exchanging email and enjoying a Web community. The pet eventually grows its character according to the way the user communicates with it. With many kawaii details both in visual aesthetics and the game design, communicating and playing with the pets is in fact entertaining, helped by the known AI research background in Sony. (AI is used for Sony's ketai as well as for AIBO.) In that sense PostPet is one of the most advanced and entertaining alife, or growing, games available in Japan today.

When a user writes an email message to a friend, he or she sees the pet go out of the room with an envelope in its hand (i.e., the email is going out). The pet, a pink teddy bear for example, brings the envelope to the PostPet room of the destination. What would happen if the friend is away, or the computer is not on, or PostPet software has not been launched? The door of the destination is closed, so to speak, for the poor pink teddy bear. It would stay there for a while hoping the door would open. (Of course this is a metaphorical interpretation of how it is programmed.) It means that the user cannot send an email any more until his or her teddy bear comes home. It might be a little better with a cat—cats are not such patient animals—but can be almost a tragedy with a turtle.

If the friend happens to be there and using the software, the teddy bear has access to the door of the room of the friend's PostPet. The friend will see the pink teddy bear enter the room with an envelope. Hence the email is delivered. However, after delivering the message, the pink teddy bear might decide not to come back immediately, as it wants to stay there and play with the other PostPet, which can be another bear or a hamster or a penguin, or something else. They are friends since they have been meeting every now and then for deliveries. It means that the user cannot send another email until the teddy bear returns.

What would happen then, if the user gets tired of all these situations and stops using the software, or does not send the PostPet for mail delivery frequently enough? The PostPet will get bored if there is nothing to do, and it will start writing and sending email by itself. Furthermore, if the user is not eager to communicate or play with the pet, the pet leaves the room permanently to go to PostPet Park, a theme park and community of the virtual pets who decided to live on their own. A pet will also leave the user when it is aged. A user can visit PostPet Park, join the community, and chat with other members, who not only talk about their former pets but also about themselves. Like dog owners who start talking to each other as they take their dogs to a park, the lost pets give humans the opportunity to start communicating with each other, with topics they share.

PostPet is different from the concept of an agent or an avatar that represents the user on the network. The pets are not designed to act exactly according to the mission given by the users. Also, it is not meant as a practical, useful software package. A user cannot enjoy it without having a sense of humor and curiosity. The fun is in enjoying the unexpected behavior of the virtual pets, communicating with them on an equal basis, giving up one's position as the master of the pet. It is the opposite of the master-slave kind of relationship, as in case of traditional robotics. Each pet has its own life and character, which grows out of autonomous behavior and influences from the user and his or her friends. In fact, it is parallel to having real pets such as dogs or cats. In most cases they are not taken for convenience or practical purposes. Rather, keeping a pet might even bring expected or unexpected troubles as well as pleasure. Still pet owners enjoy interacting with them, observe certain personalities, and try to understand them. Then why not apply such model to virtual pets?

Although it looks pop and funny, the concept of PostPet is derived from a deeper understanding of the changing nature of telecommunication. Like the way the young generation uses ketai for chatting and exchanging messages for the sake of communication—rather than exchanging necessary information—communication can be an entertainment (and "healing") by itself, and an entertainment can be used to promote communication. Probably that has been always true in our history. Because digital communication technologies were rather expensive and mainly used for business purposes, until recently, engineers and developers tended to focus on practical issues such as efficiency rather than exploring a playful use of the technology. PostPet was conceived and appeared on the market exactly when access to the Internet and the use of email became available for wider population, including young people. It showed clearly that a new approach was needed to understand the meaning of the network for the younger generation. We can see that development of ketai followed the similar process.

GIVING A PHYSICAL FORM TO A VIRTUAL CHARACTER

On a side street facing PARCO, a famous fashion mall, stands PostPet House. The signboard on the roof reads "Popteen Station." In the town of Shibuya, Tokyo, crowded with young people, this is exactly the corner where they hung around. Apparently PostPet is a valid attraction for them here. Inside the shop one finds an exhibition of PostPet stuffed characters everywhere. More than several "Print Club" systems are there as well, inviting visitors to take photos inside the booth and have them printed with PostPet characters and messages from them. Machines similar to UFO Catcher are everywhere, with stuffed PostPet characters inside the transparent domes. Teens are manipulating the robot arm to catch "special models" that are difficult to find elsewhere. In fact, PostPet characters are available as stuffed toys in various sizes or plastic models. Soft stuffed toys come in various sizes. Smaller ones are often attached a school bags, key chains, or mobile phones. Why are they so popular? How may the phenomenon be interpreted?

Keeping favorite virtual characters in physical forms have several meanings. First, these items function as a communication medium in their own right. Since it represents a subject of interest to the owner, it helps start conversations. It is why there are many "funny" ketai straps, such as miniature pizza. It can be regarded as the contemporary version of a known Japanese tradition of admiring Netsuke, miniature sculptures to be worn with Kimono. (Because there is no pocket on Kimono, one's purse is kept inside the Obi belt. A netsuke is attached to the purse so that it wouldn't slip off, and can be easily located when needed. Netsuke became a major accessory for men and a favorite conversation starter. Netsuke has been a collected item because of its artistic quality and imaginative motives.) The tradition is now revived. There is an incredible variety of ketai straps on the market, game characters being an important part of it.

Attaching one's favorite small item to a "personal" belonging such as a school bag, a ketai, or a car, is an act of "personalizing" these things that are industrially produced. Of course it helps identifying "mine" from others', since these are not unique objects by nature. However, it has more than a practical purpose. Certain objects become a part of one's life as they travel together. Adding a personal taste is important in making the object truly personal.

Physical toys play another important role in the users' psychology. Miniature toys of PostPet or other characters bridge the two worlds, imaginary and real. This, essentially, is not particularly Japanese. Both traditional dolls or stuffed animals, and current characters , are based on our wish for physical representation of imaginary characters. What is particular to Japan is that such character business has been strongly connected to manga and anime. These are not merely meant for kids, but are part of Japanese pop culture. It means that physical versions of virtual characters, such as Momo of PostPet, are used by those who can afford ketai or computers or cars. However it does not mean that they are simple enough to mix the real and the virtual. They enjoy chatting with Momo knowing it is a game and that Momo does not exist in reality. Still, there is a feeling that something like Momo exists somewhere in cyberspace. (This has been an internationally shared feeling among online gamers for many years.) Physical toys help the user enjoy the borderland between the real and the virtual by staying and traveling with the user in daily life. Thus a girl will chat with her Post-Pet on the screen, which is an active yet nonphysical form of representation, then go to bed with a larger, warm, tactile but silent version of it. In her minds these two versions are integrated into one—her PostPet.

In fact SCN organizes PostPet Fair every now and then in major cities, building mock-ups of Momo's room and filling the space with real objects such as furniture or tableware—physical version of what users see on their TV, PC, ketai or Pocket PostPet screens. By seeing them in physical forms, PostPet and its world becomes more concrete.

EVERYTHING GOES TO KETAI (MOBILE PHONE)

Karaoke has been popular entertainment on home game platforms. Takara released a low cost karaoke set made in the shape of microphone that became a big hit. Now mobile phones can be used for practicing karaoke. Karaoke service is a part of the standard menu one finds on an Internet mobile phone, such as i-mode from Docomo. By connecting to the server and selecting a favorite song, the sound comes from the phone while the text is shown on the screen as in normal karaoke. It is not only useful for practicing but it creates a new form of karaoke, such as mobile outdoor karaoke with friends.

Mobile phone networks with an Internet connection such as "i-mode," "Vodafone," and "au" have already become the most popular platform among the young generation for sending email and browsing the Web. The Japanese mobile phones has already formed a culture of its own, with new ways of exchanging email, meeting friends, using all kinds of services from checking the train timetable to finding a restaurant in the area (with PHS or GPS networks, the server knows the user's location), and enjoying games while waiting for friends or taking trains. Instead of seeing people speaking on their mobile phones on trains, now we see them moving their fingers on the push buttons at an amazing speed, either sending messages or downloading services or playing games. Such phenomenon has taken place only recently, around the end of 1999 in big cities.

These mobile phones are in fact handheld computers with graphic capabilities. Although mobile phones may become "intelligent phones" in the near future worldwide, there is a specific reason why mobile phone became "wearable computers" in Japan, ahead of many other countries. It comes from the nature of Japanese language. To write in Japanese, two different types of Japanese phonetic alphabets, Chinese characters (Kanji) and Western numbers are needed. Western alphabets are used as well. Chinese characters, which are numerous in number and consist of too many strokes, cannot be entered from a normal keypad. Thus words are entered phonetically using one of the alphabets and then transformed into appropriate sets of Kanji among possible candidates. The process is required not only for entering sentences but also for writing names of people or places. Therefore, even to have an address book feature, a mobile phone needs to have a word processing function and a high-resolution display that can show Kanji in readable manner. Sending a message on a mobile phone means a word processing engine is involved. Such needs have made Japanese mobile phones evolve quickly. In a way it is only a small step from a usable mobile phone supporting textural messaging function to a multifunctional mini-sized computer with a wireless telephone connection. Now a typical mobile phone in Japan has a fairly large color display, push buttons so one can enter any alphabets, cursor keys to select menus and play games, polyphony sound for ring tones and music, in addition to the other functions needed as a telephone. Some services support the use of a still or video camera equipped with the phone. GPS phones are on the market as well. Here are some facts on mobile phones in Japan.

In the fall of 2003, over 80 million mobile phones were in use in Japan, including over 40 million i-mode phones, 14.5 million Vodafone, and 10 million third-generation phones (W-CDMA and CDMA2000 1x). This number means more than 60 percent of the whole population use mobile phones. (Japan has a population of 127 million people, 50 million households.) These numbers change from time to time, according to the services available and the cost, yet the above statistics would be enough to see how mobile phones, or, "smart phones" with Internet connectivity, are widely used in Japan.

As the mobile phone became commonplace—at the rate of more than 1.6 units per household—its social role has changed, as well as what it called. Officially named "Keitai denwa" (portable phone) and written in Chinese characters (Kanji) when it was known as a business tool, people started calling it "keitai" as it became commonplace. When the young generation became its core user, they started to call it "ketai" with two syllables instead of four, written in Katakana (the Japanese alphabet) instead of Kanji, which is far easier to pronounce or write. Now the word "ketai" is a part of our daily language. Ketai is no longer a mobile "phone." It is a multimedia wearable device that is used to create, exchange, and retrieve visual, textual, and audible information, as well as being a tool for amusement. The major part of the transition took place within only a few years.

"KETAI CONTENT"

Today, practically all sorts of services and information available on the Internet are also found on mobile phones. Especially, game content available on mobile phones is exploding. In addition to all kinds of board games, classic video games, virtual sports playing, fortune telling, train simulator and others, simulation games such as *SimCity*, role playing games such as *Legends of Zelda* or *Final Fantasy*, and a rich variety of growing games are attracting mobile phone users. Online games are also becoming popular. It is not too much exaggeration to say almost all games available on PCs and game platforms are now found on ketai. Of course the screen size of ketai is limited, but ketai has other advantages to compensate, such as mobility, ease of downloading and updating, cost, and so forth. Online connectivity is by nature one of the advantages ketai has. The online golf match has been popular among businessmen. As connection speed and accessibility become better, and connection cost becomes lower, online games attract more attention. However, online entertainment is not only distributed by the industry. The online haiku (Japanese short poem) party is another popular activity, taking the tradition in haiku where people go for a picnic together and organize a competition on the spot, and turning it into a virtual online party. Collaborative activities among users such as interactive storytelling with graphic images could be also found at the early stage. People are finding their own ways of using mobile phones for entertainment.

In fact, an important feature behind Japanese ketai culture is the richness of ketai content created by normal people. One of the reasons why i-mode attracted many users is the content—the Web sites a user can browse using i-mode. The language used in building a Web site for i-mode is C-html (Compact HTML), which is basically a subset of regular HTML. Therefore normal Web sites written in HTML can be easily modified for i-mode access. Building a new Web site for i-mode is not difficult for those who have experience with Web designing. What makes i-mode exciting is not just the services provided by commercial parties. Small businesses and individuals make their own Web sites, including things such as a photo gallery of one's own pet, virtual gallery of illustrations, free download of one's music composition, so and so forth.

Today major Web design tools support templates and output formats for major mobile phone carriers including i-mode. Mobile phones with cameras (or video cameras) are handy tools people use to create digital content. Some people are already experimenting with Weblog software for mobile phones. Soon mobile phones and the Internet will be more closely interrelated.

FROM ENTERTAINMENT TO CULTURE

Japanese games and game culture have developed on the network of influence among different forms of entertainment, visual art, technology, and people's desire for communication. Such interaction has been made possible partly because there were no solid walls built between art, entertainment, and technology, as well as between high art and low art, or fine art and applied art. Positive thought toward amusement in every aspect of daily life is behind the absence of borders. While art can be enjoyed in daily life on furniture or dishes, entertainment can be a part of cultural and artistic activities. The highly functional and beautifully designed mobile phones seem to prove the tradition continues today and supports the gaming culture in Japan. At the same time, we should realize the power of entertainment—including communication as entertainment—that made it possible to design such a sophisticated machine packed in a slim, light, and stylish body. The same can be said with the entertainment robots such as AIBO, PINO, or ASIMO. Entertainment has been pushing the limit of digital media technology and turning it into culture. Our desire to play is an essential element of creativity. Games and gaming culture have already proven it.

Notes
1 Often in remote regions (such as Hokkaido) wooden cards were used instead of paper cards for the players, probably because printed cards were not easily available at the frontier lands. The game is much harsher than one might imagine from its elegant nature, because speed matters in gaining the cards. Paper cards are soon worn out.
2 Many of the selected poems are of those of love, since exchanging short poems was the manner in medieval Japan. (One can find similarities in the medieval European court, as we know from literature.) Because of that, playing the traditional card sets was considered too decadent during World

War II. The authorities edited a new version named "Aikoku (i.e., patriotic) Hyakunin Isshu," which consisted of poems reflecting "correct" ethics.

3 The idea came from China. However, such idea is not far from the traditional learning system in Europe. In France, for example, elementary school children were forced to memorize verses.

4 Taking the model of the poem cards, different versions of card sets based on texts such as proverbs have been edited and published from time to time, including those for younger children. Playing these cards used to be a New Year's tradition, among other family entertainment such as flying kites, playing spins, and "Hanetsuki," which is the Japanese equivalent of badminton. Western cards are brought to Japan once again when Japan opened its border in the nineteenth century. Western card sets and card games are called "trump" in Japan and became a typical pastime among young people (especially during school trips) and families in Japan. Among the traditional card games besides the poem cards, there is another card game named "hanafuda" (flower cards) that consists of a set of cards that are beautifully illustrated with flowers and animals. This card game was played mainly among adults, often in the entertainment quarters or for gambling along with dice games, as can be seen in Yakuza (Japanese equivalent of "mafia") films. Because of such history, playing hanafuda was usually not considered as a part of traditional family entertainment. Nintendo has been the major publisher of these card sets.

5 In most Japanese households, "living-dining" room is the central place of the family, where a TV set sits on one corner of the room, opposite but not too far from the dinner table. Richer families with bigger homes might separate the living room from the dining room.

6 Many children take courses outside their school to prepare for entrance exams.

7 Masuyama, Hiroshi. (2000). Bit Generation 2000/'TV-games'. Exhibition Catalog. Kobe Fashion Museum/TV Game Museum.

8 Since April 2001 the game has been revived in Japan for a popular palmtop, ZAURUS, from Sharp.

9 Because of such background, NAMCO developed robots including Mappy, a mouse robot that would try to find its way through maze—a cutting edge experiment at that time. It also developed driving simulation projects in collaboration with MAZDA and with the Police Department of Kanagawa Prefecture.

10 When Japan's first commercial computer graphics studio, JCGL (Japan Computer Graphics Laboratory, founded in 1981), went out of business in 1989, NAMCO, which already had collaborated with JCGL in game creation, decided to inherit the asset by hiring most of the designers and engineers who are trained in creating high-end images of 3D virtual worlds for film and TV. Also, as I described before, NAMCO supports its engineers and designers in producing their own artwork, which have been selected at SIGGRAPH, Ars Electronica, and other festivals every

year. They can use the company's system for creating artwork, but they should work outside their regular working hours. As PCs have become powerful enough, they often use their own machines at home these days, which means that the role of the company in supporting their work is less important than it used to be. Still the artists say that there remains an atmosphere at NAMCO to respect these artists, which makes them feel more comfortable at work. The company profits from their creativity by having the NAMCO credit on their work, and it helps to attract young, ambitious artists as they recruit. Quite a few ex-NAMCO artists and engineers work outside Japan.

11 The company that developed and distributed *Aquazone* changed its name a few times. Before it was developed and published from 9003 Inc. Now (January 2002) the game is published from Cinomix Inc. and DigiCube Inc. The concept of the game influenced other games that came later, including Tamagotchi. The company 9003 Inc. also developed a bird growing game named Piina, which is also still on the market with five different types of birds. Yutaka Saito, who later created another fish tank simulation game, Seaman, was a game designer of 9003 Inc. Seaman is thus based upon his experience with Aquazone.

12 The game was available until recently. The last version of the game, *Princess Maker 3*, ran on Sega's Dreamcast. Because Dreamcast was withdrawn from the market, Princess Maker is currently unavailable at the time of this writing. Like other successful games on Dreamcast that have been recently available on PlayStation 2, it might come back on another game platform. For more information about the game, see http://www.gainax.co.jp/soft/catalog/pri1.html

The story is partly based on an old Japanese tale from the medieval age that every Japanese person knows ("The Tale of Taketori"). The story is about a baby girl found and adopted by an old couple, who then grows up and is revealed to be the princess of the Moon. The theme of the game sounds like a mixture of the Japanese tale and the Broadway musical "My Fair Lady"—rather than its original version "Pygmalion" by George Bernard Shaw. In Pygmalion, the woman leaves the man who has "educated" her, as she feels more independent and cannot stand the man's class-oriented mind. It sounds like a story by the ironical socialist Bernard Shaw. Broadway took the story, but changed the ending—the woman comes back to him.

13 This is not an exaggeration. Because of the different religious background, children are considered to be given their life by their parents, not by God. This leads to the concept that the parents have the right for the life and body of their children. Historically this is the common philosophical notion in China, Korea, and Japan.

14 Tamagotchi measured approx. 5 cm by 4 cm by 1.5 cm and had a chain to be used as a key holder. The screen size was 2 by 2.2 cm. Even a little

child could hold it easily. The body of Tamagotchi came in different colors. Fifteen models were released in two years, each of them in different colors, transparencies, patterns, or even with some little toys. More important versions are those with "genders" (male and female Tamagotchi, to communicate through the infrared communication) and Angel's Tamagotchi. Collecting different models or toys became a part of the Tamagotchi boom.

15 "Kawaii" is a key word in understanding today's Japanese culture. A kawaii object usually is small, round in shape rather than square, light both in weight and color, and simple in function. Tamagotchi was designed exactly according to such idea. The love for small objects has a long tradition in Japanese culture, which can be traced back to the medieval age. Japanese keitai (mobile phones) also developed along such aesthetics.

16 In both Aquazone and Tamagotchi a user would raise an egg and take care of the virtual creatures by feeding them and keeping the environment comfortable. However, while Aquazone was based on simulation and visual reality, Tamagotchi had a more direct expression with visual and acoustic impact that would appeal to children.

For example, Aquazone users would check the water quality with virtual laboratory equipment, but Tamagotchi users had to remove the "poop" as soon as possible, when a steaming warm pile appears on the screen. Removal is accomplished by clicking a button.

17 The notion of angel in Japan is flexible, as a religious background does not bind it.

18 It was provided for Sega's Dreamcast. Now it is available on PS2. This version (version 2) was developed by Vivarium and ASCII, as ASCII transferred the program to PS2. The English version was available on Dreamcast.

19 Not only the photorealism, but also the maintenance system for the fish tank and the "food" tank simulate real environment, as in Aquazone.

OTAKU

Lawrence Eng

Otaku culture, a type of obsessive fan culture, was first described in Japan in the early 1980s. Since that time, the exact definition of "otaku" has been varied and contested by different parties. Although some consider the term insulting and degrading, others wear it as a badge of honor. Otaku culture has similarities to geek and hacker cultures. The subcultural categorization most similar to otaku, however, is probably "anorak" (the British term used to describe obsessive fans). Although "otaku" broadly describes obsessive fans of anything, it has most commonly been used to describe fans of anime (Japanese animation) and manga (Japanese comics). This common use of the term is especially prevalent among anime and manga fans in the United States.

Although similar to "otaku," terms such as "geek," "hacker," and "anorak" have their own unique connotations that are constantly changing, so it is important not to place too much emphasis on trying to translate "otaku." Due to its varied connotations, "otaku" is an especially difficult term to define. Most simply, we can think of otaku as extreme fans. They can be fans of anything. Although the term is most often used to describe fans of Japanese animation, otaku can be fans of computers, comic books, televisions shows, video games, music stars, cars, goldfish, and so forth. Otaku are not primarily defined by their chosen objects of interest, but by the level of devotion and expertise they have regarding those objects. Otaku are fans, but not in any casual sense. Experts in the objects of everyday life (such as television shows, comic books, and pets), otaku invest an enormous amount of time and energy into activities that other people might view as "hobbies."

OTAKU ACTIVITIES

Even though otaku are highly engaged with popular culture and mass media products, they are not merely a consumer culture. Their expertise and information-gathering abilities make them exceptionally informed consumers, oftentimes more informed than media producers expect or want. In some cases, otaku knowledge surpasses the knowledge of the producers. Such mastery over the information surrounding mass media products gives otaku a certain kind of power. Otaku, instead of being driven by marketing forces, are able to enjoy the products of popular culture on their own terms.

With their knowledge, otaku participate in an underground information economy, developing powerful alliances and status depending on the depth of their expertise. Within otaku culture, the value of objects is not defined by mainstream metrics, such as Manufacturers Suggested Retail Price (MSRP), but by the subculture's own determinants of value. In some cases, mainstream channels of consumption are avoided completely. Otaku routinely participate in black-market economies that often deal in the trade of illicitly copied, pirated, or unlicensed items, and other goods not intended for sale on the mass market or at all.

Otaku do not merely enjoy products as they are sold to the public. Instead, otaku are said to "change, manipulate, and subvert ready-made products."[1] They also produce their own products to be enjoyed and traded as well, another way of becoming more independent of mainstream producers of popular culture. An example of this type of activity is the production of *doujinshi*, or fanzines that are produced and sold within otaku culture. Most often, these *doujinshi* are comics that portray preexisting characters in non-official stories, some of which are very far removed from the original material. For example, pornographic depictions of anime and manga characters (from non-pornographic anime and manga) are very common. Even though otaku enjoy and support the products of popular culture, they also use those products for their own, often subversive, ends.

Due to otaku culture's emphasis on information, much of otaku daily activity is conducted online. Otaku also attend conventions and other gatherings such as anime screenings at local clubs.

THE ORIGIN OF THE WORD "OTAKU" AS USED AMONG FANS

We should note the etymology of "otaku.".[2] Literally and originally, it means "your house," and more generally it is also a very polite (distancing and non-imposing as opposed to familiar) way of saying "you." In the anime Otaku no Video, AnimEigo uses "thou" instead of "you" to translate "otaku," indicating the term's archaic formality. In everyday mainstream Japanese conversation, calling a person you know "otaku" would be viewed as strange or possibly sarcastic. It would be like calling one's friends "Ma'am" or "Sir."

Takashi Murakami, the otaku/pop artist, cites his friend Toshio Okada, an expert on otaku culture, in explaining where the usage of "otaku" among fans came from. Okada, Murakami says, links "otaku" to Shoji Kawamori and Haruhiko Mikimoto, the creators of the anime *Super Dimensional Fortress Macross* (1982), at Studio Nue. Kawamori and Mikimoto were students at Keio University in the early 1980s when they started working on *Macross*.

> Keio is known as one of the more upstanding and relatively upper-class institutes of learning in Japan. In tune with their somewhat aristocratic surroundings, Kawamori and Mikimoto used the classical, refined second-person form of address, "otaku," in preference to "anata," the usual form of address. Fans of the studio's work began using the term to show respect toward Studio Nue's creators, and it entered common use among the fans who gathered at comic markets, fanzine meetings, and all-night line parties before anime movie releases.[3]

Tomohiro Machiyama suggests that the use of "otaku" as a form of address among anime fans was mimicked from the *Macross* anime directly. Machiyama says that the main character, Hikaru Ichijoe, frequently uses the extra-polite "otaku" when talking to other characters.

In a 2003 lecture at MIT, Toshio Okada discussed this subject further. According to Okada, at science fiction conventions in Japan (in the late 1970s and early 1980s), otaku from various places (i.e., anime clubs at different universities) would meet. Out of respect for each other's clubs, they would refer to each other using "otaku," the extra-polite form of address. It is possible that Kawamori and Mikimoto were part of this particular fan culture.

MAINSTREAM PERCEPTIONS OF OTAKU

According to Frederick Schodt, the first published report on the usage of "otaku" among fans appeared in 1983. Akio Nakamori wrote a series of articles called "Otaku no Kenkyu" (Studies of Otaku) in Manga Burikko. He called those hardcore fans who called each other "otaku" the "otaku-zoku" ("zoku" meaning tribe). His was perhaps the first article stereotyping otaku as being antisocial, unkempt, and unpopular.

The "otaku panic," as described by Sharon Kinsella, didn't really occur until after the infamous Tsutomu Miyazaki incident in 1989. Miyazaki (who was twenty-six, and in no way to be confused with acclaimed anime director Hayao Miyazaki) kidnapped and murdered four little girls. When he was arrested, the police found a huge collection of various anime and manga, some of it pornographic, in his apartment.

The media picked up on this and repeatedly referred to Miyazaki as an otaku, thereby exposing the term to the public at large. As such, otaku became associated with sociopaths like Miyazaki, and in the panic, many in the media tried to blame Miyazaki's deviant behavior on anime and manga.

Not unlike American adult society, but perhaps taken to greater extremes, Japanese adult society has long had anxieties about its youth culture becoming more individualistic and isolated and less interested in fulfilling mainstream social duty. The Miyazaki incident was both a cause for further anxiety and an outlet for the media to deal with preexisting anxiety by pointing a blaming finger at anime and manga subculture.

OTAKU DEFINED AND REDEFINED

Since the Miyazaki incident, the mainstream Japanese usage of "otaku" has been mostly derogatory, with a certain amount of fear and loathing. The typical negative stereotype of otaku generally portrays a young man in his teens or twenties who is either overweight or skinny, is unkempt, and lacks social graces, leading to social isolation (except among other otaku). Beyond these negative stereotypes, however, many have tried to discuss the positive and distinctive aspects of otaku culture.

"What defines an otaku?" is a complicated question that resists quick and easy answers. Media sensationalism aside, "otaku" has gone from simply being what hardcore fans used to call each other to being a general concept of how individuals use information for their own ends. William Gibson calls otaku "passionate obsessive(s)." Volker Grassmuck describes them as "information fetishists." In the most basic sense, an otaku is someone who is highly dedicated to something and uses information from anywhere and everywhere to further his or her understanding of that thing for fun and maybe even profit. Lawrence Eng has described otaku in terms of an "Otaku Ethic," highlighting their particular philosophy of information, their mode of resistance as "reluctant insiders," and their quasi-scientific activities with an emphasis on technology.[4] As people have come to recognize the significance of otaku culture, it has increasingly become a subject of academic study.

THE POPULARIZATION OF OTAKU CULTURE IN JAPAN

Even in Japan, where the term "otaku" still carries a number of negative connotations, there are champions of otaku culture. One of the biggest proponents of otaku culture in Japan is Toshio Okada, affectionately known as the Otaking, who was one of the founders of the anime studio Gainax. Okada left Gainax in 1992 to write books about otaku culture, and he has even lectured on the subject at Tokyo University (one of Japan's most prestigious schools).

The Gainax anime *Otaku no Video*, which came out several years after the Miyazaki incident, portrayed otaku in a humorous and self-mocking way, but with a healthy dose of pride as well. Although the otaku portrayed might have been shown to be a little eccentric at times, they were also harmless—a far cry from the frightening image of the child-killing sociopath the Japanese media had presented just a few years before. *Otaku no Video* also apparently made it a point to show the diversity of those called "otaku," demonstrating that otaku can't be so easily stereotyped.

Takashi Murakami's "Poku" (pop + otaku) art style has achieved much acclaim in Japan and abroad. Murakami's work has highlighted and helped to reduce the discrimination shown toward otaku in Japan.

Due to these and other efforts to educate (and entertain) the public, otaku culture has achieved international recognition, and perhaps more importantly, a little more acceptance domestically (though acceptance of otaku culture in Japan varies depending on who you talk to and the prevailing media attitude toward otaku). A more recent group of troubled youth being discussed in Japan are the *hikikomori*, shut-ins who have cut off all social contact with their peers and even family members. As many of the *hikikomori* spend their time playing video games, watching anime, and reading manga, they have often been associated with otaku, even though there are important differences between otaku and *hikikomori*.

THE POPULARIZATION OF OTAKU CULTURE
INTERNATIONALLY

With the international spread of anime and manga, otaku culture has spread as well, infused by local culture to form all new expressions of otaku-ism. There are groups that identify themselves as otaku all over the world. The United States is one country where otaku culture has been growing rapidly.

Organized anime fandom in the United States emerged in the late 1970s—at around the same time that organized anime fandom showed up in Japan. Since then, as anime has become more popular, otaku culture has flourished in the United States. The American video release of the aforementioned *Otaku no Video* (1991) was probably very influential in introducing the concept of otaku to many American anime fans. Otaku in America do many of the same things that Japanese otaku do: attend conventions, create fanzines, dress up in costumes, attend screenings, interact with each other on the internet, and, create fan Web sites, etc. One major difference between Japanese and American otaku is that the term "otaku" in the United States lacks most of the negative connotations that surround the mainstream usage of "otaku" in Japan. At the same time, "otaku" in the United States is commonly used to simply mean "fan of anime and manga," which is fairly generic and indistinctive. Some American anime and manga fans have rejected the term "otaku" as a positive or neutral term, preferring to emphasize the mainstream Japanese usage of the term, which is mostly negative. On the other hand, there are some otaku in America who have tried to emphasize the expert nature of otaku, highlighting the positive aspects of the subculture.

Notes
1 See Grassmuck.
2 See Grassmuck.
3 See Murakami, 62.
4 See Eng.

Resources

Books

Gainax. (1991). *Otaku no Video 1982 and More Otaku no Video 1985* [VHS]. Tokyo: Youmex. Translated by AnimEigo.

Kinsella, S. (2000). *Adult manga: Culture and power in contemporary Japanese society.* Honolulu: University of Hawai'i Press.

Macias, P., & Machiyama, T. (2004). *Cruising the anime city: An otaku guide to Neo Tokyo.* Berkeley, CA: Stone Bridge Press.

Murakami, T. (2001). Impotence culture-anime. In D. Frankel, F. Brabenec Hart, & S. Schwartz (Eds.). *My reality—contemporary art and the culture of Japanese animation* (pp. 58–66). Des Moines, IA: Des Moines Art Center.

Schodt, F. L. (1996). *Dreamland Japan: Writings on modern manga, Japanese comics for otaku.* Berkeley, CA: Stone Bridge Press.

Web Sites

Eng, L. (2002, May). Otak-who? Technoculture, youth, consumption, and resistance. American representations of a Japanese youth subculture. Retrieved February 11, 2005 from http://www.rpi.edu/~engl/otaku.pdf

Gibson, W. (2001, April). Modern boys and mobile girls. Retrieved February 11, 2005 from http://observer.guardian.co.uk/life/story/ 0,6903,466391,00.html

Grassmuck, V. (1990, December). "I'm alone, but not lonely": Japanese otaku-kids colonize the realm of information and media, a tale of sex and crime from a faraway place. Retrieved February 11, 2005 from http:// www.cjas.org/~leng/otaku-e.htm

MANGA

Michele Knobel and Colin Lankshear

Manga is a stylized graphic genre generally referred to as "Japanese comics." Manga can be dated back to the often humorous outline drawings done by sixth century Shintoist monks to illustrate calendar scrolls. The term "manga" itself (which translates roughly into "whimsical pictures" in English) wasn't used to describe a particular style of illustration until the late seventeenth-century, when Japanese artist Hokusai rebelled against traditional woodblock style Japanese printmaking and drew on French and Dutch art and art theory to develop the art of drawing finely detailed, free-flowing characters and landscapes as part of creating a meaningful *and* entertaining art piece. Manga really came into its own, however, in the late 1940s and early 1950s with the work of Osamu Tezuko. Comic strips were popular in Japan soon after they first began appearing in U.S. newspapers early in the twentieth century. However, the growing worldwide popularity of Disney animations and cinema techniques, and the ready availability of Marvel and DC comics in Japan after World War II helped to shape manga into a distinct and highly popular graphic-and-text genre.

Early manga tended to focus on action-packed adventure or sci-fi stories for boys (shonen manga) or romance stories for girls (shojo manga). In Japan in the 1970s, manga for adult readers became available, and included much more violent and "dark" manga, pornographic manga, and homoerotic manga, as well as much more prosaic instruction manual manga, textbook manga, and so on. Storylines in narrative manga generally include flawed or thoroughly ordinary heroes (e.g., "office lady" manga is a popular reading choice in Japan), eccentric secondary characters, androgynous characters, and sometimes sharp social critique. By the end of the twentieth century, manga—whether serialized or collected together in graphic novel form—comprised 40 percent of Japan's book and magazine sales. Manga continues to distinguish itself by its careful attention to art *and* story *and* entertainment as a seamless whole: "Cinematic and iconographic, [manga] allow for focusing on the minutiae of daily life and [offer] a quick read." According to Lent, key themes found in popular manga include loyalty, intelligence, beauty, and cuteness.

Manga began to be translated into English during the late 1990s, and quickly caught on as popular reading texts for young English-speaking people (especially the *Yu-Gi-Oh* and *Dragon-Ball Z* graphic novels, and the *Shonen Jump* serial collections). In English-speaking countries, manga fans (known as *otaku*) tend to be adolescents and young adults, with females making up a sizeable proportion of readers. The largest market for manga outside Japan is the United States, which spent approximately $100 million on manga in 2002, at a time "when book sales overall are growing 1–2 percent yearly, manga sales show triple-digit increases." Manga have attracted criticism from parents and educators for being too violent or for "dulling readers' minds." However, manga are complex texts, and require English-language readers to learn to read comic frames from right to left and to recognize the significance of different-sized-frames. For example, a narrow, page-length frame can denote time passing or direction in a journey, and a two-page single frame can signal something momentous is about to happen. The illustrator can also shift the reader's point of view or stance from that of "outsider, looking in" to "viewing the scene from the perspective of the different characters in the story" and the reader needs to be able to keep up with changing points of view.

As with fan fiction, popular manga have generated a subculture of what are referred to as "amateur manga"—manga drawn by fans that add to or produce new versions of existing manga—and which, in Japan and the United States at least, are distributed at manga markets or comics conventions. These gatherings have also become an important source of feedback on drawing techniques (e.g., fine-tuning perspective, facial expressions, hair, etc.) and plot developments for amateur manga writers. Amateur manga writers are particularly serious about their artwork and regularly form "circles" or distributed groups (especially online) devoted to constructively critiquing each other's manga drawings. Most highly prized within these circles are original drawings, rather than copies of existing manga artwork. Documenting amateur manga feedback online, Kelly Chandler-Olcott and Donna Mahar provide excellent examples of the kind of art-focused critique that takes place between manga fans in their case study of Eileen, a thirteen-year-old aspiring manga artist. Eileen scans and posts an original drawing she had done to an email discussion list, and receives the following feedback:

> The background is kinda simple, which is actually a pretty good idea. You might want to add something towards the bottom of the picture to balance all the items you have floating around at the top. . . . Also, his chest is either really small, or really smushed. Either way, it's not a good look with large biceps (those are the ones on the top of the arms, right? I get confused sometimes). Not to be crude, but he needs more

shading in the crotch area. It seems there's nothing there from knee to knee. Otherwise I love the expression, specially the grin. It totally sets the mood to scare some people. Or freak them out, whatever. And like usual, nice shiny hair, Very pretty.

MANGA RESEARCH FOCI

Key research approaches to studying manga tend to include text-based content and thematic analysis of commercial manga. Manga tend to be researched in terms of the following:

- Artwork and/or as an art style, including the cinematic qualities of manga drawings and art education
- Being an historical barometer
- Gender and identity and/or sexuality
- Ideology and propaganda
- Being a popular culture artifact
- Reading material and learning resources
- Amateur manga production as a subculture
- Social practice

GAPS IN RESEARCH

The main foci of manga-oriented research to date have been analyses of artistic techniques employed in manga drawing, content analyses of manga texts, and examination of manga texts as leisure reading choices or as reading resources for classrooms. In particular, manga studies have tended to focus on women's manga reading preferences and on analyses of identity or subjectivity. Much of the extant manga-oriented research focuses on adult manga readers and writers. This is slowly beginning to change as researchers turn their attention to studying online amateur manga writing/drawing sites, as well as young people's engagement with animated manga or animè. Few studies, however, focus on amateur manga production as a process involving the blurring of plotlines, dialogue, and illustration. Even fewer studies focus on young people's engagement with manga as readers and writers/artists in relation to their other media engagement and social relations, despite research evidence suggesting that this orientation towards young people's media use (e.g., television, video games) and literacy practices is significantly complex and has important implications for how media and literacy are approached in schools. Other noticeable absences in the research literature include studies that explore the complexity of manga texts themselves and their popularity as leisure reading texts, even among many young people who struggle with reading within school contexts.

STATE OF KNOWLEDGE

It is clear from the available research that manga reading, writing, and drawing is very much tied to identity, popular culture preferences, and historical moments. A key contribution manga studies are making at present is a greater understanding of the role older and younger women are playing in shaping the content and direction of what traditionally has been a male-oriented genre. However, the majority of manga studies treat manga as somewhat static popular culture artifacts, rather than aspects of social and cultural practice. More recent ethnographic-type studies that promote contextualized understandings of manga engagement emphasize the importance of paying attention to the *fluidity* of students' engagement with manga (and animé) that spans paper-based, television, video game and internet media.

Resources

Allen, K., & Ingulsrud, J. (2003). Manga literacy: Popular culture and the reading habits of Japanese college students. *Journal of Adolescent & Adult Literacy,* 46 (8), 674–683.

Chandler-Olcott, K., & Mahar, D. (2003). Adolescents' anime-inspired "fanfictions": An exploration of multiliteracies. *Journal of Adolescent & Adult Literacy,* 46 (7), 556–566.

Lent, A. (2003). Far out *and* mundane: The mammoth world of manga. *Phi Delta Kappa Forum,* 84 (3), 28–41.

Sanchez, F. (2003). HIST 101: History of manga. AnimeInfo.org—Anime University. Retrieved November 24, 2003 from http://animeinfo.org/animeu/hist102-11.html

ANIME

Lien Shen

Anime (an-nee-may) is a Japanese word derived from the French word for "animated," and is well known as "Japanese animation" among English speakers. Anime works include everything that Western audiences are accustomed to seeing in live-action film, romance, comedy, tragedy, adventure, horror, and so on. Many scholars consider anime to be a medium rather than a genre in film because anime itself has various genres. Appealing to various groups of audiences, anime plays a remarkable role in Japanese popular culture and occupies a huge amount of Japan's export of cultural industry.

The earliest Japanese animation was by individual film hobbyists inspired by American and European pioneer animators. Japanese animation began emerging after World War II, and the industry grew during the 1960s and 1970s. In 1964, the Japanese animation series *Astro Boy* by Osamu Tezuka premiered on NBC and stunned American audiences. Through his animated images, Tezuka presented a new visual style of animation to American audiences with Japan's "internal contradiction" after World War II and the "external resistance" to American cultural production. Although animation is originally from the West, Tezuka led Japanese animation toward its own aesthetic and embraced more complicated concepts of culture within his works.

In 1988, the anime film *Akira* became an international hit by giving the world a blast with the graphically violent and gruesome anime. According to Japanese culture and literature scholar Susan Napier, *Akira* is "unquestionably a masterpiece of technical animation" and "a complex and challenging work of art that provoked, bewildered, and inspired its audiences."[1] The worldwide success of *Akira* made it a landmark of Japanese animation, and since then fans have started to use the term "anime" instead of "Japanese animation" to refer to such visual aesthetic experiences. Around the same time, anime began to be distributed and licensed widely in the United States. Anime has slowly gained Western audiences' attention since the late 1980s, and become an extension of mainstream animation after several U.S. box office records in the mid-1990s, including Mamoru Oshii's *Ghost in the Shell* (1996) and Hayao Miyazaki's *Princess Mononoke* (1997). Whereas anime used to be seen as a part of subculture in the United States, Hollywood has begun to integrate "anime aesthetics" in recent action movies due to its popularity and influences. For instance, *Animatrix* (2003), a collection of several animations detailing the back-story of the universe within the film *Matrix* (1999), was commissioned and produced by the Wachowski Brothers with Japanese and Korean anime directors. The Wachowski Brothers even claim their film *Matrix* was highly influenced by *Akira*. Another recent example of anime influence is in the film *Kill Bill* (2003). Its director, Quentin Tarantino, includes a short anime to represent one character's bloody past. Clearly, anime is blooming in the United States.

Napier claims that anime is "the ideal artistic vehicle for expressing the hopes and nightmares of our uneasy contemporary world."[2] Anime not only maintains artistic value in the Japanese tradition and presents a transcultural aesthetic in the global world, but also expresses the internal human struggles and playfulness in contemporary society. "Anime," the word itself, connotes a whole complex of interwoven cultural and aesthetic values. The relationship between anime and Western animation is always interwoven and unsettled. "Animation" is defined as a set of moving images in which imagery and motion are created, rather than recorded.

Maureen Furniss emphasizes that animation is "the art of movements" formed by the artist's rendering of successive images. In the United States, animation studios can receive bigger budgets on their production costs, which enable animators to render more drawings per second thus creating smoother and more fluid images. For instance, Disney used twenty-four images per second to simulate film-quality motion in *Snow White*. This ideal fluidity of motion is situated on Furniss's emphasis: animation as "the art of movements." However, due to technical limitations and financial constraints, Japanese animators had to limit the drawings within five or six frames per second during the 1960s–1970s. Thomas Lamarre argues that due to economic reasons in Japanese animation production, animators strategically use fewer drawings to illustrate motion that develops a specific aesthetic for Japanese anime. In contrast to Western animation, which emphasizes "drawing movements," anime deliberately conveys its aesthetic by "moving drawings"—the art of drawings that move.

Under such historical and socioeconomic circumstances, anime has become a culturally and aesthetically hybridized term for animation, implying a certain kind of visual and aesthetic style originally from Japan. One may claim that the characteristics of anime are a reaction to these circumstances. For instance, characters are designed with large eyes because the animators want to drive the viewers' attention to the characters' emotion instead of their action. Whereas animators strategically used the same plots and shots to save production costs, anime tends to incorporate deeper and more sophisticated storylines in order to extend the market and attract various audiences.

MANGA

Manga (mahn-gah), literally meaning "humorous picture," refers to comic books in Japan. Rooted in Japanese traditional art, manga depicts the complexity of human dramas in graphic narrative. Most manga works are printed in monochromatic tones (i.e., pictures are black and white) on inexpensive, low-quality recycled paper, and are published as periodicals in a weekly, biweekly, and monthly format. Manga in Japan is targeted to various groups of readers, and can be loosely categorized as *shōnen* manga (boys' comics), *shōjo* manga (girls' comics), and *seinen* manga (adult comics). In general, each of them has a distinctive visual and narrative style to attract the specified group.

Japan is a country situated on many pictocentric traditions. The origin of manga can be traced back to the temple scrolls "chojugiga"—humorous pictures of birds and animals—in the twelfth century. In the early eighteenth century, the style of graphic narratives was developed in the woodblock prints, ukiyo-e or "floating world," which featured not only actors and courtesans of the time, but also imaginative subject matters, such as demons, ghosts, and extremely creative pornography. On the basis of such a historical and cultural background, manga artists began to incorporate the styles in American comics and Disney animation with the graphic narratives in Japanese traditions after

World War II. Since then, the "formality" of contemporary manga has been developed, what Toku calls "the grammar of manga." The elements of formality in manga include (1) pictures (depicting objects and figures), (2) words (including onomatopoeia), (3) balloons (indicating the position of words), and (4) frames (transiting from panels to panels). Both American comic artists and manga artists strategically use these elements to create composite narratives with images and texts. However, their strategies are very different. Many scholars and commentators use the term "graphic novel" instead of "comic" in order to stress the significance of this narrative form. The term "graphic novel" emphasizes the narrative form as a "novel with graphics," mirroring the privileged textual culture in Western society, whereas manga values "visual narrative" as a Japanese aesthetic that highlights the pictorial throughout history. Because Japan is a society situated on the visual, a quality manga work should be able to tell a story through the visual while minimizing the written words. The reading habit is another reason causing the difference between American comics and manga. Major manga magazines are often published weekly, and they can be as large as a metropolitan telephone book, reaching 1,000 or more pages. Most popular manga usually feature extendable serialized stories, collected in more than twenty volumes. Manga is intended to be a narrative form that allows readers to access it quickly and easily. According to Schodt, manga artists draw in a style of calligraphy with visual effects of quick brush painting that allows readers to only spend about 3.75 seconds per page.

OTAKU

Otaku is a term often used to refer to obsessive fans of anime and manga. In Japanese the original meaning of the word "otaku" is "your residence," or a polite way of saying "you" or "thou." It connotes the meanings of detachment and isolation from society. The closest English equivalent would be "nerds" or "geeks"—to describe someone who is somewhat antisocial in a negative sense.

In the 1980s, among amateur manga artists and fans, otaku refers to their excessive fans, who are serious about manga cultures, often self-proclaimed information-fetishists of manga. The sense of the selfish otaku generation has typified contemporary Japanese society, which is developing more eccentric and individualisic behavior, similar to Western attitudes. Between the 1960s and 1990s, the Japanese youth experienced no poverty and no postwar difficulties, were comfortable in seeking their own pleasure, and had become less interested in intellectual development and aesthetic tastes. The new breed of generations in postwar Japan developed a sense of "pleasure over pain," "recreation over work," "consumption over production," and "appreciation over creation,"[3] which are being critiqued as "passionless," "empty," and "neurotic," but preoccupied with their own cabin-style lives. In this sense, otaku culture has represented the socially unhealthy portion of anime and manga.

DÔJINSHI

The term "dôjinshi," originally applied to manga-like fanzines, refers to the hobby magazines and comic books produced by amateurs. "Dôjin" means folks who share the same taste and "shi" means magazine. It is very popular among manga and anime fans to self-publish fanzines and to distribute them to specific groups or communities. In 1975, dôjinshi artists began to distribute their fanzines in Comic Market, a form of convention where anime and manga fan art can be bought, sold, displayed, or exchanged.

YAOI

Yaoi means boy-to-boy love stories, a kind of erotic manga that features homosexual relationships, especially between male characters. Yaoi is a genre rooted in *shōjo* manga and emerged from female fanzines.

Notes
1 Napier, 2001, p. 5.2. From the producers' interview in the DVD of *Animatrix*. In the DVD, the Wachowski Brothers filmed a series of interviews with the directors and scholars who deal with anime, including Susan Napier.
2 Napier, 2001, p. 11.
3 Kinsella, 1998, p. 292.

Resources

Books

Furniss, M. (1998). *Art in motion: Animation aesthetics*. Bloomington, IN: Indiana University Press.

Kinsella, S. (2000). *Adult manga: Culture and power in contemporary Japanese society*. Honolulu: University of Hawaii Press.

Levi, A. (1996). *Samurai from outer space: Understanding Japanese animation*. Chicago: Open Court.

Napier, S. (2001). *Anime: From Akira to Princess Mononoke*. New York: Palgrave.

Schodt, F. (1996). *Dreamland Japan: Writings on modern manga*. Berkeley, CA: Stone Bridge Press.

———. (1986). *Manga! Manga!: The world of Japanese comics*. Tokyo: Kodansha International.

Articles

Chen, J. S. (2002). Mediating on the voiceless words of the invisible other: Young female anime fan artist—Narratives of gender images. *Social Theory in Art Education*, 24 (1), 213–233.

Kinsella, S. (1998). Japanese subculture in the 1990s: Otaku and the amateur manga movement. *Journal of Japanese Studies*, 24 (2), 289–316.

Lamarre, T. (2002). From animation to anime: Drawing movements and moving drawings. *Japan Forum*, 14 (2), 329–399.

Toku, M. (2001, March). What is manga?: The influence of pop culture in adolescent art. *Art Education*, 11–17.

Controversy in Hip Hop
(Commentary on Rap Music)

Matthew Cenac

Even though hip hop is surviving today
There is a lot of controversy around the way.
Ever since Biggie's and Tupac's lives ended badly,
And now we see there's even more tragedy
Some artists have gone to their grave
Others will be locked up and need to be saved.
Shyne is spending 10 or 20 years in jail,
Trying to call his peeps and family to get bail.
I don't know what DMX was thinking,
destroying cars, what the heck was he smoking?
Now he has to be in jail like Beanie Sigel,
Doing a lot of time, like a real criminal.
Left Eye's death would not have happened if she drove carefully,
Aaliyah would still be alive if her plane landed safely.
It was bad to hear about what happened to Big Pun
now in Terror Squad, Fat Joe is the only big one.
It was bad enough that Run DMC has been put to rest,
But how come Jam Master Jay didn't have a bulletproof vest?
Most women have been offended by the rap lyrics they have heard,
most rappers think that the women are being absurd.
Controversy is here,
Controversy is here,
and hip hop is getting dull like the edge of a spear.
Even though hip hop is going down like a sunset,
tragedy is happening,
but the hip hop era is not over yet.

Instant Messaging and Identity

Gloria E. Jacobs

Instant messaging is a text-based form of computer-mediated communication in which people use the computer to talk to another person in real time. Computer mediated communication (CMC) refers to the practice of using networked computers and alphabetic text to transmit messages between people or groups of people across space and time. Other forms of CMC include chat rooms and e-mail. Instant messaging is different from chat rooms in that only two people are engaged in a conversation at a time. It is different from e-mail in that the conversations occur in real time. Instant messaging includes three aspects: conversations, "away messages," and "profiles." Instant messaging software is constantly changing and new capabilities are constantly being added to the programs. At the end of the twentieth and the beginning of the twenty-first centuries, instant messaging was one of the most rapidly growing ways that youth stayed in touch with one another. Because instant messaging became so popular so quickly, and because it often includes spellings and abbreviations that are not part of standard written language, parents and teachers grew concerned that using instant messaging would damage young people's ability to write. Currently there is no research that indicates that this is the case. What research does show is that instant messaging is a specific type or genre of writing that is different from the writing people do in school. Furthermore, research is showing that just like speech, the way people use instant messaging is linked to their identity or type of person they want to be seen as.

Most instant messaging conversations use alphabetic text (the standard computer keyboard) as the primary form of communication. Instant messages typically are short in length; the average for each instant messaging entry is 5.1 words. Small graphics such as smiley faces (emoticons) can also be included in order to show emotion or make clear that a statement is a joke. Messages can include letter strings (such as "brb" for be right back or "lol" for laughing out loud), abbreviations (u for you, y for why) nonstandard spellings (cuz for because), little punctuation, lack of apostrophes, and limited use of capital letters. This way of writing is foreign to people who do not use instant messaging and is often thought of as bad writing. Articles in newspapers such as the *New York Times* and *Washington Post* say that it is the appearance of abbreviations and letter strings in school writing that concern parents and teachers. At the same time, educators such as Lelia Christenbury, past president of the National Council of Teachers of English, argue that instant messaging helps young people write because it gives them more experience with turning their thoughts into text.

Currently there is no research that indicates that instant messaging really does hurt writing skills, but there is also no research that indicates that it helps writing either. Research does indicate that people who use instant messaging change the way they write and spell depending upon who they are talking to. Lewis and Fabos found that if a person wants to be considered part of a group or to become closer friends with the person they are instant messaging, they will consciously imitate that person's writing style. This might include using letter strings, abbreviations, and other nonstandard writing forms, or it might require that the messages be written using language close to standard written English. Sometimes close friends will adopt each other's way of writing, although this is not always the case. Jacobs found that if people see themselves as being a particular type of person, they may resist what friends do and write the way they want to. The way people write when using instant messaging also depends on their experience and self-image as a writer. For example, Jacobs found that a young woman who writes a great deal, has won awards for her writing, and is thinking about majoring in English in college does not use a high number of abbreviations and letter strings in her instant messaging. Younger adolescents who are just learning to use instant messaging and who are experimenting with their identity as teens use more nonstandard spellings and other writing forms. In other words, contrary to what is popularly believed, the use of nonstandard forms is not always part of instant messaging.

Screen names and buddy icons are another aspect of instant messaging that is part of the identity a person projects through instant messaging. Each screen name within an instant messaging service (such as America Online Instant Messenger (AIM), ICQ, iChat, etc.) must be unique. Some people use variations on their real names. Other people come up with names that reflect their hobbies, their pets, their religious faith, their sense of humor, or any other number of aspects of their lives. Screen names tend to be long lasting because it can be cumbersome to change a name. Every time a person changes their screen name, they have to let all their online buddies know about the new name. It is not uncommon, however, for instant messaging users to have more than one screen. This appears to be most common among younger adolescents. By the time people reach their upper teens, their screen names tend to be stable. However, people may change screen names such as when they switch Internet providers and they are unable to take their old screen name with them.

Buddy icons are small pictures that appear in the receiver's instant messaging window. These icons help the receiver identify who they are conversing with. Instant messaging services such as AIM provide a large number of cartoons, drawings, and pictures from popular movies and video games that their subscribers can use as buddy icons. Buddy icons are also available through other Web sites. Although buddy icons are a visual representation of a person and as such seem to be an important part of identity, people often forget what icon they have selected. This is because it is not visible to the sender. To date, no research has been conducted about how people select or interpret buddy icons so it is unclear how buddy icons are connected to a person's identity.

Instant messaging software also lets users post "away messages" if the user has an always-on Internet connection. Once the Internet connection is broken, the away message is closed down. Away messages allow users to stay connected to their friends without having to sit at their computer. Away messages are similar to the outgoing messages people leave on their telephone answering machines and voice mail in that the messages let people know that the user is not able to respond to messages at the moment. They differ from answering machines in that away messages must be posted intentionally. Users tend to change their away messages frequently. For example, they might post that they are at dinner, and then when they are done eating, they might change their away message to something about homework.

As students gets older and busier, away messages play an important role in keeping friends in touch and aware of each other's plans. Reading friends' away messages is used as a form of procrastination and serves to connect people to their friends by letting them know that their friends are struggling with the same things they are. People use away messages to ask for homework help, to post plans, and to indicate mood. By keeping their friends informed, their friends can provide the type of support that is needed the most. For example, an away message that indicates that someone is in a bad or sad mood causes friends to leave messages of support or to call the person. An away message that indicates that the person is struggling with homework or has a question about homework can lead people to leave messages or to call with information. Posting these types of messages also helps the instant messaging user solidify their identity as a member of their group of friends. Messages about homework also help the user create an identity that they are a person who is concerned about school.

Away messages are not always informative. Sometimes they are humorous and playful, sometimes they can be ironic, and other times they can hide what a person is really doing by containing information that is not true. The type of messages a person posts is part of the identity they want to project. At the same time, it is necessary for the reader to know the person so that they are able to understand the humor or irony in the message. For example, college students often use away messages to make their lives seem more exciting than they really are or to make fun of the lack of excitement in their lives. For example, a college student may really be staying in and watching television or doing homework, but he may put up an away message saying he is out on a fantastic date. Although on the surface the message may make it look as if the person lives an exciting life, those who really know the person would understand the humor or irony of the posting.

Another way that people can use instant messaging to help create their identity is through profiles. Profiles are fairly static. That is, once they are written and posted, they tend to stay the same for quite some time. In AIM, it takes some effort to change a profile because the user has to go through several screens. The profile interface contains an option in which the user can establish an identity within the larger Internet community by posting biographical information and selecting areas of interest. Selecting this option makes the instant messaging user open to being contacted by other AIM users whom they may or may not know. If users do not choose to publicly post information, they can still use a text area into which they can enter any text they wish. A user's profile can be accessed only when they are signed on to the instant messaging system. Research into how instant message users make use of profiles has not yet been studied.

Resources
Books

Baron, N. (2000). *Alphabet to e-mail: How written English evolved and where it's heading*. London: Routledge.

Crystal, D. (2001). *Language and the Internet*. Cambridge, MA: Cambridge University Press.

Turkle, S. (1995). *Life on the screen: Identity in the age of the internet*. New York: Touchstone.

Articles

Axtman, K. (2002, December 12). 'r u online?': The evolving lexicon of wired teens. *Christian Science Monitor*.

Baron, N. (1984). Computer-mediated communication as a force in language change. *Visible Language*, 18 (2), 118–141.

———. (1998). Writing in the age of email: the impact of ideology versus technology. *Language and Communication*, 32 (1), 35–53.

Bedell, D. (2002, July 17). Messaging shapes language with a ;) and a smile. *Dallas Morning News*.

Cobb, C. (2002, October 12). Kewl or 2 much. *Orlando Sentinel*.

Erickson, T. (1999). Persistent conversation: an introduction. *Journal of Computer Mediated Communication*, 4 (4).

Garcia, A., & Jacobs, J. (1999). The eyes of the beholder: Understanding the turn-taking system in quasi-synchronous computer mediated communication. *Research on Language and Social Interaction*, 32 (4), 337–367.

Hard af Segerstad, Y. (2002). Instant messaging with WebWho. *International Journal of Human-Computer Studies*, 56, 147–171.

Helderman, R. (2003, May 20). Click by click, teens polish writing. *Washington Post*. p. 1.

Jacobs, G. (2004). Complicating contexts: Issues of methodology in researching the language and literacies of instant messaging. *Reading Research Quarterly*, 39 (4), 394–406.

Lam, W. S. E. (2000). Literacy and the design of the self: a case study of a teenage writing on the internet. *TESOL Quarterly, 34* (3), 457–482.

Lee, J. (2002, September 19). Nu shortcuts in school r 2 much 4 teachers. *New York Times*.

Lewis, C., & Fabos, B. (2000). But will it work in the heartland? A response and illustration. *Journal of Adolescent and Adult Literacy, 43* (5), 462–469.

Web Sites

Baron, N., Squires, L., Tench, S., & Thompson, M. *Tethered or mobile? Use of away messages in instant messaging by American college students, 22–24 June 2003.* Retrieved September 29, 2004 from http://www.american.edu/tesol/Grimstad-Baron.pdf

Herbsleb, J. D., Atkins, D. L., Boyer, D. G., Handel, M., & Finholt, T. A. (2002). *Introducing instant messaging and chat in the workplace.* Retrieved September 29, 2004 from http://www.cs.uoregon.edu/~datkins/papers/chi-rvm.pdf

Lenhart, A., Rainie, L., & Lewis, O. *Teenage life online: The rise of the instant-message generation and the Internet's impact on friendships and family relationships.* Pew Internet & American Life Project 2001. Retrieved September 29, 2004 from http://www.pewinternet.org/reports/toc.asp?Report=36

Livingstone, S., & Bovill, M. (2001). *Families and the Internet: An observational study of children and young people's Internet use.* London School of Economics and Political Science. Retrieved September 29, 2004 from http://www.lse.ac.uk/collections/media@lse/whosWho/sonia LivingstonePublications2.htm

———. (2001). *Young people, new media* [Summary report]. London School of Economics and Political Science. Retrieved September 29, 2004 from http://www.lse.ac.uk/collections/media@lse/pdf/young_people_report.pdf

Nardi, B., Whittaker, S., & Bradner, E. (2000). *Interaction and outeraction: Instant messaging in action.* Association for Computing Machinery. Retrieved September 29, 2004 from http://portal.acm.org/citation.cfm?id=358975

Randall, N. (2002). *Lingo online: A report on the language of the keyboard generation.* MSNCA. Retrieved September 29, 2004 from http://www.arts.uwaterloo.ca/~nrandall/LingoOnline-finalreport.pdf

Schiano, D., Chen, C. P., Ginsberg, J., Gretarsdottir, U., Huddleston, M., & Isaacs, E. (2002). *Teen use of messaging media.* Retrieved September 29, 2004 from http://portal.acm.org/citation.cfm?doid=506443.506500

Voida, A., Newstetter, W. C., & Mynatt, E. D. (2002). *When conventions collide: The tensions of instant messaging attributed.* Retrieved September 29, 2004 from http://portal.acm.org/citation. cfm? id= 503376.503410

CYBERCHICKS AND NETGRRLS: FEMALE NET CULTURE

Birgit Richard

Styles analyzed in this encyclopedia under "Girl Culture," are those that have existed over the last two decades. These female youth cultures are all equally present in the World Wide Web. These Web sites of youth cultures deal with the main topics of the scene and, for the first time, allow us to take a look into the youth cultures' "scientific" activities of collecting and organizing outside their visual appearance on the street. Existing infrastructures of "real life" are enhanced and expanded by virtual means. The scenes offer archives, collections, images, sounds, stories, concert reviews, and online magazines. The history of the style is reconstructed, its icons and symbols are reappraised and recycled. New means of communication such as chats, forums, and newsgroups, dealing with the respective important topics of the youth culture, supplement the range.

The techno and house scene's predominant feature is the presence and relevance of events, while the gothic and punk sites focus on the history of the style, whose graphical presentation is quite different. The Internet offers older styles the opportunity to vividly demonstrate their style in its historical dimensions to later generations as well, thereby revitalizing it and, by making it public, call it back to mind.

The innovative forms developing on the Internet are only partially linked to real youth cultures. An imaginary sphere is constituted, which functions in an entirely different way than street-spheres. On the Net, the youth cultures are not represented as street styles, and street credibility is quite unnecessary. Apart from the fact that punk became ossified at a certain stage, only a few girls can "live" it in reality. Here, the Web might make up for that lacking chance. Strangers to the "streetstyle," who only want to listen to music at home, also get the opportunity to exchange information, a particular advantage for women who like punk music, but do not want to wear the outfit or live that life in public.

Owing to the construction of the style, the gothic girls are more isolated than other youth cultures. The blacks, in the definable reality, are no "street style" that stresses public presentation and confrontation. Thus, the Net offers outstanding opportunities to present their own stylistic concepts and images. For the community of the lonely and shy, the Internet is the ideal means of communication. It allows for contact and exchange, but lets the participants remains physically detached. The characterization of the techno and house scene and their female members on the Net is difficult.

There are quite a lot of sites offering additional information on parties, images, flyers, or sounds. In contrast to other youth cultures this is a pure dance floor movement, which means that members have to experience the parties and listen to the music there themselves: the girlie is obliged to dance. The abstract participation on the screen via webcams—the magazine *Prinz*, for example, in March 1999 offered insight into three parties in Hamburg—cannot convey the scene's actual way of life. The music is produced for the context of the party and requires the individual's physical presence. It is not suitable for silent participation at home.

Therefore, the Internet is no indication for a detachment from or a transfer of "street styles." The street cannot be replaced by virtual spheres. Despite the urban metaphors, it is a sphere organized in a completely different way, requiring different competences. The virtual spheres on the Internet show a de-localized pattern, which structurally supports forming autonomous cultures on the Net: "girls become gypsies in inner space, rather than exiles on Main Street."

When girl cultures use the Internet, they, as usually, operate from their private spheres. This private place/sphere is the most important sphere from which girls have always stepped into virtual cultures. The Internet takes up familiar, imaginary spheres of communication, constituted, for example, by the telephone. Sadie Plant asserts that the Net has female structures per se and offers opportunities especially for the realization of projects by women. There is the "equal opportunity" to define female territories in this virtual sphere. The Net, as a structural basic requirement of the medium, offers autonomous access, the unregulated creation of information, its dissemination and communication by e-mail, chats, forums, and newsgroups. On the Net, girls appreciate the instant dissemination of information and the possibility of an "instant response."

Female Net competence and Net credibility return to the development of the competence to use the structures offered by the media, to present offers and click away annoying offers by the male Net community. Women also appreciate the self-chosen invisibility on the Internet, which, on the one hand, offers advantages for interaction in the medium. An undesired visual contact, a voyeuristic scrutiny is impossible.

There is, on the other hand, an unwelcome side to invisibility on the Internet. The image of femininity is explicitly defined sexually. This surrogate-world of images, superimposed on other worlds of images, carries male connotations. Men not only occupy the street, they also occupy virtual spheres. They were able to occupy large parts of virtual spheres and to keep women away by pornographic writings and pictures.

However, women are not deterred. New forms of communication and organization have developed: netchicks, netgrrls, cybergrrls, and so on. This indicates that the structures of classic youth cultures—with the exception of sites purely for fans of music—are left behind. The Internet can promote the development from female punks to riot grrls, from gothic woman to cyberwitch and from techno-girlie to netgirlie, though not in a direct genealogy, but by cross-references, "links."

Female sites have the distinctive feature that most networks explicitly female call themselves girls or girlie. This implies a preadolescent, female, rebellious freshness. However, queries on the Internet using these terms in search engines make the whole extent of male definition of the contents, though not the structures of the medium, visible: a query results in 70 percent sexually explicit sites (using www.hotbot.com), followed by 20 percent girlie magazines (meaning simply magazines for girls, not pornography), and only 10 percent of the sites found use the term in its emancipatory meaning.

This clearly shows the danger of playing around with these stereotypes and clichés. Furthermore, it demonstrates that this form of "drag" on the Internet as a medium is highly ambiguous, since here the process of gender-switching is not a visual one, but is carried out via the linguistic, imaginary level of arbitrary determination of gender. On the Internet, age and gender can be freely chosen. There, the term "girlie" means "fresh" goods in a business of Lolita- and teen-sex pictures.

NETPUNKS

When we consider punk Web sites on the Internet, we must ask whether the style is brought up-to-date here or visually remains stuck in its beginning stage. As it seems, the common motifs of punk are repeated.

The Web sites bear witness to an existing, lively scene, predominantly in the United States of America. This is also demonstrated by screen shots from a new punk film (*SLC Punk*). The World Wide Punk Directory provides information on the scene, its history and contemporary manifestation (http://www.worldwidepunk.com). The Web represents, as it does with other styles, an immaterial archive and a storage room for the most important icons and protagonists of the scene.

The commercial infrastructure is expanded. It is especially the small home-business sites (e.g. for the sale of records or T-shirts of the scene) for which the Web extends the range. New bands get new opportunities. They can make their songs available to a worldwide audience, without having to send out a number of demo tapes. For the development of the fanzine culture the Web is the ideal and least expensive medium of distribution. In the 1990s, the new structures in the media change the original style of fanzines. The blackmail-letter style, the chaotic collage, is not suitable for being produced on computers. To compensate for that, fonts reminiscent of handwriting are used fairly often. The so-called e-zines (electronic magazines) of the punks, however, still prefer the raw and unfinished, counteracting the smooth perfection of other Web sites. The culture of personal magazines is thus transferred from a print medium to an electronic one. An e-zine produces a mixture of global leadership and regional personal authorship. What is lost is the "face-to-face" contact of selling fanzines on concerts, formerly what the makers of fanzines wanted. On the other hand, they can now reach out to a worldwide punk community.

Concerning the inclusion of women, the Web sites are rather an expression of nostalgia: for example, on sites that reconstruct the history of female punk bands in the 1970s. They bear witness to a time when women participated in rock business, which we will not see again in the near future. In addition, on the sites dealing with riot grrl culture punk presents itself as the motor and primer for the riot grrls, when it comes to music. The latter for the first time also use the Internet for their purposes on a grander scale. There is a link between riot grrl and punk as regards technology and content.

BLACK NETWORLD: FEMALE GOTH CULTURE

The Internet as a new medium of communication through international links selectively does away with the individual isolation. The existing "black nets," which were launched on festivals and by fanzines, are expanded. The Web offers the opportunity to communicate directly and exchange information with like-minded people (e.g., information on concerts and records, gothic clubs and scene-boutiques, films, comics, books, poems and online-games), which is independent of physical proximity. The blacks often offer special, self-tailored clothes of the typical black aesthetics, such as at http://www.inthenik.usss.net.au/fgowo_htm (Fashion Item-Gothic Woman).

The decisive structural feature for gothics is the "link," the link to other gothic-sites (e.g., Death Homepage, 1995; The Darkening of the Light, The Dark Side, all September 1996), which guarantees that a permanent linking-up with other "blacks" all over the world can be sustained (http://our-world.compuserve.com/homepages/arleod/arlmusic.htm;1999). The gothics are a retrospective youth culture. The whole style is a complex, historically orientated form of coming to terms with melancholy and depression, mentally combining individual and collective death. The gothics have extreme and direct ways of dealing with death, which is unsettling for the rest of society. This is owing to the partial release and the removal of taboos of notions and images of death. They construct niches in various media, where the seemingly archaic, atavistic symbols and images can be circulated (e.g. picture galleries on the Web). The myths of the scene are repeated here. The desire for an ever-present encyclopedia or a genealogy of the images of the style can be realized here in an adequate fashion. The most important function of the gothic homepages on the Internet is therefore, besides the online communication, the collection and exchange of images and symbols of death. Repetition and the creation of variants on a basic repertory of images (e.g., gothic image database, gothic/images/index) turn the Net into the virtual archive of the style.

It is the keeper of the stories (e.g., about the gool, ghoul, the gravedigger) and the immaterial image-representations of the out-of-the-ordinary symbolism of the style mentioned above, so that they are constantly at the disposal of the internal autopoesis of the style.

CONCLUSION

After having considered the real scenes of youth cultures and their counterparts on the Net, we have pursued the question of whether the Internet is an extension of an existing exchange via the media or, based on the specific structures of forms of communication on the Net, if there are new manifestations of integration, which might put new niches for an autonomous self-organization at the disposal of female members of youth cultures. In conclusion, a first approach for a hypothesis was developed, which states that on the Internet, new immaterial female images of style are formed, which are independent of material manifestations like fashion and only exist in immaterial spheres.

Jammer Girl and the World Wide Web

Debra Merskin

Adolescence is an especially volatile time for girls not only because their bodies are changing but also, simultaneously, the culture forces girls to choose between one of two very different identities—good girl or bad girl. In recent years, two factors have helped make a third identity possible, one less tied to moral conformity and more to empowering young women: jammer girl. The rise of jammer girl is linked to and springs from the Internet and third wave feminism. Both of these factors are discussed in this essay.

Although boys also go through physiological changes, girls' challenges are unique. Physical development, such as widening hips, developing breasts, and emerging curves, are often inconsistent with mass media–generated and sustained images of ideal female beauty and behavior associated with being a good girl. Psychologically, long-term exposure to stereotypical role portrayals of girls (as eventual women) in the media may encourage internalization of the associated values and ideals associated with ideal female beauty.

For many girls, identity is shaped by the images they see on television, in movies, and in magazines, and by what they hear in music and see in videos. Already intensely self-conscious, girls are vulnerable targets for messages that provide solutions to personal conflict and physical challenges through the purchase of the right clothes, cosmetics, hair and body ornaments, and other beauty products.

Although physical appearance is a key component of self-esteem for girls (and mediated by peer approval), other factors contribute to a healthy (or unhealthy) sense of self. For example, feelings of competence are tied to how much or how little parents and teachers respect the opinions of girls. Outcomes related to shaky self-image include dropping out of school and the associated stresses of dating violence, sexual assault, and pregnancy. Depression is another concern as the rate of depression and suicide is higher among girls than among boys.

Through a combination of these factors, girls often find themselves labeled as either" "good" or "bad." If a girl is thought of as "good" she has the blessings of the entire culture because she has learned to meet the criteria of acceptability for what is considered to be "feminine." A good girl learns to shop, particularly for brand-name products, and to spend time and money on her appearance. The media help in the training process, teaching a girl how to be good, pretty, quiet, compliant, and orderly. Meeting these nebulous goals requires intense self-scrutiny and surveillance of other girls to maintain the role of pretty and popular as a position of power. Maintenance of good girl status often pits girls against one another.

Conversely, the stereotypical bad girl wears too much or the wrong kind of makeup, too little or the wrong kind of clothing, rejects authority, is angry, aggressive, loud, and uses bad language. So-called "bad girls" are often more ashamed than they are angry about not fitting in, feeling popular, or, ultimately, not feeling respected. If not in life at least in the mass media, the division between "good" and "bad" is increasingly blurred, and few healthy compromises are presented. Contradictions are abundant in role models presented in popular culture. For example, is Britney pure and wholesome or lusty and loose? According to Lyn Mikel Brown, based on hundreds of interviews, a common theme runs through the stories of girls. "It's a story about containment and dismissal that gets acted out by girls on each other because this is the safest and easiest outlet for girls' outrage and frustration. Simply put, girls' treatment of other girls is too often a reflection of and a reaction to the way society sees and treats them."

Are there only two alternatives available to girls? To be good or to be bad? Not any longer. Enter jammer girl. A jammer girl is defined as a pre-adolescent or adolescent girl whose identity is not based on physical appearance and passivity, but on health and social activism. Her third wave feminist views about beauty, diversity, and empowerment are articulated on and often motivated by the Internet. She rejects, in healthy ways, the confines of good versus bad girl femininity. Jammer girls know that the good girl/bad girl dichotomy is false because "the world doesn't work that way; people are never so simple." Girls can be each other's best friends who watch (as well as stab) each other's backs. The goal is nurturing the first reality while working to neutralize the second.

Most girls are initiated early into American cultural values based on gender, sexuality, physical appearance, and consumerism but later on, some girls reject them. These jammer girls choose, in healthy ways, to reject the confines of good versus bad girl femininity. They speak out and want to be taken seriously, even if they are sometimes ostracized as "weird" or "unusual" or ignored because they voice often powerful opinions. These teen girls are not taken in by advertising messages that state self-worth, value, popularity, and agency come from conforming by buying the right products. Jammer girls seek choice, change, place, and media that celebrate the individual, physical, *and* intellectual qualities of girl-ness, and speak out about the damage done to girls by the steady stream of commercial messages.

Over the past decade, the rise of jammer girl coincides with and has been facilitated by two changes, one sociological and one technological. Sociologically, jammer girl identity is consistent with the rise of third wave feminism, defined as a response by young women to media generated perceptions of feminism and as a movement for global social justice to combat inequities based on age, sexual orientation, economics, education, race and ethnicity.

Technologically, the ascension of jammer girl coincides with girls' access to and increased usage of the Internet. Riot grrls, paper zines, and bands such as Bikini Kill and Bratmobile preceded the Internet, but the compulsion to create them was, and remains, the same. Just as riot grrls did not shy away from difficult issues and painful topics, jammer girls answer a similar call to action. Riot and other girl/gurl/grrrls are examples of the independent, assertive, and empowering beliefs of many young women entering previously male-dominated fields are clear they have every right to be there.

Unlike teen girl magazines that continue to emphasize beauty, consumerism, and passive interaction with the medium, the Internet allows girls to interact, interpret, and negotiate their worlds. Web sites have a narrower focus compared with the broader view of other media. The Internet facilitates intimate, transactional, informational relationships for young women, particularly in their search for knowledge about personal topics. Girls' use of the Internet affords ways of negotiating social relationships that are personalized, self-directed, and self-paced. The accessibility and privacy of Web-based information offers personal and private space in which to explore questions about bodies and minds. The Internet facilitates a social life of shared common joys as well as trials and tribulations. It also provides a mechanism with which to maintain friendships while avoiding face-to-face contact. The Net is also a place where girls can enjoy a sense of freedom, control, privacy, and fun. The World Wide Web provides an avenue for girls to speak out about their rejection of mainstream views of who a girl can become.

Whereas feminism of the 1960s to 1980s (second wave) forged the way for other active feminist groups to extend their reach and claim virtual, electronic space, third wave feminism has refined and broadened the reach of feminism going beyond white or middle class feminism. Just as girl zines were often designed to resist or oppose representations of gender, sexuality, class, race, and age found in mainstream culture, today, several Internet sites openly critique and criticize dominant ways of thinking about female adolescence reproduced in mainstream teen girl magazines, particularly the advertising.

Most Web sites provide Net-savvy teens with a heavy dose of popular culture (fan sites, fashion, and advice), there has been an increase in the number of sites promoting 'culture jamming' as a viable and effective form of social activism. Lampooning, critiquing, and parodying mainstream media representations are forms of culture jamming. The Web makes the space for activism. Simultaneously, *Adbusters,* the magazine and the Web site (http://adbusters.org/home), is best known for spoof ads that aim to challenge corporate images through satire and social marketing campaigns such as "Buy Nothing Day" and "TV Turnoff Week." The intent is to turn the way we look at media "on its head" by actively taking an advertisement and/or brand and revealing inconsistencies and, in some cases, hypocrisy. The rise of culture jamming-focused Web sites, increased numbers of users in general and girls in particular, and more sites devoted to and created by girls, extends the hands-on aspects of girl culture activism. The sister concepts of subvertising and culture jamming are strategies embraced by jammer girl activism and illustrated on Web sites such as AdiosBarbie.com, About-Face.org.

Briefly, AdiosBarbie.com encourages jammer girl activism through the use of humor interactivity, with a focus on body image, as reflected on the homepage welcome:

> Welcome to AdiosBarbie.com, a body image site for every body. No matter what your size or background, we hope to inspire you to love your body through thick and thin!

A popular, interactive component of the site is the "Feed the model" game where the user, equipped with sixteen food items (apples to apple pie) each of a different weight, tries to make the model eat by "throwing" food at her. The goal is to "Save the starving fashion model!" by having her gain at least 240 pounds by the time she hits the runway. The food items are to be tossed into the mouth of the eighty-pound emaciated ingénue. The blonde, pursed-lipped, walks back and forth across the curtained stage while audience member's cameras flash. A newspaper image, *The Daily Purge* ("Gorge on our Gossip"), appears on the screen with the headline "Brazen brawl erupts between models and agents during charity banquet!!! 'I'm starving' shrieks model!"

There are also links to a journal kept by the editors of the site such as features ("how to love your body through thick and thin" and "The color of hunger," an essay about women of color and body image). The Body Outlaw link is a clear example of how third wave feminist girls can jam at the site. Description reads:

> Outlaws, as you probably know, are people who break society's rules and live on their own terms. These "body outlaws" have chosen to call the shots and live large, making the world a comfier place for us all.

This page celebrates breaking through the media clutter by telling true stories of body struggles and successes (a story by a gymnast) and popular culture fun with a mermaid page. The Media Diet page contains a list of myths told by the media about diet, body image, and advertisements that equate products with popularity and/or sex. For example "Can conditioner improve your sex life" is a critique of Pantene ads and "Is anorexia contagious? Hollywood thinks so." The Play link takes users to the Feed the Model game and a list of stickers to link to a girl's personal Web site such as "Soul Food for your Inner Goddess. AdiosBarbie.Com Resources provide lists of readings that would be useful for study or for girls writing papers on body image related topics and links where a girl can go for help. The Barbiology link is all thinks related to Barbie . . . facts, figures (so to speak) as part of the "art and science of being Barbie." Finally, the About Us link gives contact information for the site editors and an e-mail address for comments and contributions.

Whereas AdiosBarbie.com focuses mostly on written texts, About-Face.org is a visually oriented activist site. It is a Web site resource for girls and women that provides examples of and skills needed to evaluate harmful images of girls and women in advertising (particularly in fashion advertising) that help sustain the good girl/bad girl dichotomy.

About-Face.org uses a feminist pedagogical approach to guide young women through the process of making an about-face, a reversal of standpoint, when they look at advertising and media messages. The goal, according to its founders, is to get girls "to stop, turn around, and think about what they are seeing. Conversely, we agitate for an about-face in the way advertisers portray women." The founding and on-going goal of About-Face.org is to address the dozens of glossy advertisements contained in dozens of glossy magazines, ads that emphasize what women look like instead of what they think.

The site contains several links. All about us provides the history of the site; Gallery of Offenders lists advertisers along with their ads and describes why these images are problematic. Gallery of Winners is the place to see advertisements that positively portray girls and women. The "Your Voice, ""Your Letters," "Visitor Feedback," and "Your Forum" ("Visitor

Picks," a fourth link, was not operational, but is a site for submission of images) encourage girls to submit their ideas and their art work as a way of encouraging activism. Activism in the form of protests, letter writing, and boycotting are all described at the "Making Changes" link. For example, a success story is told when individuals and a school group wrote to the parent company of Fetish perfume to complain about the violent sexist image used in their advertising (a girl with a black eye and the headline "when no means yes." The ad was pulled and the letter from the company describing this is also posted. Facts, links, articles, and other information are available at the "Resources" link and "Contact Us" is the place to go to e-mail or write About-Face.org.

Web sites such as AdiosBarbie.com, About-Face.org, GirlsInc.org, and Girlscando.com provide places and spaces for jammer girls to be heard by providing information and encouraging the submission of original art and essays that give voice to the concerns and ideas of young women.

Resources

Books

Brown, L. M. (1991). *Girlfighting: Betrayal and rejection among girls.* New York: New York University Press.

Driscoll, C. (2002). *Girls: Feminine adolescence in popular culture and cultural theory.* New York: Columbia University Press.

Kilbourne, J. (1999). *Can't buy my love: How advertising changes the way we think and feel.* New York: Simon & Schuster.

Merskin, D. (in press). Making an about-face: Jammer girls and the World Wide Web. In S. Mazzarella (Ed.). *Girl Wide Web: Reflections on girls and the Internet.* New York: Peter Lang Publishers.

ONLINE HIP HOP CULTURE

Jannis Androutsopoulos

In the past two decades, studies of youth culture have moved away from conceptions of class-based youth subcultures in Western societies to approaches that emphasize the diversity of youth-cultural expressions worldwide. This is coupled with a shift of focus from resistance to dominant culture and deviation from mainstream norms to lifestyle choices in a variety of ethnic groups and local communities. Based on ethnographically derived categories, current research is concerned with situated communities emerging around aesthetic preferences, hobbies and commodities such as music styles or video games. Although the globalization of cultural commodities and the subsequent homogenization tendencies in youth culture are not denied, there is a concern with the ways in which globally available resources are actively and creatively appropriated by young actors in local contexts. Youth cultures are thereby treated not as substitutes for an adult status that is not yet achieved, but as practices in their own right. These developments also affect our view of the relation between youth cultures and the media. In early studies the media were conceived of as an institution external to "authentic" youth culture, but current views recognize that media are an integral part of the formation and articulation of youth cultures. With the Internet, the articulation of youth culture and the media becomes even more dense and intricate. However, still little is known about how youth culture is constructed, reproduced, negotiated on the Web through online text and talk. Though young people's use of new media is attentively followed by both market surveys and scholarly research, their authentic online communication has largely been neglected. Analysis of text and talk is an established part of research on computer-mediated communication, but not widely noticed in studies on youth and the new media.

This entry will examine communicative practices in an online youth-cultural community. I will discuss how young fans, artists, and activists create a new discursive space in ways that extend youth-cultural uses of media. Unlike many studies of youth culture, my emphasis will be placed on online text and talk. This is due not only to my academic background in sociolinguistics, but also to the feeling that this aspect of youth culture deserves much more attention in the era of the Web. An understanding of online community requires paying attention to the texts and discourses produced by this community. Consequently, the focus of attention moves away from second-hand reconstructions to first-hand observations and analyses of online communicative activities. My exploration of the relation between youth culture and online communication will use hip hop in Germany as an area of practice, and draw on the notions of literacy and style in examining this practice as a culturally specific use of the new media in communicative action. Studies of social literacy, i.e. the culturally specific use of writing and reading, are increasingly interested in the importance of the written word in cyber culture. Style is an interdisciplinary meeting point of cultural studies, where it is a keyword since the beginning and sociolinguistics. Definitions of style in sociolinguistics and cultural studies converge in viewing style as an orchestration of symbolic resources in the construction of situated identities for particular audiences. Style work is an act of identity. It involves creating an image, which declares affiliation to an audience, a social world, using available semiotic resources. Investigating style on the Web implies a focus on subtleties of language use, though without neglecting the other semiotic resources participants have at their disposal in constructing identities.

Hip hop is a well-suited arena to pursue this question because it fore-grounds the relation between cultural globalization and local appropria-tion and the role of the media in this process. My research is concerned with local instantiations of hip hop culture in Germany, the discourse of which develops around "local" (i.e., German) events and productions, using the local language. However, these local instances are connected to a global frame of reference (i.e., U.S. hip hop), and this connection is mani-fested both in discourse and in language style. Hip hop's popularity in Ger-many, which is together with France and Italy the biggest market for rap and hip hop in Europe since the early 1990s, is reflected in the amount of computer-mediated activity by its fans and artists. These adolescents and young adults—mostly, but not exclusively, males—use the Internet as one additional means of articulating cultural affiliation and involvement, of "representing" their social context (i.e. city, neighborhood, clique, or ethnic group). Their activities, such as reading online magazines dedicated to hip hop, posting to affiliated bulletin boards, chatting with other fans or mak-ing a personal homepage, are extending offline youth culture into cyber space, though without the aim of replacing real-life engagement.

RESEARCH BACKGROUND

The research this entry is based on used a combination of linguistic anal-ysis and ethnography of online practices. Ethnographic observation makes it possible to describe the structures and communicative processes of social formations such as mailing lists, newsgroups, or e-chat groups from the participants' point of view. Genre analysis generally aims at reconstructing pre-patterned ways of solving communicative problems. For instance, the genre of a personal homepage involves typical ways of solving the problem of self-presentation in cyberspace. Following the framework outlined by Günthner & Knoblauch, I analyze genres as configurations of "internal" (i.e., linguistic, but also typographic and non-verbal means), "external" (social and institutional embedding), and "situative" (referring to commu-nicative processes) features. The other linguistic method used in the project, that is, variation analysis, has a much narrower scope. It examines the relative frequency of particular linguistic features across genres as well as across speakers with different social characteristics. Empirical issues include the relation between oral and written features according to genre, or the amount of English used by German youth on various discussion boards.

The research process unfolded in three steps, framing linguistic analysis with two layers of online ethnography. The starting point was the observa-tion of CMC activities related to hip hop in Germany. A sum of nineteen interviews were conducted, of which ten were face-to-face and nine by phone or e-mail. The examples used in this essay will draw on fieldwork with the following individuals: "Anita," a fifteen-year-old female high school student who maintained a personal homepage; "Luke," a texter and graphic designer in his early twenties who was involved in various online activities; and "Alex," in his mid twenties, owner and Webmaster of a Web portal dedicated to rap music. The constant moving to and fro between field observation, interview data, and linguistic text offers insights that could not be gained by a purely ethnographic or purely linguistic approach, such as the reconstruction of the online field, participant's literacy practices, and their awareness of language style in the field.

HIP HOP ON THE WEB: DELIMITING THE FIELD

Although my research pays close attention to the details of signifying practices in Web site texts and online interactions, it also aims at reconstructing the "big picture," that is, the structure of the online field in which these practices are embedded. The notion of field originates in the work of Pierre Bourdieu, and was further developed by Fairclough. A field is a structured space of positions for the articulation of a social discourse, in which the value of individual participants depends on their location vis-à-vis other participants. In analogy, *an online field may be defined as a set of Web sites and interaction platforms, which are socially, discursively, and hypertextually interconnected*. The components of a field are linked to each other in a network pattern, whereby some nodes may be more central to the network than others. Online fields are relatively "autonomous" public spheres dedicated to the discourse of a specific social world. The self-categorization of individual sites and hypertextual connections between sites are important criteria in the reconstruction of an online field. On the social level, the Web sites and interaction platforms that make up a field are produced and consumed by individuals and groups with similar lifestyles. As for German hip hop, the mzee.com link project listed 480 German-speaking sites in several categories in spring 2002, and 831 sites in summer 2003. The figures of another large directory, webbeatz.de, were 263 and 458, respectively. The fact that there is significant overlapping between these directories suggests that they include a significant part of the field components. In the study of online fields, the tension between *community* and *competition* may be expected to play an important part. Online activities in the field generally aim at generating and enhancing community. However, individual practices and their outcomes, e.g. homepages, also stand in competition to one another. For instance, guest-book entries are sometimes quite critical with regard to the media style of the host. Style is created in the tension between converging towards the community's norms, and trying to establish individuality and originality in a market of competing productions.

Just as in many other countries around the world, hip hop in Germany has gone online. The accessibility and interactivity of the Web offers a platform for self-expression and interaction among fans.

As one participant puts it:

The Internet is just another medium which hip hop appears in. Just as printed media, radio and tv. I don't see any difference in that; there exists both bad and good Web sites. However, the Internet goes a step further [than other media], here on this board, for instance, I can talk with people from all over Germany.

Web portals, online magazines, and bulletin boards (the latter usually called forums in German) are core components of the online field, because they attract the most visitors and are most widely known. Web portals are the most professional and resource-demanding type of Web site in the field, because they functionally integrate various types of service: They provide infrastructure for boards and chats, and some also provide free Web space for members' homepages. Moreover, they offer link directories of smaller Web sites and personal homepages, thus building a starting point to explore the field. They also provide some edited content (e.g. interviews reviews and reports) and often an online shop. Few portals offer this whole range of services, rap.de and hiphop.de being the ones mentioned by several interview partners. Online magazines range from amateur projects with a regionally restricted scope up to online versions of established printed magazines. Typically run by young adults who have been socialized in hip hop, they combine at their best traditional media content with community contributions and multimedia features, such as downloadable songs, streaming audio and video interviews. While the mzee.com link directory features more than 60 entries, the actual number of frequently updated hip hop e-zines (portals not included) is considerably smaller. More than a dozen widely-known boards and chats are exclusively dedicated to hip hop in Germany. Six boards I have observed in more detail—the boards hosted by the two leading portals, rap.de and hiphop.de, as well as mzee.com, rapz.de, webbeatz.de, and deflok.de—had a sum of over 65,000 registered users in the summer of 2003 (though not all of them are active). Though this number is far surpassed by other Web services, it has more than doubled in a period of fifteen months. According to Webmasters' estimations, users range from fourteen to twenty-nine years of age, represent all types of schooling, and are mostly males, and Webmasters themselves are typically in their twenties. The largest category is the personal homepage, a Web site maintained by a private person. Judging from link collections, several hundreds of personal homepages are dedicated to hip hop in Germany. The overall purposes of their authors are to present themselves as active members of the culture, to represent the local hip hop scenes they come from, and to make connections with like-minded individuals. Most of these are artist pages by newcomer artists, some are dedicated to activities and activists from a town or region. What is culturally specific are samples of the producers' cultural productions, such as songs, lyrics, graffiti, breakdance videos, and so forth.

This note provides a base from which to assess the relation of the Web to other types of alternative media. The Web extends the grass roots use of media—for example, fanzines or pirate radio—for the creation of alternative public spheres. What is specific about the Web in youth-cultural activism can be summarized based on Gauntlett's categories. First, the Web dramatically extends the opportunity of young fans, activists and newcomers to present and express themselves. Amateur productions are much more readily available to a large public than was the case with, for example, fanzines. For newcomer bands in Germany, for instance, having a homepage is the norm rather than the exception. Moreover, the Web "brings people together, building communities." The hip hop boards and chats create a public space for fan interaction. In addition, the separation of the edited matter and fan interaction is transgressed on web portals, and new, hybrid connections between journalism and fandom are formed.

LITERACY PRACTICES IN ONLINE HIP HOP

Literacy practice, defined as a culture-specific way of utilizing written language, is a core concept in the social theory of literacy proposed by Barton and Hamilton. Literacy practices in online hip hop are multimodal and vernacular. *Multimodal literacy* refers to the growing interdependence of visual and verbal elements in the composition of media texts. Web pages are multimodal texts par excellence, i.e. visually structured compositions of text blocks and lists, graphics, images, etc. *Vernacular literacy* practices are not regulated by the formal rules and procedures of dominant social institutions, but have their origins in everyday life. They are in fact hybrid practices that draw on a range of models from different domains. Both aspects meet in the production of a personal homepage. It involves a range of activities, which are less "writing" than "composing," such as planning the overall structure, choosing a layout, collecting texts, images, and links. Fifteen-year-old Anita, for instance, draws on various genres in the construction of her homepage, combining models from private writing and mass media discourse. Some of her texts are lists with a descriptive purpose (e.g., personal facts, links); others are text blocks in a narrative mode (e.g., personal welcome text). She also features a photo album, song texts, a guest book, and a forum. Anita spends much of time updating the page's design and in particular her logo, which she wants to be as individual as possible.

Naming is a practice of great importance, including the site's name and author's nickname(s). Although there is some research on chat nicknames, less is known about other naming patterns. On the following page are some personal nicknames of Web site authors (1) as well as names and slogans of hip hop magazines and portals (2).

Many online nicknames in my data attempt to combine the original first or nickname with some sort of reference to hip hop. This is achieved

(1)

| – | Waldemar/Walde/Wall-Dee | Florian/Flo/flow |
| – | Chris/ChrizzFX | Lion/Lea-wun/Lea One |

(2)

–	blackwax.de: Die Hiphop Seite	germanhiphop.de: The B@sement
–	wicked.de: hip hop magazin	hiphopsite.de: the #1 in hiphop culture beatz & information
–	hiphopstation.ch: HipHopCommunity	mzee.com: HIP HOP NETWORK
–	rap.de: ROCKIN' YOU SINCE 1998	rapz.de: Yo REAL HipHop Community

through intertextual references and allusions, puns, and other modifications. For instance, Florian substitutes his usual nickname, "Flo," through "Flow," a core term in hip hop art. Waldemar turns his usual nickname, "Walde," into "Wall-Dee," which follows a usual naming pattern of U.S. rap artists (cf. Ice-T or Public Enemy's Chuck D). Several Web site names use the terms "hip hop" and "rap," others prefer hip hop slang (wicked, yo, real), metonyms for music (blackwax), as well as the notion of a community of producers and recipients, which is conveyed by items such as community and network. We also find glimpses of colloquial English (cf. beatz, rockin'). In both areas, the dominance of English as a naming resource is striking. Although these authors address a German-speaking audience, and the language of copy text is German, English is preferred for emblematic purposes. Anita's statement, "German in the title sounds boring," is something obviously many youngsters in the hip hop field agree with.

In order to attract visitors, homepage producers have to promote their site. While Web portals and online magazines use professional tools such as ad banners, authors of personal homepages develop do-it-yourself procedures. Some informants create their own banners and offer them to visitors who'd like to link to their site. Others register their site in link collections, and write advertisement entries in big boards and guest-books. This is a popular technique, because it promises that the homepage address will be visible for every visitor on the board. The numerous boards provide ample space for online discussions on all relevant issues of hip hop, such as new releases, artists and events, regional connections and so on. These discussions are quite illuminating with respect to the way hip hop relates to broader discourses of youth in relation to gender, ethnicity, politics and social institutions. A steady preoccupation is the borderline between "true" hip hop and its commercial adaptations (cf. next section). However, the original purpose of these boards inevitably gets at odds with the attitude of teenage rebellion. The reduced responsibility of authorship and the widespread anonymity in boards and chats makes them a space of liminality. In conditions of liminality, participants cross certain borders of social behavior and experiment with social identities in ways that are clearly outside their normal, everyday repertoire. In the German hip hop context, this involves appropriations of the imagery of African American hip hop, including the "gangsta" type of tough guy. However, anonymity also invites some adolescent on-liners to extensive "flaming" and insulting. Judging from interviews and postings, the figure of an adolescent joining a board just to cause disruption with nonsense or aggressive postings is a quite familiar one. The reality of teenage appropriation of the Web often does not meet expectations of what online discussions should look like.

Boards and chats differ in terms of typical communicative actions and interactional modality. Whereas boards are (at least expected to be) issue-centered, e-chats and guest-books provide more space for expressive, interpersonal communication. The homepage of Anita, for instance, offers visitors both a forum and a guest-book. However, the youngsters avoid the forum, which they judge suitable for serious matters and longer texts. The guest-book on the other hand, is a meeting point for the local clique and, in a sense, an extension of expressive school yard interaction. The opposite of the expressive freedom that is characteristic for chats and boards is the literacy practice of writing content for a Webzine or portal. Portals are run by young adults, but most of their edited content, for example, reports, reviews and interviews, is contributed by young freelance writers (in their late teens or early twenties). Interviews with portal administrators reveal a clear awareness of the language style they consider appropriate for freelancers. What is expected from them is not the oral, vernacular style prevailing in boards and chats, but rather "*gutes schriftdeutsch,*" as a Webmaster put it, that is, solid skills in standard German.

These literacy practices are not mutually exclusive, as illustrated by the example of Luke, a Web activist in his early twenties. Luke is a member of de.alt.music.hiphop, the oldest and most important newsgroup on hip hop in Germany, operating since 1997. He is also a member of other boards, such as mzee.com. Luke is member of a rap band and in charge of the band's homepage. The band also maintains a smaller homepage on a hip hop promotion platform. Finally, Luke is also a freelance writer for hiphop.de, one of the largest Web portals. This range of practices goes hand-in-hand with the differentiation of writing styles according to activity. Although this is indeed an exceptional richness of online literacy practices, smaller scale combinations, such as making a personal homepage and participating in a board or chat, seem to be quite usual among my interview partners.

SEPARATING 'TRUE' FROM 'FAKE' HIP HOP IN BOARD DISCUSSIONS

Hip Hop in Germany became increasingly popular in the late 1990s. Fanzine authors and board members, regarding themselves as representants of "true" hip hop, frequently comment on the way hip hop is constructed for a mainstream audience. In doing so, they reinforce the borderline between "true" and "fake" culture. The excerpt presented here is part of such a discussion, which was sparkled by "Hip Hop Schule," a feature by *Bravo* magazine.

These six entries, which appeared some three hours after discussion started, display a number of strategies for dealing with "fake" representations of hip hop. Quite expectedly, discussants are straightforwardly devaluing, or dissing, the feature's authors. The author of (1) demands for them a death penalty, while the author of (3) calls them "Toys," a term from graffiti talk for inexperienced beginners. Moreover, the author of (1) devalues the *Bravo* feature through irony. He pastes in excerpts from the *Bravo* feature and parenthetically comments them with exaggerated statements of agreement, smileys, discourse interjections, and simulated shouting. This juxtaposition of original voice and ironic commentary is rhetorically much more elegant and powerful than a simple reporting of the feature's claims. While Andi criticizes the *Bravo* feature in terms of its content, Dan (5) comments on the feature's language style (try to sound hip hop wise / *ein auf HipHop tun*), using as an example the utterance "Ferris had to hang around in jail," which refers to a German rapper's trouble with the police. This use of *abhängen* (hanging out), a popular verb in German youth language, which refers to leisure activities and usually collocates with items such as "café," "record shop," and "at home," is pragmatically odd. What is presumably an attempt by the *Bravo* editors to a playful use of slang is rejected here by insider recipients. Dan's reaction is, again, irony, that is, he tops the utterance with an even odder formulation: Ferris was chilling in jail.

(3) Excerpt from the thread "Hip Hop Schuleby Bravo" on mzee.com (URL: http://www.mzee.com/forum/showthread.php?threadid= 26223; numbering added for reference purposes)

[1]*Posted by Andi on DATE at 21:59:*

God is a DJ! His name is DJ Tomekk! Every MC wants to make a track with him (sure, they're fighting for it) D like DJ: Indispensable in Hip Hop! The turntable turners are in charge for fat beats and cool samples. The absolute king among the turntable specialists: DJ Tomekk (*ahem* *ahem*)! This Berlin guy has the coolest connections (AAAHHHHH-HHH). Even USA rap stars like GZA, KRS-One or Grandmaster Flash are delighted to rap for DJ Tomekk. Other great DJ's: Plattenpapzt, DJ Friction, DJ Mad, DJ Emilio.

What a pity the death sentence is forbidden nowadays, these bloody editors really deserve it for this statement, don't they **** how stupid are they really!!??!

OOOPPPSSS right now I see someone else has posted this one before, well whatever...

[2]*Posted by Ben on DATE at 22:09:*

These Bravo editors certainly had fun writing this feature

[3]*Posted by Carl on DATE at 22:16:*

I think my d***'s exploding this can't be serious these toys from bravo.de really think they could define hip hop or sum it up in such a bloody alphabetic a–z feature

[4]*Posted by Andi on DATE at 22:31:*

I think my d***'s exploding

I think my d***'s exploding

This surely is the best one-liner I've ever heard

I think I'll say that tomorrow to my teachers if they stress me out

"Ms B. I think my d***'s exploding" *lol*

[5]*Posted by Dan on DATE at 22:33:*

They even try to sound hip hop wise! "Ferris had to hang around in jail" Why don't they just write "Ferris was chilling in jail"

[6]*Posted by Emil on DATE at 22:38:*

I knew this topic would make it to the board's nr 1 topic in a few hours...

In an excurse from the main topic, posting (4) blends in a scenario of rebellious behavior at school. Andi picks up Carl's opening one-liner, "I think my d***'s exploding," transfers it in the school setting, and fictionally addresses it to the teacher. This staging of teenage rebellion is probably a source of entertainment for the thread readers, and brings in an association of hip hop with images of school rebellion. Finally, note how posting (2) attempts at disentangling the feature's editors from the media institution they write for. While Andi and Carl discredit the editors ("stupid," "toys"), Ben implies they might be conscious of the fact that their representation is a gross simplification from an insider point of view. He suggests that these editors may be forced to write this way in order to cater for an inexperienced mass public. He implicitly redirects the participant's critique towards the institution as opposed to the individual actors.

STYLE RESOURCES

While language is the main symbolic resource participants work with in online communication, other types of resources may be relevant as well, depending on the activity at hand. For homepage producers, software can be a powerful style resource, which allows them to demonstrate their technical skills in coding and Web design. However, symbolic capital is gained not only through mastering technology but also through a conscious avoidance of it. A simple Web site, combined with appropriate discourse, is perfectly capable of expressing a respectful stance. What counts in the hip hop field is not technical excellence by any means, but the individuality of the end result. For instance, hand coding is highly valued, while the use of commercially available page templates is devalued. Scripts (e.g. PHP, java, or flash) are necessary for the construction and maintenance of larger Web sites with a community base (portals, forums, magazines), but less widespread in homepages, where their use marks out individuals with some formal training or with ambitions to an ITC career.

The multimodality of Web literacies implies that participants may draw on a variety of nonverbal material with cultural significance. For instance, many Web sites feature a pictorial representation of the "four elements" of hip hop, which is best described as a *visual synecdoche*: A spray can represents graffiti, sneakers stand for dancing, a microphone for rapping and a turntable for DJ-ing/scratching. This basic relation occurs in numerous individual variations in terms of colour and iconography. Cultural symbolism also extends to the use of colour and typography. The Webmaster of the hiphop.de portal justified his use of colour by referring to "the colour of hip hop." Another widespread colour symbolism is the relation of a black background to an "underground" orientation. In the interviews, authors of Web sites with a black background refer to a white background as typical for "a medical forum" (*Ärzteforum*) or "a site that sells washing machines", thus connecting the choice of white background to institutions and the mainstream commercial arena. In typography, there is a widespread use of graffiti/tag style for emblematic purposes (i.e., Web site logo, ad banners, navigation bars). These items are expected to be as individual as possible, so that digitalization of hand-made tags is preferred over the use of custom computer fonts.

Out of the variety of linguistic resources, three categories seem more relevant in this context: First, orientation to spoken discourse, involving patterns of informal spoken language on various levels of linguistic analysis (syntax, lexicon, discourse markers, spelling). Second, "hip hop slang": vocabulary, idioms, and formulaic speech, which are referentially or intertextually related to hip hop culture. These resources are almost completely of English origin. They include both major class items (i.e., nouns, verbs and adjectives) with various grades of morphological integration into German, and instances of code-switching (i.e., whole utterances or turns in English). Third, spelling variation with no correspondence to phonetic features, as in "4" (for), "ph" for "f," "$" for "S." These spellings exploit the distance from the orthographic norm to attract attention (e.g., in advertising) or to contextualize an attitude towards the referent of the lexical item they operate on, or to index sub-cultural affiliations. Although these types of resources are not specific to hip hop, but have wide currency in several youth and sub-cultural fields, they also form the bottom line of a writing style that is typical for hip hop. Their co-presence in online discourse is by the following example (numbering added for reference purposes):

(4)

(a) Jo! (b) Mach beatz and cutz. (c) Bock drauf zu rappen? (d) Dann mailt mir ma. (e) Wär cool.

Gloss: (a) Yo! (b) [I] make beats and cuts. (c) [Would you] like to rap on them? (d) Just mail me. (e) [It] would be cool. (Material in square brackets is omitted in the original message.)

Features of this message that are typical for online interaction in the hip hop field include orality features in spelling (e.g., reductions *mache > mach*, *mal > ma, wäre > wär*) and in syntax (deletion of subject pronoun *ich* in (b), of verbal phrase *hast du* in (c), of pronoun *das* in (e); dialogical orientation, i.e. the entry is directed to the community; informal greeting *Jo!* from hip hop slang in (a); colloquial and non-standard expressions such as *bock drauf* (c) and *cool* (e); English items referring to music, e.g. beats, cuts, rappen in (b, c); and spelling choices such as the -z ending in *beatz* and *cutz*.

WORKING ON LANGUAGE STYLE

Far from being homogeneous, language style in the hip hop field crucially depends on the various communicative activities participants engage in. Monological and interactive genres generally differ in their orientation to literate versus oral patterns of speech. Contributions to boards, chats, and guest-books are largely unplanned and informal, and display a strong orientation to the oral mode. In contrast, many Web site texts originate in traditional media or private literacy, and their language retains features of traditional written style.

In concluding this essay, I will demonstrate the complexity of online language use on a single Web site with two examples. The first is about the use and awareness of spelling markers, the second will discuss activity-related writing styles. The arena for both examples is www.rapz.de, a board with a large community base (2050 registered members in summer 2003, 950 in spring 2002), of which 90 percent are male adolescents. The Web site also offers some edited content and an online record shop. Alex, the site's owner, is a twenty-six-year-old hip hop activist, active since 1988, based in an East German town. He views the Web site as a "100% commercial" enterprise, and maintains strong relations to the relevant segment of the music industry.

In the e-mail interview, Alex points out some linguistic features he considers typical for "hip hop slang," and provides an interpretation of their sociolinguistic function:

> The ending –er is spelt as –a. All endings with –s are spelt as –z. Some hardcore rap freaks even respell every S as Z oder double ZZ within words. This is judged as "underground" affiliation.

Both features mentioned by the Webmaster are global stereotypes for African American vernacular and hip hop slang: the substitution of -er by -a, as in "gangsta," and of -s by -z, as in "tapez." The genetic relationship of English and German favors their adaptation in the host language. The -a ending is also a phonetic spelling with respect to German, and the -z variant can be added to German nouns as well, as in *Jungz* (boys). The Webmaster also notes further variants in the use of -z, and points out their social meaning (*judged as "underground" affiliation*).

The following example, part of a discussion of a recent record release, illustrates a heavy use of both features. It includes a systematic substitution of -er endings through -a (*eina, bessa, aba*) and of -s to -z (*Lyricz, Beatz, alz*). Significantly, the author extends the distribution of -z to a German lexical item, *alz*(than).

(5) Posting on the rapz.de board, November 2001

> Um ehrlich zu sein, das Album finde ich echt dope. Afrob ist für mich sowieso eina der echt guten Texter. Sehr gute Lyricz und gute Beatz. Zwa jetzt keine Überbombe aba bessa alz andere Sachen die es zur zeit gibt, natürlich nicht so dope wie Azad aba es lohnt sich auf jeden fall mal reinzuhören.

> Gloss: To be honest, I think the album is really dope. Afrob is in my view one of the best text writers anyway. Very good lyrics and good beats. It's not the bomb, but still better than other things going on at the moment. Of course not so dope as Azad but it's worth it listening to it.

The writing practices of the site's Webmaster are more complicated. Alex is active both in the site's news center, writing news pieces, and in the community boards, participating in member discussions. He thus has a double role to play, as a journalist and as a member, and constructs this double role through appropriate shifts in his writing style, as demonstrated by the example (6) and summarized in Table (1). His news style has many features of professional news writing and follows the German spelling norms (including capitalization of nouns). However, his board style capitalizes on slang, has many typical spoken features, uses expressive punctuation, emoticons, and other CMC resources, and ignores the rule of noun capitalization. Random sampling reveals that these differences are consistent across a large number of Alex's messages. Positioning himself both as a young ITC professional and a member in a youth-cultural online community, Alex is trying to reconcile both through his different writing styles. In the interview, he positions himself on the professional side, noting that his writing style should "guarantee some quality standards for advertisers and labels," and "not shock the labels and advertisers." His board style, however, capitalizes on the kind of "hardcore slang" he attests for members' board discussions.

(10) Alex's writing styles, postings by Alex, November 2001 (translated)

News style

DJ Laz is not unknown to Miami bass freaks, for he is THE most known Bass DJ when it comes to bring Latin sound and Miami bass into fusion, and he is considered beside his colleague DJ Magic Mike to be the "King Of Bass," just as the title of his 1996 album goes. In Germany there has never been a sign of life by DJ Laz, altough he continuously released a new album every 2 years since his 1993 hit album "Journey Into Bass," but there was no distribution and only expensive import records were to be found in German bass record stores. [...]

Board style

COOL!! GREAT!! DOPE !!

When is it supposed to come out and on which label?? Universal again??

Miracle ist THE DOPE MOFUKKA, he should drop some BOUNCE Burners again and get down radically just as on the 1st record!

The spelling markers and other features of non-standard style illustrated by the previous messages (4, 5, and Alex's board style) are a popular in the field. Many German youngsters capitalize on US hip hop slang, including spelling variants, as an easy way of demonstrating group affiliation and cultural expertise. This is how Anita and her friend Tim judge *z*, *tha* and other

Table 1: *Style contrasts in the writing of the www.rapz.de Webmaster*
news styleboard stylesyntax

-      longer texts

-      longer, more complex clauses

-      shorter texts

-      fragmented, context-dependent syntax

-      more simple and elliptical clauses

-      anaphoric relations to other entries lexicon

-      music style categorizations (*Latin Sound, King of Bass*)

-      anaphoric relations to other entries lexicon

-      music style categorizations (*Latin Sound, King of Bass*)

-      fan categorizations ?(*Miami Bass Freaks*)

-      evaluative (English) slang

-      conceptually oral vocabulary

-      emoticons, representations of laughterspelling

-      noun capitalizing throughout

-      no expressive use of punctuation

-      lack of noun capitalizing

-      expressive punctuation, e.g. "*!!!*", "*???*"

-      spelling variation

formal markers of African American English: it is cool, it looks better this way, it is not used by everyone, it demarcates. In contrast to institutional orthographic norms, chats, boards, and guest-books are sites of what Mark Sebba calls "spelling rebellion." However, this strategy of identity marking is not unchallenged within the field as well as from a scholarly point of view (cf. Richardson/Lewis 2000). Some participants (e.g., Luke) reject spelling markers as nonprofessional and overused, others reject a construction of identity that relies on superficial features alone, pointing out that being a "real" member takes more than words. This challenging and diverging inter- pretation of signifying practices is a characteristic of hip hop discourse. Far from unanimously reproducing a single stance, participants continuously debate about the meaning and appropriateness of resources and techniques for creating style. The constant challenge from within makes hip hop a lively, dynamic, fast-changing culture, both off and online.

CONCLUSION

In conclusion, the main points of this essay may be summarized as follows:

(1) Computer-mediated communication demands a new look at the relation between young people, youth culture, and the new media, in which the productive appropriation of media plays a central part. We need to conceive the new media as a tool young people use in constructing youth culture.

(2) This essay proposes the concept of an online field to describe the representation of youth cultures on the Web. Field analysis includes a distinction between various types of participation and literacy practices, which can then be related to various language styles. The field notion may help us grasp large social formations in cyberspace, which frame smaller virtual networks and individual practices.

(3) Young people on the Web constantly work on their style, that is, the way they construct themselves online, using a variety of multimodal resources. Linguistic resources that are characteristic for the field as a whole: the shift to the oral mode of expression in writing, marking off the activity as a vernacular, non-institutional one; the special register of hip hop terminology, indexing the global dimension of hip hop; and spelling variation, which is a particularly popular technique for marking membership. As in real-life interaction and other kinds of media discourse, language is strategically used as a resource of self-presentation in the online field. Different online activities, as well as different stances within youth-cultural discourse, are expressed through a variety of resources, whereby face-to-face resources and specific written ones are combined in new hybrid forms.

Resources
Books
Abbott, C. (1998). Making connections: Young people and the Internet. In J. Sefton-Green (Ed.), *Digital diversions: Youth culture in the age of multimedia* (pp. 84–105). London: UCL Press.

Amid-Talai, V., & Wulff, H. (Eds.), (1995). *Youth cultures: A cross-cultural perspective*. London: Routledge.

Androutsopoulos, J. (in print). Musikszenen im Netz: Felder, Nutzer, Codes. In H. Merkens & J. Zinnecker (Eds.). *Jahrbuch Jugendforschung 3*. Opladen: Leske and Budrich.

Androutsopoulos, J., & Scholz, A. (2003). Spaghetti funk: Appropriations of hip-hop culture and rap music in Europe. *Popular Music and Society*, 26.4, 463–480.

Atton, C. (2002). *Alternative media*. London: Sage.

Barton, D., & Hamilton, M. (1998). *Local literacies. Reading and writing in one community*. London, New York: Routledge

Baym, N. K. (2000). *Tune in, log on: Soaps, fandom, and on-line community*. Thousand Oaks, CA: Sage.

Bourdieu, P. (1991). *Language and symbolic power.* Oxford: Polity Press.

Choi, I. (2002). *Their own voices: Vernacular literacies in the Lives of Young People.* Unpublished doctoral thesis, Lancaster University.

Danet, B. (2001). *Cyberpl@y. Communicating online.* Oxford: Berg.

Döring, N. (2003). *Sozialpsychologie des Internet.* Göttingen: Hogrefe.

Eckert, P., & Rickford, J. (Eds.). (2001). *Style and sociolinguistic variation.* Oxford: Blackwell.

Fairclough, N. (1995). *Media discourse.* London: Arnold.

Gauntlett, D. (Ed.). (2000). *Web.studies. Rewiring media studies for the digital age.* London: Arnold.

Hawisher, G. E., & Selfe, C. L. (Eds.). (2000). *Global literacies and the World Wide Web.* London: Routledge.

Hebdige, D. (1979). *Subculture. The meaning of style.* London: Methuen.

Hine, C. (2000). *Virtual ethnography.* London: Sage.

Karlsson, A.-M. (2002). *Skriftbruk I föröndring. En semiotisk studie av den personliga hemsidan.* Stockholm: Almqvist & Wiksell.

———. (2002). To write a page and colour a text. Concepts and practices of homepage use. In P. Coppock (Ed.). *The semiotics of writing.* Turnhout, Belgium: Brepols.

Livingstone, S. (2002). *Young people and new media.* London: Sage.

Meikle, G. (2002). *Future active: Media activism and the Internet.* London: Routledge.

Mitchell, T. (Ed.). (2001). *Global noise. Rap and hip-hop outside the USA.* Middletown, CT: Wesleyan University Press.

Pullen, K. (2000). I-love-Xena.com: Creating online fan communities. In D. Gauntlett (Ed.). *Web.studies. Rewiring media studies for the digital age* (pp. 52–61). London: Arnold.

Richard, B. (2000). Schwarze Netze statt Netzstrümpfe? Weibliche Kommunikationsräume in Jugendkulturen im Internet. In W. Marotzki, et al. (Eds.). *Zum Bildungswert des Internet* (pp. 341–362). Opladen: Leske and Budrich.

Richardson, E., & Lewis, S. (2000). "Flippin' the Script" / "Blowin' up the Spot": puttin' Hip-Hop online in (African) America and South Africa. In G. E. Hawisher & C. L. Selfe (Eds.). *Global Literacies and the World Wide Web* (pp. 251–276). New York: Routledge.

Sebba, M. (2003). Spelling rebellion. In J. Androutsopoulos & A. Georgakopoulou (Eds.). *Discourse constructions of youth identities* (pp. 151–172). Amsterdam: Benjamins.

———. (in press). Will the real impersonator please stand up? Language and identity in the Ali G websites. In B. Kettemann (Ed.). *Arbeiten aus Anglistik and Amerikanistik.* Tübingen, Germany: Gunter Narr.

Shelton, T., & Valentine, G. (1998). *Cool places. Geographies of youth cultures.* London: Routledge.

Snyder, I. (Ed.). (2002). *Silicon literacies. Communication, innovation and education in the electronic age*. London: Routledge.

Sutton, L. A. (1999). All media are created equal. Do-it-yourself identity in alternative publishing. In M. Bucholtz, A. C. Liang, & L. Sutton (Eds.). *Reinventing identities: The gendered self in discourse* (pp. 163–180). Oxford: Oxford University Press.

Thornton, S. (1995). *Club cultures. Music, media and subcultural capital*. Cambridge: Polity Press.

Articles

Günthner, S., & Knoblauch, H. (1994). Culturally patterned speaking practices—The analysis of communicative genres. *Pragmatics, 5* (1), 1–32.

Paolillo, J. (2001). Language variation on Internet Relay Chat: A social network approach. *Journal of Sociolinguistics, 5* (2), 180–213.

Web Sites

Chandler, D. (1998). Personal home pages and the construction of identities on the Web. Retrieved August 6, 2005 from http://www.aber.ac.uk/media/Documents/short/webident.html

Chandler, D., & Roberts-Young, D. (1998). The construction of identity in the personal homepages of adolescents. Retrieved August 6, 2005 from http://www.aber.ac.uk/media/Documents/short/strasbourg.html

Döring, N. (2002). Personal home pages on the Web: A review of research. *Journal of Computer-Mediated Communication, 7* (3). Retrieved August 6, 2005 from http://www.ascusc.org/jcmc/vol7/issue3/doering.html

Karlsson, A.-M. (2002). Web literacy, web literacies or just literacies on the web? Reflections from a study of personal homepages. *The Reading Matrix, 2* (2). Retrieved August 6, 2005 from http://www.reading matrix.com/articles/karlsson/index.html

Mitra, A. (1999). Characteristics of the WWW text: Tracing discursive strategies. *Journal of Computer-Mediated Communication, 5* (1). Retrieved August 6, 2005 from www.ascusc.org/jcmc/vol5/issue1/mitra.html

KINDERCULTURE AND MARKETING: FROM TOYS TO HARRY POTTER

Peter Pericles Trifonas and Effie Balomenos

Many teens love comics and superheroes.

The power of marketing for children gives new meaning to the phrase "shock and awe" since everyone who is old enough to watch the orchestrated jibes and gimmicks for getting your pound, euro, dollar, peso, or yen that we call "advertising campaigns" is fair game. Only during the last ten years have marketers realized what toy manufacturers have known for a long time: From babies to teenagers, children are important consumers. They exert tremendous influence on those who advocate for them economically—parents. Children have needs, wants, and desires that have to be fulfilled, because, let us not forget, they are people too. Just because a child cannot walk or talk yet does not mean that the child doesn't participate in the economic gravy train of consumer culture. Parents just buy things for them until they are ready to do it for themselves.

Starting from relatively humble beginnings—the simple idea that children need to be entertained—toys have become products of unimaginable power and influence. In *Homo Ludens*, the historian Johan Huizinga characterizes all of human life as a form of play. We can see the role of contests and games at work in the fields of law, economics, politics, epistemology, and the arts that define the social and ethical foundations of culture and civilization. In *kinderculture*—the culture of children—play is a type of challenge that validates existence and teaches you how to relate to rules and to others. It is not a matter of ironic political commentary or ideological exclusion. A recent toy craze has had kids around the globe downright battling each other within the walls of tabletop stadiums. The Beyblade, a spinning top by Hasbro, has had competing manufacturers scrambling to create facsimiles that might hitch a ride on the marketing bandwagon of this commercial success. The allure of the toy is the opportunity it provides to be destructive and creative, to destroy and rebuild, without hurting anyone, then to start over again. You have to put together the Beyblade from component parts and launch it with a rip cord. The parts are interchangeable between models. You battle an opponent with another spinning top and the last one left standing wins. Parents and kids alike have felt the impact of an effective marketing campaign by the Hasbro advertising intelligentsia. The buying frenzy created by the advertising, media coverage, and an animated series featuring Beyblades has generated immense interest in the toy. Using the motifs of a post-nuclear, teenage techno-wasteland, it depicts vagabond kids traveling around the world in search of opponents to challenge, tournaments to win, and glory to be gained. The music is loud and catchy, and the plots are based around simple morality plays of good versus evil. The characters are easy to identify with and live through vicariously, because they have the same concerns as all kids—finding friends and having a good time. Everyone wants to be a hero, at least in a secret life of make-believe. The cartoon animations give children a context for living out their fantasy lives while making them want more Beyblades too! Pokémon, the phenomenon that most closely parallels the marketing prowess of Beyblades, says it best through its theme song: "Gotta Catch 'em All."

The concept of play is inextricably tied to commercial interests and the buying power of the child consumer. Even parents are inclined to take note of the commercials and listen in on the complex, quasi-religious language of Beybladism, so that they are not left behind when their youngsters use the cult-like jargon native to their favorite pastime. But, like adults, kids are teased with the appeal of new choices that often move in on the consumer radar so quickly that there is little time to realize what has hit the fan. The commercial media pump out a continuous stream of gimmicks and clever sales initiatives to entice the unsuspecting pool of youth that form the gaming culture of today and the adult shoppers who are willing to buy toys, cereals and lunch boxes as the cost of a child's entertainment. The synergy of media outlets and clever advertising gives the items a magical persona, tying the fantasy to the product. Each child dreams of having a piece of this make believe world in their hot little hands. To believe that children's tastes and behavior are not affected by advertising is an escapist view of the desire produced and advocated by marketing. The power of the media images kids see cannot be denied as consumerism promises to bring the virtual to life. The young and naive are often hit the hardest because they have not yet developed the defensive auto-immune strategies adults use to fight off at least some of the market appeal of every single item they are hit with by advertising. For that very reason, the effect of mass advertising and commercialism becomes a major influence on children's tastes, their material world, and their behavior. Why? Because children are consumers.

Kids from the ages of eight to fourteen spent a staggering 300 billion U.S. dollars worldwide during 2002 on appearances, entertainment, and food. In the book *BRANDchild*, marketing consultants Martin Lindstrom and Patricia Seybold call this group the tween generation—no longer tykes but not teens either. These kids are described as "smart consumers," based on the fact that they learn to identify brands at an early age, and in the process have become sophisticated consumers of culture, keenly attuned to the marketing strategies aimed directly at their disposable income. Tweens are also described as avid users of technology, including *Playstation 2*, *X Box*, mobile phones, DVDs, and music downloaded from the Internet. This skill is supposed to situate them well as consumers in a global marketplace. Tweens, we are told, also often suffer from social and cultural dislocation as members of broken homes or neglectful parents. Otherwise, how would these kids watch the 22,000 commercials that marketers claim they do each year. There are some other judgments about tweens beside the fact that they are brand slaves without individuality: they love rewards, like secrets, have a mind of their own, are moody, competitive, and exemplify the transition between the comfortable and familiar and the new and exciting. Sounds a lot like Harry Potter. Even the consumer habits of the young wizard and his friends fall in line, if we consider that some brands of magical broomsticks are better than others.

Could the fact that Harry Potter resembles a tween account for the popularity of the novels among children aged eight to fourteen? Can it also explain their phenomenal marketability?

Books are cultural commodities—pieces of history that are bought and sold. Books are also works of artistic flair we call "literature" that comment on society and reflect cultural preoccupations and concerns. The *Harry Potter* series has sold in excess of 200 million books around the world and is being furiously translated into every major and minor language on the planet. Children's novels are not supposed to do that! The sales of the book are rivaled only by some of the largest grossing best sellers and the greatest literary works in the English language. J. K. Rowling, like Stephen King or David Mamet, is not Shakespeare. But then again, no other writer dead or alive can compete with the literary clout of the Bard. The American literary critic Harold Bloom believes that the way we define our cultural selves is by reading and studying stories of the human condition. Best seller lists don't lie, however. If popularity is any indication of public taste and value, then the tales of Harry Potter's childhood adventures are to be considered masterpieces of literary genius that touch the human soul.

Children love the books because they see themselves in the otherwise ordinary protagonist. Harry Potter is a powerless child who is an orphan, lives with an unloving surrogate family, looks like a nerd, but discovers he has the heart of a lion. Oh, and to his delight, he also turns out to be a wizard. Harry Potter is an underdog who has fears and insecurities like all children, but he faces them head on and gives young readers a fantasy hero to identify with and live through. When the underdog becomes a hero, it is empowering. The popularity of the novels is great, owing to the fact that schools and critics have urged kids and adults alike to buy and read the books. *Harry Potter* has become a modern day vehicle for promoting literacy across cultures. Reading books helps develop lexical decoding skills no matter what the age and language. We hear amazing accounts of primary-school kids reading Rowling's 600-page book in two sittings. Stories abound of parents desperately trying to wrestle the novels out of the hands of their enchanted children at bedtime. These well-known urban legends are no doubt substantiated by examples of adults who are seen clutching copies of *Harry Potter*. Holding the book out in front of them, as if in prayer, they are unable to let go of the force of the fictional dream—to be children again. By all accounts, it would seem these novels are the cultural elixir of educational tools for creating a literate society, something that educational systems have had a hard time doing. But there is another side to the books: spin-off products and marketing.

Having achieved cult-like levels of popularity usually reserved only for rock stars and tele-evangelists, J. K. Rowling fills football stadiums for book readings. Literary admirers, young and old, dressed in the traditional wizardry garb of long flowing capes, tall pointy hats, and magic wands hang breathlessly on every syllable of the writer-prophet's words. Demand for the books is so great that facilities where the manuscripts are printed, bound, and stored are patrolled round the clock by armed security guards to prevent a copy being stolen and a paragraph or two being leaked before its time to hungry readers. But at the same time the dramatization rights to the novels have been sold to movie studios, and the spin-off product licensing deals to manufacturers have resulted in everything from Harry Potter glasses to Every Flavor Beans, Harry Potter frogs to board games, not to mention action figures, phone covers, clocks, mugs, T-shirts, shoes, play clothes, and birthday supplies, etc. The list goes on and on and on. The spin-off deals have generated more profits than the *Harry Potter* books themselves. An estimated 2 billion U.S. dollars of projected box-office and product tie-in deals was generated from the first movie for AOL Time Warner, who also marketed the film in its magazines (e.g., *Time* and *People*). *Harry Potter* mania has created its own self-sustaining universe of fans of the novels, but at the same time admirers and critics have been repelled by the extent of the commercialization. One can only hope in the name of good taste that the tween generation develops the media-savvy discretion to recognize the over-saturation of a theme. Otherwise, sighting a whole crowd of eleven year olds in Harry Potter designer glasses, wearing Ron Weasly T-shirts, drinking "Live the Magic" Coca Cola, and carrying Albus Dumbledore backpacks might not be so far-fetched.

As one would expect, *BRANDchild* is more or less a manual for marketers on how to advertise to kids who, in addition to their own spending, generate another 350 billion U.S. dollars, spent by their parents, essentially by nagging. There could be something to it. The tweens seem to exist as just another gimmick to be sold to advertising executives who are looking for a phantom demographic group to hang a hat on when making a pitch. After all, we do have the "Boomers," the "Busters," the "Echoes," and of course, "Generation X." As Martin Lindstrom says, "Kids want something to believe in. If you can't believe in families, you can believe in brands."

Resources
Klein, N. (2001). *No logo.* New York: Picador.
Lindstrom, M., & Seygold, P. B. (2003). *BRANDchild: Insights into the minds of today's global kids.* New York: Kogan Page.

DISNEY AND CONSUMER CULTURE

Christine Quail

Most adults, youth, and children in America—and across the globe—have come into contact with the Disney Corporation, its products, and its celebrities. In fact, Disney has come to symbolize, for many, the very notion of childhood innocence and magical fantasy that characterizes youth. Disney is one of the foundations of American culture, with its characters the icons of generations. Although this prevailing image and ideology may exist, one can look deeper at Disney in order to understand how this image of Disney is just that—an image, a social construction. It is possible to think about the social, political, and cultural power infused in the business of Disney and its cultural texts. This essay will highlight some of the central critiques made about this cultural construction through a critique of The Disney Store. This extended example will illustrate how Disney operates along the lines of consumer culture, gender stereotypes, and racial bias.

I visited the Disney Store at a mall in a mid-sized Northwestern city, three times. The first time I visited was a brief visit that consisted of a quick browse; the second visit consisted of a closer look at the merchandise. During this last visit, I took a notebook and made extensive notes on the products and the store. I also spoke to the manager on the final visit.

Disney is one of the largest media companies in the world. As Bettig and Hall outline in *Big Media, Big Money,* they own film production studios, a vast film library, The Disney Channel, cable systems, ABC, television distribution companies, comic books, Radio Disney, book publishing, magazines, resorts and conference centers, Celebration—a town in Florida, Disneyland, Disney World, and Disney Stores. The company is known for its successes in the film department and for its characters such as Mickey and Minnie Mouse, Donald Duck, Pluto, and more recently, Nemo, Lizzie McGuire, and Lilo & Stitch.

While the company does earn much revenue from box office receipts and video rentals, they also make money from licensing its characters for merchandise. The company's merchandise is sold in many stores, on the Disney Web site, through catalogues, and in The Disney Store, which opened in 1987. The number of stores worldwide has been steadily increasing since then, mostly located in malls in the U.S. In 1998, there were 478 Disney Stores in North America, 107 in Europe, and 96 in Asia/Pacific. The revenues from The Disney Store were high but were lagging towards the end of the 1990s, as detailed by Janet Wasko in *Understanding Disney*.

The spread of Disney merchandise across the globe is testament to both the imagination Disney has colonized, as well as the aggressive nature of its marketing. As critiques of consumer culture attest, identifying oneself with popular culture texts and characters creates an identity based on corporate culture rather than local culture or personal relationships. Identifying oneself as a "Pooh" collector, or a Mickey freak, sutures those characters deep into the psyche and life of the fan. Disney is meaningful to those who consume it. It fills a desire, even if a desire to see a lovable character that reminds one of youth. But it is also important to think about how Disney merchandise perpetuates a culture where consumption of trinkets and novelty items that are inherently linked to "fun" and "innocence" speaks to the larger cultural desires to find fun and innocence in life. What happens, though, to desires for fun and innocence when the contradictions of Disney become apparent? What is it that we're consuming?

Let us describe and analyze The Disney Store as a way of thinking through this issue. Unlike most other stores, The Disney Store's front window displays do not show what is for sale inside the store. No mannequins exhibit clothes, there's no shoe display, no coffee on trays, sleeping pets in cages, or cans of beans beside a sale price. Rather, the windows' structure is that of a glass bubble, bulging from the wall, with a filmstrip of Mickey painted around the bubble. The protuberance suggests a nonthreatening atmosphere in its roundness, part of the classic Disney style, echoed in the round bodies of popular characters. The right window is a seemingly permanent ceramic display of a wonderland where ceramic Mickey hangs playfully from a clock, and Minnie, Goofy, Donald are in there leaning forward, as if to call shoppers into the store. No products are featured at all. The front left window, on the other hand, is a dark blue, purple, and black display—arranged as an underwater world—with cardboard cut-outs of "Atlantis" characters advertising the movie premiere. Although this is an advertisement for a Disney product, the movie itself is not on sale in the store. Atlantis merchandise is on sale, as well (obviously) as many products featuring Mickey, Minnie, Donald, and Goofy, but the front windows do not display *actual* products that are for sale inside. They merely establish the aura of Disney and hence sell the "idea" of Disney (cute, childlike, round, colorful, fun, and imaginative). You have to enter to see what's for sale . . . This strategy points to the ubiquity and image of Disney in American culture. The characters' popularity and the company's film ads are enough to entice customers into the store. The public's strong identification with Disney from youth keeps bringing people back time and time again.

As soon as I entered the store, I was overcome with the loud music playing from "Bear in the Big Blue House." Its repetitiveness and volume seemed to attempt to create a fun party atmosphere. A quick glance around turned up brightly colored ceramics around the entire perimeter of the store's upper level—above the merchandise sat more of the ceramic scenes like the front window contains—Belle and the Beast about to dance, the teacup with a scroll reading, "Be Our Guest!", another Donald, Mickey and Minnie, etc. The music, it turns out, emanates from the back of the store, as a giant-screen monitor displays advertisements for Disney films, Disney World ("Dreams come true . . . life is a happy holiday . . . we'll share enchantment all the way . . . Take a look at a world that's just for you . . . Just make a wish and close your eyes: dreams come true"), Disney television shows (*Bear in the Big Blue House*, *Jo Jo's Circus*, *Doodlebops*, *Kim Possible*, etc.), Disney DVDs and videos. One montage edited shots of animated Disney babies (such as Dumbo and Bambi) with real human photographed babies of different ethnicities and races, while the Dumbo song "Baby of Mine" plays. The fast-paced editing is reminiscent of MTV's music videos. These elements suggest that the store is creating a fun

A popular icon makes the brick walls

Disney makes it on to urban walls

and exciting *family* and child-centered aura, one that is hip and fun, youthful and energetic.

The cacophony of the music, video, and decor contrasts the orderliness of the store's product displays much like the contradiction between the popular image of Disney and a critical reflection of its business and representation. The front left portion of the store could be considered a tee-shirt corner, as it is filled with adult and children's tops. Screen-printed Poohs and Mickeys for adults (for $14.99), fleeces for $19.99, and kids' *Atlantis* tees for $7.99 line the wall. In the middle of the floor stands a baby toy carousel with Pooh-Rings ($8.00), Pooh diaper bags, and Pooh bath toys for infants.

The front right corner displays a Disney movie marquis alerting customers to new videos: *The Emperor's New Groove, 102 Dalmatians, Remember the Titans,* and *Lady and the Tramp 2.* Along the sidewall are beach and pool accessories: plastic beach/pool bags in neon colors brandishing Minnie, Ariel, and Tinkerbell. Sandals and girls' beach coverups and swimsuits ($20.00) also embed Minnie and Ariel. Out from the wall sits another girls' apparel rack containing bohemian style girls' clothes—denims and paisleys replicating the simple, made-from-scratch dresses of the 1960s and 70s. They sell for $10.00 and have Pooh embroidered on the front.

The front middle section is the only *active* toys section. It is filled with Buzz Lightyear walkie talkies, hoop toss games, and talking figures (the fastest store item to sell out, according to the manager). This section is disheveled and apparently popular with young shoppers, as opposed to adults.

Catty-corner to this stand sits the Disney Princess display. This line combines almost all the Disney heroines—Cinderella, Snow White, Ariel, Sleeping Beauty, Jasmine, Pocahontas, and their images, mixes in a lot of pink, and has a new line of products. Items such as the Princess Piano, spindancers (dolls that spin), talking tea set (for $28.00), soccer balls, softballs, Magical Princess Crown (it lights up!), the Princess Fuzzy Phone (that speaks: "It's so nice to hear from you!"), Barbie-like dolls, character gift sets, clocks, purses, dish sets, photo albums, T-shirts, nightgowns, underwear sets (one each of every heroine!), books, lunch boxes, pens, tote bags, and the princess dresses. The princess dress looks like a nightgown, but could possibly be worn as a dress or nightgown. They are for little girls, and come in white, pink, and turquoise—each with a different Disney Princess on the bosom. Behind the Princess racks are the Princess and Minnie jewelry, hair clips, combs, nail polish, bracelets, lip gloss. Pooh shows up again with glow-in-the-dark stickers of Pooh and Piglet that you adorn a plastic ring with, then throw out and replace that sticker with a new character sticker. Everything is pink, most of it is fuzzy. These are traditional constructs of girl culture or femininity. Disney's construct of girls is in line with this traditional construct of pink and frills.

Behind the girls' apparel is (apparently) the boys' apparel. It is not marked, "boys" but is in stark contrast to the girls' in style (buttons and collars rather than fluff, lace, and fuzz), colors, and characters, so I determine that it is more for boys, although girls could certainly wear it (as well as boys wearing the girls', but this, as in most things in life, is somehow more of a big deal than girls wearing boys' clothes). These T-shirts and shorts sets are in khakis, tans, dark greens (contrasted with the pinks and turquoises for girls). Many of these shirts are decorated with *Nemo* and *Atlantis* characters (rather than Princesses and Minnie), and are underwater scenes. These are hats, T-shirts, and shorts. Behind this rests a watch case that sits directly to the right of the cash wrap—watches with Tigger, Pooh, Mickey, and Minnie must be unlocked to examine and try on. Much like the construct of "girl," the "boy" of Disney is a traditional blue-and-khaki, water-playing person.

Across the store, the left middle wall contains cups and mugs, plates, and art. The art includes cells, photographs, and paintings. Those with prices are anywhere from $100 to $500. The stands contain snow globes, picture frames, cookie jars, and a few food products such as syrup and ice cream sprinkles. These items are very expensive and point to the lengths that some fans go to consume Disney culture. The prized possessions are exclusive, not the "utopian" and common culture Disney likes to present itself as. Additionally, these household items suggest that one can infuse Disney into any aspect of one's life, even into the syrup you pour on your frozen waffle.

Not to exclude any generation, the back-middle left of the store is the baby section. All the colors in this section are tempered pastels and natural materials. Both Classic Pooh and the new Disney Pooh are visible. The Classic characters are on the Baby's memory book, the plush toys, onesies, hats, and socks, and the colors are in muted pinks, blues, and yellows. Also, a few other characters make up the baby section. Bambi is on the pink clothes, and Thumper on the blue. Mickey is on the blue-striped clothes. Past the newborn clothes are the toddlers' clothes. Jean jumpers with Bear (from "Bear in the Big Blue House"), Mickey, and Pooh logos could be considered masculine, as they are simple and geometric (for $17.99). More boys' clothes are in dark blues, khakis, greens, and jungle prints, with animals golfing. Toddler girls have the same red paisleys as in the little girls' section. The girls' jumpers (as defined by the flowers behind the characters) are also $17.99. To continue the gender analysis, we see here that even baby Disney fans can express themselves through gender-appropriate attire.

In the middle of the store are the where the knick-knacks are displayed. This includes key chains, pencils, bendable pets for $5.99 (cats from *Aristocats*, Pluto, Lady, Tramp, Dalmatians, etc.), more picture frames. An entire Mickey graduation section has different graduation-related merchandise, from stuffed Mickeys wearing the mortarboard cap and holding a diploma, to picture frames for teachers, with an apple producing a frame. Customers can express their identification with Disney through these simple key chains, or allow Mickey to help them celebrate their graduation. Again, we see how ingrained identification with Disney characters becomes.

The back-middle right is the cash wrap. It has two TV screens on either side of it, playing Disney videos, and a painted scene behind on the wall of Cinderella reading to many different Disney animals with the castle in the background. The back left of the store is the women's adult apparel (besides the T-shirts, which were located in the front of the store, as mentioned). There is no adult men's section, just the T-shirts in the front (which are actually unisex). Ladies' pajamas and nightgowns in silky polyester show sophisticated designs with tasteful (small, thinly drawn) Poohs. Also more comfort-designed tanks and cotton pant pajama sets play "find the hidden Mickeys" with citrus fruits and cherries in the shape of Mickey's head/ears. The strangest part of these pajamas is that, sold separately, they match smelly plush toys of Minnie—either a pink cherry-scented (for the cherries pajamas) or a green apple-scented (for the citrus, I presume) dolls for $30.00. Finally, women's boxers display the frog prince ("Kiss me, I'm yours!") Sleeping Beauty designs.

The back center is where the TV screen sits, as mentioned. Spilling out from the bottom of the screen is a four-tiered, rounded stuffed animal extravaganza. Largest toys in the back, and Mickeys toward the middle, the display holds Dalmatians, bears, all of the dwarfs, Dumbo, the Aristocats, Bear of the Big Blue House and his friends, and Classic and New Disney Pooh, Eeyore, Piglet, and Tigger.

The back right contains more toys and games and leads into computer games and videos that border the left portion of the cash wrap. Directly bordering the stuffed animals sits all of the *Atlantis* merchandise, from cars, coloring books, walkie-talkies, and a boat launcher, to the main character dolls, Milo and Kida. Next to this are the kitchen toys—play mixers and a "Mouse around the House" toy, a set of plastic food in the shape of Mickey's ears (waffles, eggs, etc.). Curving around are the Mickey Play-doh sets. Inflatable plastic water toys (Eeyore and Tigger) and sand toys (buckets, shovels, etc). Next are the videos. Most of the videos are the Disney animated films, but also there are other children's films such as *Mary Poppins* and *Life Size*, as well as a few adult films, such as *Remember the Titans* and *Meet Joe Young*. A small DVD collection is also for sale. Computer games rest on the wall. These games are categorized on the package as being either "Girls," "Creative," "Games," "Learning," "Preschool," "Kindergarten," and "1st Grade." This section shows how Disney attempts to market itself as educational, as well as entertaining.

To recap some of the critiques: As some of the above description indicates, The Disney Store has a strong delineation of "girls'" stuff—pinks, fluffy, fuzzy clothes, and "girls" computer games where you choreograph a dance or color a picture, rather than chase, jump, or rescue another character, as happens in the "games" category. They define women, too, with lots of clothes for bed! Is Disney sexy? Are we to think that women wear these

Disney nighties and pajamas because sleeping involves dreaming and innocent play, or because bed is also associated with sex and therefore the slinky nightgown is sexual? There is no men's sleepwear in the store. Colors also give indication of the meaning of these gendered products. The store itself contains lots of colors, but pastels are reserved for babies (soft, sedate, calm), and pinks for girls, blues/greens/plaids/khakis for boys. Further, the kitchen toys are marketed to girls, and the activities reserved for boys versus girls suggests that traditional roles in the kitchen are for girls, as are coloring and dancing, where boys' toys include walkie talkies. This presents Disney's construction of girls—even girls who play soccer are referred to as "Princess," and their ball is pink.

The merchandise is not a representative of all the Disney characters. Pooh was everywhere (less so for Tigger, even less for Eeyore and Piglet; Kanga, Roo, and Rabbit were nowhere). Mickey was also popular. But there was no Jiminy Cricket, no Pinocchio, no Alice in Wonderland, barely any Dumbo (video and stuffed animal), barely any Jasmine and Pocahontas, and barely any other characters from *Aladin, Pocahontas,* or *Beauty and the Beast* (there were no Beasts for sale) and no Peter Pan or Wendy (a few Tinkerbells scattered about on swimwear and flip flops). The Disney heroines are packaged together not as heroines but as princesses. Why do they not have much Lion King merchandise? What happened to all that *Hercules* stuff? Besides that—nothing about the other holdings of Disney. The store acts as though Disney were still the previous nonconglomerate corporation. No products having anything to do with ESPN, ABC, or any other Disney holding were represented. This gives the image of the traditional, Classic Disney of Walt himself. This tends to sediment the myth of the Walt Disney genius as well as Disney's "innocent" roots. By calling attention to its subsidiaries, the store would lose some of its "magical" appeal. But also, by ignoring some of its classic characters and focusing on what will sell the most merchandise today locally, the store is even misrepresenting its span of films and characters and pushing the brand image by focusing on a select group of characters.

The most abundant product was the clothing, then household items, then accessories. Every age group was represented in the clothing, as well as the toys. But, do babies need designer clothes? Is the look of babies' clothes for the child or for the parents? Does a parent love Pooh so much that they would spend $20 on a Pooh T-shirt, size 3–6 months? Thus, the commodification of children's clothes is interesting, especially in terms of branding children. Babies are no longer unmarked with simple T-shirts, hand-me-downs, or clothes from Goodwill, but are being branded by Disney's trademarked logos. Is this "fun and enchantment?" Most kids don't particularly enjoy shopping for clothes or take much stock in their clothes. If part of the Disney image is "fun," then the store's overabundance of clothing does not seem to suggest fun. Rather, the store was a contradiction: at once loud, busy, and overdone, much like an amusement park funhouse—while at the same time boring and sterile: Active toys were less represented. This is intriguing, considering that all the kids I saw in the store seemed to *want* to be actively doing something. One kid was tossing around a stuffed Pooh, one was running behind clothes racks and making her mom look for her, one was jumping on a display for the Tigger pool toy. Two were fighting over who got to look at the Buzz Lightyear talking figure—which was the only active toy actually out. But is this an active toy? Programmed toys are less imaginative—the Buzz speaks, the tea set talks—you don't even have to play tea-party anymore, you can just use the Disney set, push some buttons, and it's all done for you. If one of Disney's characteristics is "imagination," then these toys discourage part of Disney's mission.

Mostly, the Disney character logo seems to be planted, attached like a parasite, on items that it has nothing to do with. Any one of those jean jumpers without the Tigger would look exactly like any other pair of jeans. Thus, the commercialization of other products is a process central to the Disney Store.

Beyond the products, the workers in the store are also part of the text, as are the customers. Two workers were there every time I visited—two women, the manager and an associate sales clerk. Both were white women in their forties. The manager was very lively—she smiled a lot, laughed loudly, and chatted with children and adults alike. The associate was not as smiley, but was the one who approached all the customers in the front of the store. She walked around the store, tidying up, but did not make conversation with customers. At one point, the manager sent her to a group of teenage girls to speak with them, but this was the only time she approached anyone beyond greeting them. Customers consisted of several groups of moms with kids (all white) and one group of a woman with her kids and mother (Hispanic, the adults speaking Spanish and the kids English). As I mentioned, the contrast between the types of activity kids were doing did not fit well with the products for sale. The manager seemed to try to embody an image of fun, but the other worker seemed particularly unthrilled with her job. Thus, the notion of Disney as a magical employer is not fulfilled.

Before I interviewed the store manager, I overheard her talking to her sales associate. She encouraged her to approach a group of teenaged girls and ask them why they weren't in school (it was a Friday, around 11 am). The clerk said, "I already greeted them." But the manager wanted her to specifically ask why they were at the mall at all. So she returned and asked them, and they simply said, "We're on a field trip." I don't know many schools that take field trips to the mall, but that seemed to suffice for the clerk. Linda, from across the store, listened in, and replied, "What a fun field trip!"

When another customer arrived, she smiled and said loudly, "It's not Wednesday! What are you doing here today?" Apparently, this customer only shops in the store on Wednesday. Later, at the cash wrap, this woman was explaining that she lives in a nearby city and there's no Disney Store there, so she always comes to this one, and she has to come down on Wednesdays for some reason. This is devotion: a weekly, out-of-town trip.

A mother holding a small child, probably a year old, led her three-year-old blonde, curly haired daughter to the princess dresses. "What pretty dresses!" she exclaimed, and asked the girl which one she liked. "This one fits perfectly!" the *three-year-old* said, holding up the Tinkerbell gown. "WOOOOOW! But you need extra extra extra small!" the mom exclaimed, and grabbed a pink one. "Perfect," the daughter agreed. Now, this seemed like an odd interchange, where a very young girl knew so much about shopping, and had a linguistic schema for showing her approval for a dress. The mother seemed to take joy in the fact that her daughter was so small.

The three teenaged girls (probably about thirteen or fourteen) were looking at the mugs, snow globes, picture frames, and sleepwear. They seemed particularly interested in the picture frames involving Pooh, and were saying "Cute! Say 'cheese'!" and pretending to take pictures of one another.

Another girl (probably three) was missing. A mom was calling for her, and then she popped out from inside a clothes rack laughing. The mother was not mad, but they left the store after the mother had located her daughter.

A few boys were jumping on an inflated Tigger pool toy, and the three-year-old-girl was biting its ear. Another boy was tossing around a stuffed Pooh bear and watching the TV with glossy eyes.

A Hispanic family came in, the two women speaking in Spanish, and their two boys in English. The boys were trying to get the Buzz Lightyear talking doll to work, and they were fighting over who got to try it.

There were no men in the store when I was there. I thought maybe there just weren't as many men at the mall, considering that it is more common for a mom to work inside the home and have childcare as the primary caregiver. However, as I walked through the mall, I saw many dads with children, and several couples with children or a small group of adults and several children. Therefore, it was more obvious that the men just weren't shopping in the store.

My interview with Dana, the manager, was fascinating. She was very bubbly and smiley. She wore an *Atlantis* T-shirt and was careful not to ignore her other customers while talking with me. She has been working at The Disney Store for "quite a few years" and loves her job. Sometimes it's difficult, she said, but so are other jobs. As manager, she is in charge of scheduling, but she has no control over her inventory—regional managers take care of that. She bemoaned that fact, and added that it was nice that a new President of the Disney Stores was just named—because the long absence of a leader was distressing to her segment of the company. She hopes that things will be back on track. She was glad, however, that the company spent so much time selecting the right person—this shows that the company cares about having the best person for the job, she said. They provide good benefits and wages, she offered.

Dana told me that only certain people can work for Disney. "They have a certain image to protect, and you have to be the right kind of image." And she *is* Disney, innately, she said, as she smiled and giggled. She didn't articulate exactly what that image is, but I can deduce that she's talking about clean, wholesome, and fun, and nice—the image that Disney tries to portray. In so doing, the company has strict rules for employees' clothing, hair color/length, fingernail length, jewelry, and hygiene routines. Is this the image of fun fantasy, or a company that exerts high levels of control?

I asked her why there were only certain characters in the store—for instance there wasn't much Snow White. She replied that the most popular characters were represented in the store, like Ariel and there's always Mickey. Buzz Lightyear was big, and they had a hard time keeping the talking Buzz stocked. Other fun items she particularly likes are the "hidden Mickey" pajamas and matching smelly Minnies.

This analysis is consistent with other critiques of the contradiction of Disney—what they claim to be, and the reality of what they actually are. Taken as a whole, the store seems to embody commodification of fun and fantasy, the representation of gender stereotypes, and the erasure of ethnic/racial difference. In the Media Education Foundation's film, *Mickey Mouse Monopoly*, Disney's films present women as damsels in distress, and contain racial undertones that privilege white culture over a variety of different ethnicities and races. Their attempt to monopolize "fun," "innocence," and "magic," prevents them from telling real stories about Pocahontas, for example, or from presenting positive images of, say, Arabs or African Americans. Although this essay did not attempt to deconstruct these negative representations, the critique of the Disney Store is inherently a critique beyond consumer culture to include how gender and racial power are implicated in consumer culture. Disney's toys and clothes reinforce the filmic representations and create instant recognition for them as they are carried on lunchboxes, beach towels, or jean pockets. Disney has indeed achieved the goal of selling products, and its impact on cultural practices, kids' play, and gender and racial representations is dubious. Youth of every culture participate in a "cult" of Disney interest. One can easily find teenagers in every country sporting Mickey or Minnie clothing and paraphernalia on any street or in any school.

Resources
Books

Bettig, R., & Hall, J. (2003). *Big media, big money: Political economics and cultural texts.* New York: Rowman & Littlefield.

Byrne, E., & McQuillan, M. (2001). *Deconstructing Disney.* London: Pluto Press.

Geertz, C. (1973). *The interpretation of cultures: Selected essays.* New York: Basic Books.

Giroux, H. A. (1999). *The mouse that roared: Disney and the end of innocence.* Boulder, CO: Rowman & Littlefield Publishers.

Haas, L., Bell, E., & Sells, L. (Eds.). (1995). *From mouse to mermaid: The politics of film, gender, and culture.* Bloomington: Indiana University Press.

Hall, S. (Ed.). (1997). *Representation: Cultural representations and signifying practices.* London: Sage.

Ross, A. (1999). *The celebration chronicles: Life, liberty and the pursuit of property value in Disney's new town.* New York: Ballantine Books.

Smoodin, E. (1994). *Disney discourse: Producing the Magic Kingdom.* New York: Routledge.

Steinberg, S., & Kincheloe, J. (Eds.). (2003). *Kinderculture: The corporate construction of childhood* (2nd ed.). Boulder, CO: Westview.

Wasko, J. (2001). *Understanding Disney: The manufacture of fantasy.* Cambridge: Polity.

Wasko, J., Meehan, E., & Phillips, M. (Eds.). (2001). *Dazzled by Disney: The global Disney audience project.* London: Leicester University Press.

Articles

Steeves, H. L. (1987). Feminist theories and media studies. *Critical Studies in Mass Communication*, 4 (2), 95–135.

CRIPQUEERS IN THE LAND OF MAKE BELIEVE

Santiago Solis

Through their representation of disability and homosexuality, books for children and youth have the potential to contribute toward their appreciation. Previously established definitions—medical, criminal, and religious— deriving from the dominant culture about what it means to be disabled or homosexual can be contested and ultimately redefined. As young people's books capture—and celebrate—alternative physical and sexual identities, youth can begin (or continue) to generate new understanding not just about disability and homosexuality as abstract concepts, but about the disabled and homosexual people that these images depict. In other words, alternative representations of disabled and homosexual characters creates a consciousness in youth that demands the possibility to question the ways in which disabled and homosexual people are socially constructed. Both disability studies and queer theory challenge corporal, mental, sexual, social and cultural norms. Modern (re)presentations of disabled and homosexual characters in books, then, can reopen the interpretation of disability and homosexuality for further inquiry. For example, what should be the function of the "picture book" in shaping young people's perceptions about disability and/or homosexuality? What sorts of reactions do new images of disability and homosexuality provoke? How should students use recent representations as a springboard to generate discussions about interpretation? As we look at childrens' books, we can see the context in which youth create their opinions of the disabled.

This essay looks at some of the ways in which disability and homosexuality are represented within the sphere of children's books in the twenty-first century. It examines the differences as well as the similarities between these two socially constructed entities—between their representation as grotesquely deviant and their counter-representation as restrictively normalizing. Ten picture books are analyzed in order to uncover a continuum that offers less fixed and confined ways to study children's books. I argue that both corpo-normative and hetero-normative perspectives have prejudiced a considerable portion of the pictorial language from which these ten picture books draw. Specifically, I contend that disability and homosexuality are depoliticized through regulated and restricted forms of representation in an effort to normalize—as much as possible—disabled and homosexual bodies.

In the ten picture books examined here, confinement inhibits necessary and meaningful ways of presenting disability and homosexuality. The prescription of "acceptable" or "sanctioned" types of representation limits their freedom of artistic interpretation. Hence, by adhering to subtle methods of constraint, these picture books are forced to submit to institutional disableism and homophobia. In turn the restricted representation of disability and homosexuality in this set of picture books perpetuates and fortifies corpo-normative and hetero-normative perspectives. For instance, censorship forces the writer and illustrator to the creative use of suggestion and metaphor saturated with hidden meanings. Censorship, then, shapes the representation of disability and homosexuality in picture books—specifically, censorship restricts the ways in which disabled and homosexual characters are able to manifest their sexuality. The forbiddance of particular sexual behaviors and sexualized expressions is therefore problematic.

Using the ten picture books selected for this esssay, I intend to illustrate some of the societal and institutional restrictions that have informed the invisibility of cripqueer—both disabled and homosexual—sexuality in children's books. To reiterate, my goal is to analyze how disableism and homophobia contribute to a general assumption that any depiction of cripqueer sexuality is repulsive—and therefore unworthy of representation. It is this act of censorship that demands further investigation. To begin with, the belief that cripqueer sex is an unspeakable act must be understood in relation to that which this sexual manifestation challenges.

LEADING FRAMEWORK

Within this framework of prohibitive representation, both disabled and homosexual characters are infantilized—depicted as childlike and therefore asexual. As a result, this chapter's leading framework will follow the idea that any regulation of artistic representation automatically provokes some sort of reaction. A cripqueer political stance, then, refuses corporeal conformity and questions the legitimacy of "appropriate," "acceptable," "moral," and "normal" sexual behavior. For this reason, ten picture books are examined in order to gage how we might use picture books to disrupt ableist and heterosexist structures. In other words, I explore the ways in which we can utilize picture books to confront the fear of uncertainty, embrace change, and question corpo-normative and hetero-normative ideologies. The intent of this chapter, therefore, is to encourage awareness and pride in cripqueer sexuality; emphasis is on the identity of the cripqueer as a sexual being.

However, any examination of a picture book must be situated and studied within a broad set of societal ideologies. In picture books, the expanded systems—ableism and heterosexism—embedded in society have framed cripqueer sexuality as immoral, abnormal, shameful and repugnant. Any manifestation of cripqueer sexuality in picture books is therefore seen as outright illogical. Consequently, modern representations of disability and homosexuality in picture books generate new expressions of censorship that students must learn to decipher. Hence, what is unsaid—the omitted, the invisible—becomes as important as what is said.

SELECTION PROCESS AND ORGANIZATIONAL STRUCTURE

Rather than accommodate all bodies into a prescribed sexual norm based on able-bodiedness and heterosexuality, a cripqueer perspective attempts to rearticulate the "isms" of institutionalization deriving from society. Consequently, a cripqueer approach will involve trying to find new ways of analyzing the ten picture books that I chose for this chapter. This particular set of picture books was selected from multiple mainstream Internet sources. So in outlining the selection of the ten picture books, I am more than simply presenting a representative sample, I am bringing to the forefront picture books that conspicuously attempt to resist shame and silence. Here, then, is the list of ten picture books published between 2000 and 2004 divided into four main categories:

Picturebooks Containing Two Moms
> 2000 *MAMA EAT ANT, YUCK!* by Barbara Lynn Edmonds, illustrated by Matthew Daniele
> 2004 *Molly's Family* by Nancy Garden, illustrated by Sharon Wooding

Picturebooks Containing Two Dads
> 2000 *King & King* by Linda de Haan & Stern Nijland
> 2004 *King & King & Family* by Linda de Haan & Stern Nijland

2003 *How My Family Came to Be—Daddy, Papa and Me* by Andrew R. Aldrich, illustrated by Mike Motz

Picturebooks about Different Types of Families
2000 *ABC A Family Alphabet Book* by Bobbie Combs, illustrated by Desiree Keane & Brian Rappa
2000 *123 A Family Counting Book* by Bobbie Combs, illustrated by Danamarie Hosler
2000 *All Families Are Different* by Sol Gordon, illustrated by Vivien Cohen

Picturebooks with Queered Animals
2001 *PUGDOG* by Andrea U'Ren
2002 *The Sissy Duckling* by Harvey Fierstein, illustrated by Henry Cole

In order to determine how censorship is negotiated within the ten selected picture books, each text will be examined individually before making connections across multiple texts. I will begin my analysis with the two picture books that contain families with two moms as the main theme. Next, I will survey the three picture books that talk specifically about families with two dads. Then, I will look at the three picture books that talk about different types of families. Finally, I will dissect the two picture books that use animals to discuss physical and attitudinal differences. Three main questions will guide my inquiry: (1) how did censorship affect the range of sexuality that these picture books encapsulate? (2) How was sexuality depicted—or eluded? (3) how might cripqueer sexuality inform future representations of disabled and homosexual characters?

PICTURE BOOKS CONTAINING TWO MOMS

Because lesbian motherhood has been mostly invisible, highly criticized, and even condemned, I would like to begin my analysis with *MAMA EAT ANT, YUCK!* (2000). This rendition begins with a picture of a happy family unit comprising Mama, Mommy, Emma, Sue, and Tommy sitting at the kitchen table during breakfast. The story centers on Emma's first words "Mama eat ant, yuck!" which she repeats throughout the book in different contexts. The fourth illustration depicts a highly rare scene encapsulating both disability and homosexuality. During a family outing to the lake, Mama and Mommy sit next to each other on a bench with Mama's arm around Mommy as they watch their kids feed the ducks. In the background, two wheelchair users also enjoy the sunny day as they play basketball with each other. Although we have yet to see extensive representations of disabled lesbian parents, this particular image manages to link two topics that are often considered to be difficult for children—disability and homosexuality. But what I want to question is whose readiness is really at stake, the children's or the adults'. For in the end, adults are most troubled by topics that raise discomforting questions and ethical dilemmas that they wish to avoid. Nevertheless, if childhood is truly a time of innocence, then the seventh illustration may also encourage unpleasant discussions, as it shows Mama and Mommy sleeping in the same bed. Consequently, this simple book is powerful because it has the potential to stimulate dialogue around complex philosophical issues.

Molly's Family (2004) takes place in Ms. Marston's kindergarten classroom. As the children help their teacher prepare the class for the upcoming Open School Night, Molly suggests that some of the children draw pictures to decorate the room. Molly decides to draw her family—Mommy, Mama Lu, and her puppy Sam. But her classmate Tommy insists that Molly's picture is not a family since it lacks a daddy. According to Tommy, Molly cannot have two moms. Even though the other children describe their varied familial configurations, they are not convinced that a family can have two moms. At home, Mommy and Mama Lu reassure Molly that in all likelihood other kids at school may also have two moms, and some might even be adopted. At school, Ms. Marston convinces Molly that there is nothing wrong with having two moms. In the end, Molly is satisfied with the adults' explanations and consents to display her drawing on the wall next to her friends' Stephen, Tanya and Tommy. During Open School Night everyone appears to be happy. Although the story challenges the traditional nuclear family, it does not promote intimacy between two women. For example, Mommy and Mama Lu fail to display any type of romantic affection toward one another. When Mommy and Mama Lu appear together, Molly is positioned as a barrier between them. Furthermore, the text indicates that they have love, but it does not directly state that the love they have is toward each other—their love for one another is only implied.

PICTURE BOOKS CONTAINING TWO DADS

King & King (2001) and *King & King & Family* (2004) will be discussed sequentially since the 2004 version is a sequel to the 2001 publication. When the Queen decides that it is time for her son to marry, the search begins for the perfect Princess. The Prince becomes sad and depressed because he is not interested in marrying a Princess, but after being pressured by the Queen, he concedes to marry. Princesses from many Kingdoms audition for the role of Queen, but the Prince is not impressed. Finally, the last Princess' brother, Prince Lee, captures the Princes' heart. They both fall in love and marry. During the very public ceremony, the Princes hold hands and happily gaze into each other's eyes. Their impassioned stare continues into the next image, as they help each other carry the wedding cake. Their love for one another is finally consummated with a kiss, which is evidenced in the last illustration. Although this enchanting fairy tale has an untraditional (queered) ending, its premise rests on the conventional notion of heterosexual and monogamous marriage. But the most disturbing part of the story is the fact that several Princesses are required to compete for one man's approval in the hopes of marrying him.

In *King & King & Family* (2004) King Bertie and King Lee go on a royal honeymoon to an exotic location. As King and King explore the jungle, they encounter different types of animals, many of which have babies. King Bertie tells King Lee that his wish is to have a baby of their own. They conclude their honeymoon uneventfully, pack their belongings and return to the castle. But to their surprise, a little girl from the jungle jumps out of the suitcase. King and King are happy to finally have the child they desire. They adopt Princess Daisy and celebrate their new family. However, the story lacks complexity or any type of multifaceted perspective. Lamentably, the main characters' sexual identities are not highlighted and explored, but mirror socially sanctioned moral models. For example, although two gay men are the principal characters, they are simply made to comply with marital norms. In addition, the arrival of their adopted daughter, Princess Daisy, is unconvincing and problematic. The implication is that gay men see each other as asexual, and are concerned only with imitating heterosexual roles. This drive to normalize homosexual behavior is what helps define and judge what is considered normal and abnormal sexuality.

In a similar vein, *How My Family Came to Be—Daddy, Papa and Me* (2003) also deals with adoption. After filling out the necessary documentation, Daddy and Papa (who are white) adopt a baby boy (who is black). They offer their new baby all that he supposedly needs: joy, comfort, care, and love. Initially, a brief statement declares that the baby's birth mom was not healthy enough to raise children. It is assumed that the mother's only alternative is to surrender her child to adoption. No mention is made of the social barriers that often prevent ill and disabled parents from properly caring for their children—this explanation is simply dismissed. In addition, other issues of race, class, and gender are overlooked. For example, the story concludes that two gay white-middle-class men are more capable of properly nurturing a black child than a single black sick-woman. But the gay men's love for their child does not completely win out. To prevent any anxiety concerning the influence that the men's sexuality might have over their son's sexual identity, the narrative mentions that the growing boy has many women to help raise him. And once again, although the family is portrayed as happy and well adjusted, the men's physical affection for each other is kept to a bare minimum. Only one illustration shows Daddy lightly placing his hands on Papa's shoulders. All other manifestations of love are directed toward the child.

PICTURE BOOKS ABOUT DIFFERENT TYPES OF FAMILIES

ABC A Family Alphabet Book (2000) is fairly heterogeneous in terms of race, gender, disability, and homosexual identity. Although the vocabulary and sentence structure are relatively simple because of the target population—ages two to five—the illustrations are sophisticated in comparison. The first image, for instance, shows two women being awakened from the same bed by their daughter. Two other displays of physical affection between women are evidenced as each couple warmheartedly embraces each other. The final representation related to homosexual desire evidences two men holding one another as they pull their daughter down a dirt road in a red wagon. However, while different types of families are exhibited performing various activities, two illustrations are particularly noteworthy due to their potential to generate insightful discussions among young readers. One shows a pregnant woman and her female partner with their son at the supermarket buying groceries. The other is also unique in that it integrates disability and lesbian motherhood by presenting a wheelchair user, her female partner, and their daughter in a public establishment buying ice cream.

Another book by the same author, Bobbie Combs, is *123 A Family Counting Book* (2000), in which various types of families are featured. In addition to presenting an assortment of multicultural gay families, this account also incorporates disability. For example, two moms, three kids (one of them a wheelchair user), and five dogs pose for a family portrait. In addition, several displays of affectionate physical contact take place in this particular publication. This book is also geared toward a young audience (ages two to five), which proves that instead of censuring complex social issues such as disability and homosexuality, picture books that embrace challenging topics have the potential to foster understanding, empathy and respect.

In *All Families Are Different* (2000), for instance, multiple delicate subject matters are addressed. The narrative begins by questioning the traditional nuclear family and talks about orphaned and adopted children, different types of problems within families, and various living situations such as foster homes. The book encourages children to define their own kind of family and offers a variety of familial configurations, including families with same sex parents. In addition, some families are described as having a family member with illness or disability (even though some of the language refers to certain disabilities in terms of deficit). The text concludes that a thing such as a "normal" or "perfect" family does not exist because all families are exceptional. The illustrations are diverse in terms of race, class, gender, disability, and sexual identity. However, when youngsters are asked to imagine the type of family that they might want as adults, a child is pictured dreaming of a family that appears to be non-disabled and heterosexual. On the other hand, while keeping in mind that this picture book is written for youth aged seven and up, asking young people to imagine their chosen family with a disabled and/or

255

homosexual family member may generate interesting discussions that challenge disableism and homophobia.

PICTURE BOOKS WITH QUEERED ANIMALS

PUGDOG (2001) is an amusing story that defies gender roles. Mike had been treating Pugdog as a male dog since Pugdog was a puppy, but when Mike discovers from the veterinarian that Pugdog is female, Mike begins to police Pugdog's behavior in order to ensure that she acts the way Mike imagines a female dog should conduct herself. During one of their daily walks in the park they encounter a poodle. Mike assumes that the poodle is female and obliges Pugdog to imitate the poodle's ladylike demeanor. But Pugdog becomes depressed and prefers to reminisce about the days when she could play rough and get dirty. After Pugdog runs away Mike realizes that in order for Pugdog to be happy he must reconsider his gendered expectations. Mike and Pugdog are reunited, but on their way home they come across the same "effeminate" poodle. To Mike's surprise the poodle is not female, but a male dog. Mike further acknowledges that he has much to learn—and to unlearn. Pugdog's non-normative habits clearly challenge the soundness of gender, which compel the questions: what is female behavior, what is male behavior? And, what sort of gendered behavior should be expected in cripqueer contexts, if any?

Another picture book that attempts to question presuppositions about normative gender and sexuality is *The Sissy Duckling* (2002). Elmer enjoys activities that traditionally have been classified as "domestic" and "feminine" in nature. However, Papa duck pressures Elmer to participate in "masculine" sports such as baseball. But Elmer is unsuccessful. Papa duck feels that his own manhood is being threatened because his son is regarded as a sissy. Elmer is confused by the term. But when Mama duck explains its meaning, she equates sissy with being special. This is an example of how "special" is often used as synonymous with "different," "abnormal," "unnatural," "anomalous," and "deviant." Elmer is tormented by his peers and disowned by his father because of his label—sissy. Hence, Elmer swims away from home and is forced to live in isolation. He is essentially sentenced to death because he fails to approximate the norm. In the end, the flock accepts Elmer only after he proves his bravery, loyalty, and ingenuity by saving his father's life. In other words, to be tolerated, Elmer himself is transformed. Elmer must first be classified as a courageous hero in order for others to rethink their hatred toward sissies. But some questions remain unanswered: what would have happened to Elmer if he had not saved his father's life? Why are the categories of "feminine" and "masculine" produced and sustained? Why are they not avoided? Should a sissy even be assigned to a gendered category, if so, which one—female, male, a third gender combining both, or something entirely new?

IMPLICATIONS AND CONCLUSIONS

Although the traditional perception associated with picture books is changing, picture books are still regarded as righteous and therefore incapable of negatively influencing students' views on serious issues. However, the ten picture books analyzed in this chapter prove otherwise. Just as these picture books have the capability to challenge and change society by destabilizing ableist and heterosexist sexual norms, they also have the ability to preserve dominant social structures based on corpo-normative and heteronormative ideologies. It is important to note that even within the limited number of picture books discussed here, a range of positive and negative textual and pictorial representations emerge. This proves that disability and homosexuality are not entirely unspeakable or unrepresentable within the sphere of picture books. The challenge lies in deciphering how overt acts of censorship and subtle forms of suppression influence what is said and represented—and what is ultimately unrevealed or kept in the closet.

That which is closeted, therefore, must be assessed in relation to that which is disclosed. What does it mean, after all, to represent disability and homosexuality? To begin with, dominant forms of able-bodiedness dictate how disability is depicted, in the same way that dominant modes of heterosexual femininity and masculinity inform how homosexuality is represented. Hence, disability and queer theorists are now unpacking how able-bodiedness, disability, heterosexuality, and homosexuality all depend on and influence each other. For this reason, representations of disability and homosexuality must be studied in reference to corpo-normativity and hetero-normativity—not because disabled and homosexual figures exemplify deviance, but because they continue to be narratively and picturesquely subordinated, or entirely discounted. In the ten picture books examined here, disability and homosexuality are mainly implied rather than explicitly discussed, and cripqueer sexuality is vague and indirect, but mostly invisible. Perhaps one of the fears is that describing cripqueer desire might generate desire for the cripqueer.

Consequently, I propose that educators and students begin (or continue) to challenge the restraint imposed by the mainstream social usage of "sexual discourse" as a protective measure against cripqueer sexuality. In other words, in order to yield to alternative conceptualizations of what it means to be a sexual human being, educators and students should learn to appropriate the images in picture books to counter the ableist and heterosexist terms that are used to police disabled and homosexual representations. Hence, I offer a new way of looking at picture books in order to frustrate the mission of restrictive representation, which aims to desexualize disabled and homosexual—cripqueer—bodies. Cripqueering, then, helps establish a critical lens with which we can identify and challenge the ongoing overlapping and melding of able-bodied, disabled, heterosexual, and homosexual identities.

Resources

Books

Aldrich, A. R. (2003). *How my family came to be—Daddy, Papa and Me.* Oakland, CA: New Family Press.

Butler, J. (1999). *Gender trouble: Feminism and the subversion of identity.* New York: Routledge.

Combs, B. (2000a). *123. A family counting book.* Ridley Park, PA: Two Lives Publishing.

———. (2000b). *ABC. A family alphabet book.* Ridley Park, PA: Two Lives Publishing.

de Haan, L., & Nijland, S. (2000). *King & King.* Berkeley, CA: Tricycle Press.

———. (2004). *King & King & family.* Berkeley, CA: Tricycle Press.

Edmonds, B. L. (2000). *MAMA EAT ANT, YUCK!* Eugene, OR: Hundredth Munchy Publications.

Fierstein, H. (2002). *The sissy duckling.* New York: Simon & Schuster Books for Young Readers.

Garden, N. (2004). *Molly's family.* New York: Farrar, Straus and Giroux.

Gordon, S. (2000). *All families are different.* Amherst, NY: Prometheus Books.

Meyer, R. (2002). *Outlaw representation: Censorship and homosexuality in twentieth-century American art.* New York: Oxford University Press.

Silin, J. G. (1995). *Sex, death, and the education of children: Our passion for ignorance in the age of AIDS.* New York: Teachers College Press.

U'Ren, A. (2001). *Pugdog.* New York: Farrar, Straus and Giroux.

Articles

McRuer, R., & Wilkerson, A. L. (Eds.). (2003). Desiring disability: Queer theory meets disability studies. *Journal of Lesbian and Gay Studies,* 9 (1–2).

Solis, S. (2004). The disabilitymaking factory: Manufacturing "differences" through children's books. *Disability Studies Quarterly,* 24 (1).

QUEER YOUTH AND THE MEDIA

Rob Linné

In the past, gay, lesbian, bisexual, and transgendered youth were seldom represented in books, films, magazines, or television shows produced for and about young people. Recently, however, as homophobia or prejudice based on sexual orientation or perceived gender nonconformity has been questioned or rejected across our society, more characters and storylines, in a range of media and genres, have focused on the experiences of young people growing up queer. Gay characters have played central roles in teen television dramas aimed at adolescent audiences such as *My So-Called Life* and *Dawson's Creek*. Popular movies such as *The Object of My Affection* and *A Home at the End of the World* have featured young Hollywood stars in gay leading roles. MTV *Real World* house casts almost always include a queer roommate, and many videos now include homoerotic imagery or gay storylines. Popular young adult fiction writers such as Francesca Lia Block and M. E. Kerr focus their novels on issues of sexuality and identity.

Many professionals who work with youth applaud this trend as tremendous progress. Young people who are lesbian, gay, or transgendered now have opportunities to see themselves portrayed in literature, art, or media in ways that may help promote healthy personal growth and self-understanding. As well, all youth—gay or straight—may learn valuable lessons about empathy, the effects of homophobia on all in our society, and the ways sexism is related to heterosexism and other forms of prejudice. However, many who study literature and the media caution against an unquestioning acceptance of the ways queer youth are being portrayed in our culture during this time of emerging acceptance and newly won freedoms and civil rights. Critics note that the ways publishers or film producers often portray the lives of queer youth are unrealistic, continue negative stereotypes, or downplay the larger societal structures that allow homophobia and sexism to continue in many ways.

Historically, the voices of lesbians, gays, and transgendered people have often been silenced by the threat of discrimination, harassment, or even brutal physical violence. Many sexual minorities have felt pressured to keep their personal lives private, to not discuss their relationships with others or their involvement with any aspect of the gay community. One effect of such repression is a sense of invisibility among many lesbian and gays, especially among youth. Because gay voices have been silenced and because gay people have been pressured to remain in the closet and in a sense invisible, many young people have grown up without positive queer role models in their communities or in their schools.

Although society as a whole recently has made tremendous strides in terms of gay rights in our laws and the rejection of heterosexism in the workplace, repression and the threat of violence remain a fact of life for many gay people in many areas of the world. Young people in urban centers with thriving gay communities may now have easy access to gay book stores and have many opportunities to meet openly gay individuals and couples. However, many feel too intimidated to explore these areas of their cities for fear of being outed or gay-bashed. Youth in many rural or suburban areas may not even know of any gay youth groups or queer cultural institutions. They may not know any openly gay individuals or experience close contact with a lesbian or gay household. The world for many youth questioning their sexuality or working through the coming-out process remains a very isolated and isolating place.

To counter such isolation many queer youth seek out books, videos, magazines, or Web sites inclusive of gay voices and experiences. Queer fictional characters are the first gay people many youth come to "know" and they serve as important role models and guides to new ways of being in the world. Alternative magazines and gay community Web sites very often become gateways through which individuals struggling to understand or create a sexual identity enter into the social aspects of queer life and culture.

With the explosion of offerings on the Internet and the World Wide Web, young people can now peruse or purchase queer book titles in the privacy of their homes or make anonymous inquiries through library computer stations. Online texts remove the fear of running into a neighbor while purchasing a gay-themed book or a lesbian audience magazine at the local bookstore. Young people questioning their sexuality or wondering how to "come out" now have the opportunity to discuss their issues safely through hundreds of alternative chatrooms. So although, many young queers remain isolated in their home communities, technology and media now offer virtually unlimited resources for learning about queer culture and making connections with other young queers.

Such heightened visibility of lesbian, gay, and transgender cultures and an emerging market for books, films, and magazines written for young audiences represents a dramatic shift in our culture at large. However, many who study literature, film and the media caution against accepting all these changes as unquestionably and wholly positive. Censorship does remain an issue on many levels, and the new wave of book publishing and film producing may offer counterproductive or confused messages. Character portrayals may reinforce negative stereotypes and plot lines may cloud the causes underlying the homophobia that continues to divide our society even today.

Each year more and more schools allow the formation of Gay/Straight Student Alliance clubs while others enact anti-harassment policies based on sexuality. However, lesbian and gay lives too often remain extracurricular, outside the everyday conversation of school curriculums. The issue of censorship regarding queer voices in school settings continues to limit the availability of films and texts in many classrooms and the effects of such silencing loudly communicate a harsh message to students and their teachers. Although many schools now allow books and films inclusive of young gay characters and storylines to be available for individual students, fewer schools actively include queer texts as part of the general classroom curriculum for all. Such selective censorship communicates the idea that while queer people may be tolerated in a private, individual way, the voices of young lesbians and gays are not truly honored as valuable contributions to our culture as a whole. Imagine a school where books with female protagonists were allowed in school libraries, but only books with male main characters were ever read in class. Consider how an African American student might feel if she could only read about her culture by doing an online search for materials.

Beyond school censorship, issues of how young queers are actually presented in the media remain a concern for many. Several problematic patterns or themes emerge when many of the new movies or films based on queer youth characters are read as a whole.

Many stories focus on the negative and portray young lesbians and gays largely as victims. A large percentage of early books and movies from the 1970s through the early 1990s ended up with gay youth either committing suicide or being killed or brutally beaten. Portrayals of gay youth often focus on depression, isolation, loneliness, substance abuse, and unsafe sex. Although isolation and gay-bashing do indeed remain as serious issues in our society, young people also need to know of the stories of empowerment and unity.

When not relying on tragedy to tell the stories of gay youth, writers often fall back on comedy. Many television shows, as well as films and books, rely on the stock character of the shallow but funny gay character. Although these nonthreatening characters have been able to make their way onto television and into the movies, thus increasing queer visibility, they do not offer well-rounded, substantive role models for young people. When the only characterizations others see of your culture are comedians or clowns, it is not likely that you will be taken seriously in real life.

Many characterizations stress the gender conformity of the gay characters, thus marginalizing the idea of young queers who may not want to "act straight." Authors and screenwriters seem to go out of their way to demonstrate that gay boys can be just as manly as straight boys, and lesbian girls can be quite feminine. Many books focus on gay male athletes while films with young lesbians make sure the actresses portray acceptably feminine girls. Although it is important that literature and film debunk stale stereotypes, the attempt to portray the majority of young queer characters as "appropriately" masculine or feminine may marginalize young people who do not fit into society's gender norms. The conformity of gender roles displayed by gay characters in effect suggests that young people can be tolerated as gay, but that they should worry not to act "too gay."

Another clear pattern observed in books, films, magazines, and TV shows is the limited portrayal of young queers as overwhelmingly white, middle-class, and often good looking. Ostensibly this theme represents an attempt on the writers' part to make the characters more mainstream or even likable. Obviously, such a strategy prejudges one group (racial or ethnic minorities) as not desirable in a misguided attempt to uplift another oppressed group. This portrayal leaves young people of color out of the picture and encourages gay youth to embrace consumerism while understanding style and shopping as central to their identities.

Some books, films, and TV shows do resist falling into the stale themes and clichés. They offer well-rounded characters, who display strength as well as vulnerability. Now films and television shows allow gays to be the main characters instead of just the comedic sidekick. Balanced portrayals of queer youth challenge accepted norms of how people are supposed to act according to their gender and explore a range of issues regarding gender and sexuality. Current authors such as Alex Sanchez and Jacqueline Woodson write about young people from diverse ethnic and cultural backgrounds.

As more young people demand to see characters that represent the range of our cultures, writers and producers are left with no choice but to create more realistic portrayals. Schools must follow through and include quality literature and film inclusive of queer voices in their curriculums. Educators have many quality resources to help choose quality literature and film as well as guide them through any potential censorship issues in the classroom.

Note

"Transgender" is an umbrella term for people whose gender identity, expression or behavior is different from those typically associated with their assigned sex at birth.

Resources

Books

Linné, R. (2002). Facing teacher fears about lesbian and gay texts in the classroom. In J. Harmon (Ed.), *Just literacy: Promoting justice through language and learning*. Albany: New York State English Council.

Sanchez, A. (2001). *Rainbow boys*. New York: Simon and Schuster.

Woodson, J. (2003). *The house you pass by on the way*. New York: Grosset & Dunlap.

Articles

Sumara, D. (1993). Gay and lesbian voices in literature, making room on the shelf. *English Quarterly*, 25 (1), 30–34.

Norton, T., & Vare, J. (2004). Literature for today's gay and lesbian teens: Subverting the culture of silence. *The English Journal*, 94 (2), 65–70.

Web Sites

Gay, Lesbian, Straight Education Network. Retrieved January 6, 2005 from www.glsen.org

The Commercial Closet. Retrieved January 6, 2005 from www.commercialcloset.org

The Gay and Lesbian Alliance Against Defamation. Retrieved January 6, 2005 from www.glaad.org

Parents, Families, and Friends of Lesbians and Gays. Retrieved January 6, 2005 from www.pflag.org

XY Magazine for Gay Youth. Retrieved January 6, 2005 from www.xy.com

Money

Maureen A. McKeever

Money, the one thing everyone needs
The one thing that turns sharing into greed
Something that keep families together
The one thing that helps you buy things based on pleasure
The thing that makes the world go round
Money turns frowns into smiles
Whether paper or coin
It's something we all try to enjoy
Unfortunately money can be your downfall
Having all the luxurious things
But nobody to call
Money can be copper, silver, or green
We all know how we feel
when we work hard and receive that money
Love can replace money
But money buys all
If this is so, how come none of us
Seem to realize that love not money conquers all?